Cultural China

China's Long
March Toward
A Market Economy

當代中國經濟改革

Jinglian Wu

LONG RIVER PRESS
San Francisco

This edition is edited and designed by the Editorial Committee of *Cultural China* series.

Managing Editors: Naiqing Xu, Youbu Wang, Ying Wu

Executive Editor: Celia Van

Interior and Cover Design: Yinchang Yuan, Jing Li, Wenqing Xue

ISBN 1-59265-063-5

Published by

Long River Press

360 Swift Ave., Suite 48

South San Francisco, CA 94080

USA

and

Shanghai Press and Publishing Development Company

1110 Huaihai Middle Road, Donghu Villa F, Shanghai, China (200031)

Computer typeset by Yuan Yinchang Design Studio, Shanghai

Printed in China by Shanghai Donnelley Printing Co. Ltd.

1   2   3   4   5   6   7   8   9   10

Foreword

The international interest in China is increasing. Not surprisingly, the China-related news is hitting the headlines of leading international media. This is well-grounded, given the fact that China is the largest developing country in the world with almost a quarter of the world's population. However, many reports on China are self-contradictory, which again reveals the complexities of a nation in a dramatic change for over a century. For the outsider, it is virtually not possible to follow China's overriding trends of change without understanding its past and present.

This book provides a chronological record of the major changes that have taken place in the Chinese economy for the past five decades. Not long after my graduation, I joined the Institute of Economics under the Chinese Academy of Social Sciences headed by Sun Yefang, the most renowned economist in China (China's highest award in economics was named after him), and began my career as an economist. Since then, my fate has been closely associated with China's reform. Roughly speaking, my understanding of reform before 1978 was confined to the framework of a planning economy, but with the deepening of China's reform and opening up, and after my systematic study of modern economics (I was a visiting scholar in Yale University between 1983-84), I became a firm advocate of a market-oriented economy in the mid-1980s, actively involved in the reform process.

The first chapter is a summary of the reform objectives and basic processes. However, the market economy is a complex system, and different sectors naturally choose different forms and have different achievements. For this reason, the book devotes eight chapters to such important areas as development of private sector, reform of enterprises, rural reform, financial reform, fiscal reform, opening-up strategy, social security system, and macroeconomic policies. The last chapter discusses the critical issues facing the establishment of the market economy and reform in the next stage.

Some writers describe the Chinese reform as "capitalism with Chinese characteristics", which appears interesting and vivid for English-speaking readers. However, as a proponent of socialist market economy, I don't favor the use of such a description. Deng Xiaoping and other Chinese leaders set the establishment of a socialist market economy as the overall objective of economic reform, in which the meaning of "socialist" is quite close to the European concept which emphasizes social justice and common wealth. For a society in a transition from a command economy in which the government and administrative functions lead the resource allocation to a modern market economy which stresses social equality, weakening the vertical power relations and emphasizing social equality are critical to China; the word "market economy" shows China's consensus on the basic role of market mechanism in resource allocation after unsuccessful trials of so many reform efforts - this is nothing different from what the western economist have advocated since the 1970s. In this sense, "market economy" is the most appropriate word to sum up China's reform objectives and guidelines.

This book is a condensed version or adaptation of a larger work, which provides a detailed discussion of China's reform. For Chinese readers, it is more than necessary; but for English-speaking readers, it might create extra burden. China is increasingly integrating with the global economy, and naturally more and more people from outside of China are interested in its economic reform. This condensed book should be helpful for all English-speaking readers with a strong interest in Chinese economy.

As the old Chinese saying goes, "When one is in the mountain, he often can't tell its true shape." An insider has advantages over an outsider, but also with limitations. In-depth analysis and understanding of China is a global effort; comments or criticisms from the readers will only be helpful for me to remedy and improve.

My student Fan Shitao and the Chinese publisher have done enormous work in creating this condensed version, and the translators have tried their best to deliver the key messages of the book. To all those who have made this book possible, I should pay tribute to their valuable contribution.

Wu Jinglian
Senior Research Fellow
Development Research Center of State Council, PRC

CHAPTER ONE

THE EVOLUTION OF
CHINA'S REFORM
STRATEGY

Economic reform in China was initiated in September 1956, when the Eighth National Congress of the Communist Party of China (CPC) decided to launch the "economic management system reform." The fundamental theme of China's reform is the transition from a centrally planned economy to a market economy.

At the very beginning, the so-called "economic management system reform" was no more than a set of policy adjustments aimed at improving the performance of the economy and "injecting vigor into the economy". It was not until the mid-1980s that a market orientation was gradually established. However, many different opinions and viewpoints had been expressed about how to achieve the goal of a market economy. As a result, a variety of measures were taken to reform the original economic system between 1956 and the present. Backed by different theories, these measures took the Chinese economy in different, sometimes opposite, directions.

This chapter divides the course of China's reform into three stages, as follows:

1. 1958 to 1978: Administrative decentralization reform with emphasis on the central government transferring power to and sharing profits with governments at lower levels.

2. 1979 to 1993: Incremental reform, or reform of "outside the system" preceding "inside the system" (i.e., focusing on non-state sectors and off-plan parts of the economy and promoting their development).

3. 1994 to present: Reform highlighted by a strategy of "overall advancement with key breakthroughs" to establish a socialist market economy.

During China's economic reform, various reform measures in various stages were often interwoven; in other words, reform measures in the previous stage often nurture something forthcoming in the subsequent stage, and reform measures in the coming stage often contained legacies of measures instituted in the preceding stage. So, the analysis in this chapter focuses on the typical reform measures of each of the three chronological stages described.

1.1
The Chinese Planned Economic System and the Raise of the Issue of Reform

In the first few years after the founding of the PRC, Chinese leaders did plan their work in accordance with the idea of "preparation for three years and construction for ten years" before taking steps toward socialism.[1] However, in 1952, the action principle changed significantly. Thus, although the General Line for the Transition Period was put forward in 1953 with an original plan to complete the socialist transformation of individual agriculture and private capitalist industry and commerce in fifteen or more years, it took only three years to establish public ownership, with state ownership and quasi-state, collective ownership as its major forms, as the only base for the national economy. On the basis of public ownership, a Soviet-style, centrally planned economic system was established nationwide.

1.1.1 The Main Characteristics of Centrally Planned Economic System
The main point of centrally planned economic system is that state ownership and economic plans formulated and executed by state organs were regarded as the

basic economic characteristics of socialism. Moreover, state ownership was considered the foundation of the entire socialist system. On the basis of this, the central planning organ organizes the whole society into a huge single factory by administrative means to allocate resources. This definition of socialism given by Stalin in 1930s clearly reflected the "blind faith in the state" that was strongly criticized by classical Marxist authors. Ruling socialist countries for over half a century, it was regarded as an unalterable principle of Marxism for a fairly long time by leaders in some socialist countries.

1.1.2 Why China Can Successfully Shift Its System into Planned Economic System

The major reasons for china's accomplishment in implementing the planned economic system in one or two years were as follows.

1. For quite a long time, it had been regarded as an unalterable principle of socialism to abolish the market system and establish a planned economy characterized by highly centralized administrative coordination, following the example of the Soviet Union. After the founding of the PRC, "Soviet experts" completely transformed the Chinese economics education by instilling Stalin's political economy and making it the only prevailing theory of economics. According to this theory, it was natural to establish a centrally planned economic system.

2. After the outbreak of the Korean War, China had to give top priority to national defense. Therefore, Chinese leaders chose the institutional arrangement that would mobilize and allocate resources through central planning so that limited resources could be used to build up heavy industry, especially its core of military industry.

3. Having borne the humiliation of being a semi-colony for one hundred years, both the Chinese leaders and the Chinese public had a strong desire to catch up with and surpass Western developed countries. They believed that by following the example of the Soviet Union, wielding state power, and mobilizing and concentrating human, financial, and material resources, China would be able to achieve modernization in a very short time.

4. China had been a country full of small peasants for quite a long time and government control over society was a deeply rooted tradition. After the founding of the PRC, Mao Zedong, by virtue of his high prestige gained in the long revolutionary struggles, established a totalist government[2] under his leadership. This laid the political foundation for accomplishing the socialist transformation and implementing the planned economic system within only a few years.

1.1.3. The Raise of the Issue of Reform in China

Upon its establishment in the whole country, the planned economic system in China met with numerous criticisms. Enterprises, which had enjoyed much autonomy in the economy of New Democracy, became subordinates to higher-level administrative organs. They lost their vigor as they were forced to give up decision-making power regarding human, financial, and material resources as well as supply, production, and marketing. Meanwhile, the decline in managerial initiative and service quality of industrial and commercial enterprises brought about many complaints from consumers.

Party and government leaders made responses to the aforementioned economic situation. Chen Yun (1905 - 1995), a party leader in charge of economic affairs, proposed that a few adjustments in economic policies should be made so as to establish a socialist economic structure with "three mains and three supplements." They were (1) in terms of industrial and commercial business, state-run and collective-run enterprises should be its main part while a certain amount of individual businesses can be supplement to state-run and collective-run enterprises; (2) in terms of production plan, planned production should be its main part while free production according to market situation within the scope allowed by the plan can be supplement to planned production; and (3) in terms of the unified socialist market, the state market should be its main part while the free market within a certain scope and guided by the state can be supplement to the state market.[3]

The most important among these responses was Mao Zedong's instructional opinion on the reform of the Soviet-style, centrally planned economic system. He pointed out in his speech "On the Ten Major Relationships," made at the meeting of the Political Bureau of the Central Committee of the Communist Party (CCCPC) in April 1956 that the major defect of this system was the over-centralization of power in the central authorities, with too much control and too little flexibility. Therefore, the fundamental measure to reform the existing system was to delegate power to governments at lower levels and enterprises. Following this guiding principle of Mao, in 1958 China started its first economic reform after the establishment of a socialist economy. In the actual implementation of this reform, some amendments were made to Mao's 1956 principle. These amendments emphasized the division of powers and benefits among administrative organs at various levels. This was the idea of "administrative decentralization," according to which China started its economic reform in 1958.

1.2
Administrative Decentralization
(1958 to 1978)

In September 1956, the First Session of the Eighth National Congress of the CPC decided to reform the economic management system under the guidance of Mao Zedong's "On the Ten Major Relationships" and to implement the reform at the beginning of 1958.

1.2.1 The Establishment of the Policy of Delegating Power to and Sharing Profit with Local Governments

The central theme of the economic management system reform of 1958 was delegating power to and sharing profit with local governments. This policy was not completely in line with Mao Zedong's original idea, proposed in "On the Ten Major Relationships," of delegating power to and sharing profit with economic units and individual workers as well as local governments. The major reason for such a change was closely related to the political situation during 1957 and 1958, which made the idea of delegating power to and sharing profit with economic units and individual workers no longer satisfy the requirement for maintaining political correctness.

First, concerning delegating power to and sharing profit with state-owned enterprises (SOEs), even before the Eighth National Congress of the CPC, many people from economic departments began with great enthusiasm to study Yugoslavia's experiment in "enterprise autonomy." and wished to learn some experience from it in China. Later in 1957, however, the CPC's attack on the theory of self-management socialism of the Yugoslavian Communist Party escalated, and enterprise autonomy was condemned as the core of "Yugoslavian revisionism." Consequently, the issue of expanding enterprise autonomy was eliminated from the CPC's reform agenda.

Second, concerning delegating power to and sharing profit with individual workers, Mao Zedong's original idea was in line with trends in other socialist countries around 1956. In addition to the aforementioned self-management socialism of Yugoslavia that implied in-service employee ownership of enterprises, in early 1956, Khrushchev, First Secretary of the Communist Party of the Soviet Union (CPSU), also proposed to enhance "material incentive" to SOE employees when he fiercely attacked Stalin's economic policies.

However, the idea of delegating power to and sharing profit with individual workers became politically problematic in 1957. At that time, not only was the CPC attacking Yugoslavian revisionism, but also a difference in opinions about Stalinism emerged between the CPC and the CPSU. In addition, Mao Zedong had been personally in favor of spiritual incentive instead of material incentive and during the Anti-Rightist Campaign of 1957, he blamed individualism as the spiritual root cause of the anti-party and anti-socialism ideology of Rightists and demanded people to "shake off the shackles of fame and wealth." At such a moment, arousing people's enthusiasm by material incentive was obviously at odds with the mainstream ideology.

In such a political environment, only local governments and officials at various levels could be the objects of power delegating and profit sharing. In other words, the central theme of the reform became the division of power and profit among administrative bodies at different levels. Thus, transferring power and, consequently, profit to local governments at various levels became the basic theme of the reform of 1958. From then on, the economic management system reform was defined as transferring administrative functions to lower levels (tizhi xiafang). Such thinking about reform had a far-reaching impact on China's economic reform and development in later days.

1.2.2 The Implementation of the Policy of Transferring Administrative Functions to Lower Levels

The Third Plenary Session of the Eighth CCCPC in September 1957 launched the Great Leap Forward Campaign and started the economic management system reform to prepare an institutional foundation for the Great Leap Forward. At the meeting, Chen Yun, head of the five-member CCCPC Economic Affairs Group, delivered the *Report on Issues of Improving the State Administrative System and Increasing Agricultural Output.* Three related documents, drafted under the leadership of Chen Yun, namely, *Provisions on Improving the Industrial Management System* (draft), *Provisions on Improving the Commercial Management System* (draft), and *Provisions on Dividing the Power of Fiscal Administration Between Central and Local Governments* (draft), were passed in principle at the meeting and were submitted to the Standing Committee of the National People's Congress. Approved by the Standing Committee on November 14, these three documents were to be implemented in 1958. The essence of these three documents was to transfer some industrial, commercial, and financial administrative functions to local administrative bodies so that the initiative and enthusiasm of both local governments and enterprises can be brought into full play and the unified planning of the state can be accomplished according to local conditions.

Specifically, the transfer of economic administrative functions to lower levels of 1958 included several key actions, as follows.

1.2.2.1 Transferring the Power of Planning

In September 1958, the CCCPC promulgated the Provisions on Improving the Planning Administration System. In the Provisions, the original planning administration system, in which unified plans were formulated and balanced by the State Planning Commission and issued successively to lower levels, was changed into a system that was based on the overall balance by regions with coordination between specialized departments and regions. In other words, the new system was centered on local authorities, and plans were formulated and balanced from lower levels successively to higher ones so that local economies could become systems of their own. Local governments were permitted to adjust their own targets of industrial and agricultural production; to make overall plans for the construction scale, projects, and distribution of investment within their regions; to regulate the use of materials and equipment within their regions; and to have at their disposal certain proportions of the over fulfilled outputs of some important products.

1.2.2.2 Transferring the Control over Enterprises

Except for a small number of important, special, or experimental ones, all enterprises belonging to Ministries of the State Council were to be transferred to local governments. On June 2, 1958, the CCCPC notified Ministries of the State Council to complete the transfer of control over enterprises to lower levels by June 15. Thus, 88 percent of the enterprises and public institutions that used to belong to Ministries were transferred to local governments at various levels, some even to subdistricts and communes. The proportion of industrial output of enterprises directly under the central government fell from 39.7 percent in 1957 to 13.8 percent in 1958.[4]

1.2.2.3 Transferring the Power of Materials and Equipment Allocation

First, both the categories and quantities of materials and equipment allocated by the State Planning Commission and administered by Ministries were reduced drastically. Categories of materials and equipment allocated by the commission and administered by Ministries were reduced from 530 in 1957 to 132 in 1959, a three-fourths reduction. The administration of these reduced categories was transferred to provinces, municipalities, and autonomous regions. Second, instead of being planned and distributed by the central government, the remaining one-fourth of materials and equipment was managed by matching demands and supplies locally and distributing balances, with the central government control limited to the distribution of balances. Third, in terms of supply, except for railroads, military industries, foreign exchanges, and national reserves, all enterprises, either central or local, should apply for materials and equipment to and get supplies from the provinces, municipalities, and autonomous regions where they were located.

1.2.2.4 Transferring the Power of Reviewing and Approving Capital Construction Projects and Credit Administration

Concerning the review and approval of capital construction projects, it was stipulated that for locally built, large-scale construction projects above the norm, only summaries of planning assignments needed to be submitted to the State Planning Commission for approval; the design and budget were to be approved by local governments. For projects below the norm, local governments could make decisions on all issues. In July 1958, the central government decided to carry out an investment responsibility system- within their scope of investment responsibility, local governments could make decisions and accumulate funds by themselves. Local governments could therefore start any business, including large-scale projects above the norm, within the limits of funds allocated from the central government and funds raised by themselves. At the same time, credit administration was transferred to local bank branches. The original, highly centralized credit system was abolished and a new system of "transferring deposits and credits to local bank branches and managing balance nationwide" was implemented. Local bank branches were allowed to "lend no matter how much is needed and no matter when it is needed" in accordance with local needs out of "production going all out."

1.2.2.5 Transferring the Power of Finance Administration and Tax Collection

To increase the financial capacity and expand the financial authority of local governments, the old system of "expenditure deciding revenue, adjusted every year" was changed into a system of "revenue deciding expenditure, management by different levels, sharing according to different categories, and fixed for five years." Seven types of taxes, such as urban real estate tax, recreation tax, and stamp tax, were reclassified as fixed revenues of local governments. Bulk taxes, such as commodity circulation tax, goods tax, business tax, and income tax, were to be shared between the central government and local governments. The old practice of no local sharing in the profits of enterprises directly under the central departments was abolished to allow local governments at the province/municipality level to have a 20-percent share in the profits of central enterprises. In addition, local governments were also given authority to reduce, exempt, and add taxes.

1.2.2.6 Transferring the Power of Labor Administration

Recruitment plans could be executed with the confirmation of provincial-level authorities, and approval of the state ministries and commissions was no longer necessary.

Although delegating power to and sharing profit with enterprises was eliminated from the publicly announced program for the reform of 1958, in reality, a few measures of delegating power to and sharing profit with enterprises were taken in addition to those delegating power to and sharing profit with local governments. First, the targets of the mandatory plan of the State Planning Commission for industrial enterprises were reduced from 12 to 4 (outputs of major products, total number of employees, total wage bill, and profits). Second, the original system of enterprise incentive fund, or factory director's fund,[5] (retaining an industry-specific proportion of profits) was replaced by a system of "full profit retention"[6] (retaining an enterprise-specific proportion of profits). Third, the power of enterprises concerning personnel assignment was enlarged. Enterprises were responsible for managing their staff except for key managerial and technical positions. Enterprises were also granted the right to adjust their organizational structures and staffing, as long as the total number of staff was unchanged. Fourth, enterprises were granted the right to adjust the use of part of their capital and to increase, reduce, or scrap fixed assets.

1.2.3 Disorder Caused by Transferring Administrative Functions to Lower Levels and Its Remediation

Together with people's communes in the countryside, the decentralized planned economic system, created by delegating power to every lower level of local governments within the overall framework of a planned economy and resource allocation by administrative orders, laid the institutional foundation for the Great Leap Forward. Supported by this foundation, local governments at all levels responded to the call of Mao Zedong "to surpass Britain in three years and to surpass America in ten years"[7] by maximally exercising their power of resource allocation to launch capital construction projects, recruit workers, and commandeer resources from peasants in attempts to accomplish impossible plan targets, such as to double steel output every year.[8] As a result, all geographic regions, departments, and units scrambled for resources, and industrial and agricultural productions were thrown into disarray. There were 1,589 large - and medium-sized projects under construction in 1958, 1,361 in 1959, and 1,815 in 1960, with the number of projects in any single year exceeding the total number of projects during the entire First Five-Year Plan period (1953 - 1957). Investment in fixed assets increased from RMB 14.33 billion in 1957 to RMB 38.87 billion in 1960, with a three-year (1958 -1960) total of RMB 100.74 billion, 71 percent more than the total of RMB 58.85 billion during the First Five-Year Plan period. Because of transferring the power of labor administration to lower levels, the number of SOE employees increased from 24.51 million at the end of 1957 to 45.32 million at the end of 1958, a net increase of 20.81 million, or 84.9 percent. By the end of 1960, the number of SOE employees had reached 59.69 million; the urban population exceeded 130 million, an addition of more than 30 million to the 99.49 million at the end of 1957.[9]

Widespread economic disorder led to deteriorating economic efficiency, and the consumption of huge amounts of resources only generated all sorts of exaggerated statistics with which local officials could please their superiors and win rewards. Facts revealed later indicate that the grain yield in China was 170 million tons in 1959, 30 million tons less than the grain yield of 200 million tons in 1958. The grain yield was further reduced to 143.5 million tons in 1960, lower than that of 143.7 million tons in 1951. Since the information of this nationwide famine was suppressed and relief measures were inadequate, cases of edema caused by malnutrition prevailed in urban areas and deaths due to famine numbered in tens of millions in rural areas. [10]

Not until the fall of 1960 did the leadership of the CCCPC finally decide to implement the policy of "readjustment, consolidation, reinforcement, and upgrading." They appointed Chen Yun as the person in command and took drastic measures to overcome the grave economic difficulties caused by the Great Leap Forward and the Anti-Right Deviation Campaign. These measures included the following:

1. In January 1962, the CCCPC convened an enlarged working conference (the so-called Conference of Seven Thousand Cadres), which was attended by cadres at the central level, central bureau level, provincial level, prefecture level, and county level. At this meeting, Mao Zedong made a gesture of taking responsibility for mistakes to cool the grievances of cadres and called on everybody to strengthen unity, discipline, and centralization to get work done and to overcome difficulties.[11] Meanwhile, the CCCPC Financial and Economic Leading Group headed by Chen Yun was restored to exercise unified leadership in the readjustment of the national economy.

2. As requested by the CCCPC Financial and Economic Leading Group, a series of measures were taken to recentralize the administration of government finance, credit, and enterprises and to establish a system even more centralized and stricter than that of 1950 when government finance and economy were unified. For example, the so-called Ten Provisions on tightening up planning discipline and a series of other decisions were made to take back the delegated power. A vertical system of leadership under the central government was exercised in banking, government finance, and statistics. Most of the enterprises transferred to local governments were brought back under the control of central departments.

3. Scarce resources were reallocated by this highly centralized administrative system. Small iron and steel mills run by the masses with either indigenous or modern methods were all dismantled; thirty million workers recruited from rural areas during the Great Leap Forward were all sent back home; and urban industrial enterprises were reorganized by closing down, suspending operations, merging, or switching production lines. The economy was stabilized after only several months of readjustment and had basically recovered by 1963.

However, as people rejoiced over the restoration of economic order, they also experienced again all the disadvantages of a centrally planned economy and started to deliberate on reform once again.

Until 1976, market-oriented reform was politically unacceptable because of the obstacle of the ideological creed that administrative order is the only way to allocate resources under socialism. As a result, transferring planning power to governments at lower levels was left as the only choice for economic reform, resulting in several attempts similar to the administrative decentralization reform of 1958. In 1970, a large-scale economic management system reform, famous for its slogan that "decentralization is a revolution and the more decentralization, the greater the revolution," was a restage of transferring administrative functions to lower levels of 1958 in a new historical setting. In 1970, Mao Zedong, based on his assessment of the international situation, assumed that another world war was imminent and the top priority then was to be prepared against a foreign enemy's full-scale invasion. As a result, the decentralization of 1970 had a clear political and military goal of making preparation for the war. The country was divided into ten cooperation regions and every cooperation region, every province, and every city was to establish an independent and integrated industrial setup, with which it could equip itself for war and meet the need of "each fighting in its own way." The consequences of this large-scale decentralization were no different at all from the decentralization of 1958. Enthusiasm to "go in for industry in a big way" and to pursue overambitious growth targets was stirred up from the cooperation region level down to the people's commune level. Concurrently, competition for resources motivated by local interests sank the national economy into disorder, just as it did in 1958.[12] After the death of Lin Biao (1907 - 1971), the economic management system was recentralized in the "Criticizing Lin and Rectification Campaign" directed by Zhou Enlai (1898 - 1976) and the "All-round Straightening Out Campaign" directed by Deng Xiaoping (1904 -1997).

In a word, reforms of transferring administrative functions to lower levels (i.e., administrative decentralization) during 1958 to 1976 always ended up in disorder and recentralization later. Decentralization and ensuing disorder was followed by recentralization and ensuing stagnancy, resulting in cycles of decentralization - disorder - recentralization - stagnancy.

1.2.4 Economic Analysis of Administrative Decentralization

During the mid-1980s, in a discussion of the advantages and disadvantages as well as the continuation or discontinuation of the revenue sharing system in the academic circles, some economists, using tools of modern economics, criticized the idea and practice of making transferring administrative functions to lower levels the main theme of reform.[13]

The basic idea of these economists was that the aim of Reform should not be defined as decentralization in general terms because there were actually two types of decentralization, namely economic decentralization (i.e., market-oriented decentralization), which was aimed at a market economy, and administrative decentralization, which maintained the framework of a planned economy. Because the direction of China's reform was to build a market economy,[14] decentralization in China could only be economic decentralization, not administrative decentralization.[15]

The economists opposing administrative decentralization demonstrated their viewpoints from the perspective of the efficient mechanism of allocating scarce resources.

First, a planned economy allocates resources by administrative orders. This mode of resource allocation demands centralization. For a planned economy to be feasible, one of the prerequisites is for the central organ to compute a centralized calculation, determine planned quotas in a unified way, and ensure the strict enforcement of orders and prohibitions. Otherwise, the whole economy will suffer disorder as a result of divided leaderships with different agendas. Therefore, a decentralized planned economy is worse than a centralized planned economy.

Second, the only way to avoid both stagnancy in a centralized planned economy and disorder in a decentralized planned economy is to conduct market-oriented reform and to build an economic system in which market plays a fundamental role in resource allocation. Independent market players in a market economy decide what to produce, how many to produce, and for whom to produce, according to price signals and their self-interest. Economic decentralization is the only right direction of reform.

Third, it is true that administrative decentralization can motivate governments at lower levels in the short term. Measures of administrative decentralization adopted after 1978, such as the fiscal responsibility system, achieved the goal of encouraging local governments to increase revenue and reduce expenditure at the beginning. However, these measures soon revealed their shortcomings of not only weakening the unified leadership crucial for a planned economy but also encouraging local protectionism. By the mid-1980s, barriers between regions, market fragmentation, and administrative protection for local enterprises had become major obstacles to the development of a unified national market so that the Chinese economy at this point was called a "vassal economy" by some scholars. At that time, local governments' protection for vested interests hindered the process of breaking down barriers between regions and establishing a unified market.[16] Institutional change is characterized by path dependence.[17] The farther one is down a path deviating from the main path, the higher the exit cost is. The exit cost may even be so high that one is locked in this deviating path. Once locked in, it is impossible to exit without great social upheaval, according to economist Douglass C. North.

Economists noticed that administrative decentralization brought about another consequence. Market relations can hardly develop in a highly centralized planned economy. While strengthening local protectionism, administrative decentralization left some room for market relations to grow in gaps of competition among regions. As a result, China did not end up in a situation similar to that of the Soviet Union in which a highly centralized planned economy left no room for the growth of non-state sectors. Township and village enterprises (TVEs) in China are good examples of this situation. The main reason for the rapid growth of TVEs in some localities is that, in pursuit of local interests, local officials used their administrative power to offer protection and convenience to TVEs in terms of financing, production, and marketing.[18] History witnessed similar situations in the birth of market relations. In autocratic oriental countries, absolute monarchical power and inadequate legal protection of private property prevented market relations from developing. In feudal Western Europe, market relations grew in gaps between different feudal manors; as market forces gradually expanded, free cities and the bourgeoisie emerged.

1.3
Incremental Reform (1979 to 1993)

China's economic development took a favorable turn after the Third Plenary Session of the 11th CCCPC in December 1978. After years of exploration, China found a new approach to reform. After the failed experiment of expanding enterprise autonomy and the stagnancy of SOE reform, China adopted some patching-up measures to keep the state sector running and switched its main effort to non-state sectors for new growth. This strategy was called incremental reform. Achievements by China's economy during the following one or two decades could be largely attributed to this strategy. However, the continuation of this strategy led to a series of problems.

1.3.1 The Emergence of the Strategy of Incremental Reform

Reform after the downfall of the "Gang of Four" in 1976 started with expanding enterprise autonomy. Ten years of the Great Cultural Revolution (1966-1976) had driven the Chinese economy to the verge of collapse. The decision of the Third Plenary Session of the 11th CCCPC in December 1978 reiterated the policies proposed by Mao Zedong in his article, "On the Ten Major Relationships," and pointed out that a major shortcoming of the old economic system lay in its over-centralization of power. "Power should be audaciously delegated to lower levels under unified leadership. Local governments as well as industrial and agricultural enterprises should have more autonomy of management under the guidance of a unified state plan," so as to "bring into play the initiative, enthusiasm, and creativity of central departments, local governments, enterprises, and individuals, thus bringing vigorous growth to all sectors of socialist economy."[19]

Inspired by this idea, Sichuan Province initiated the reform of expanding enterprise autonomy to delegate power to and share profits with enterprises. In October 1978, Sichuan Province selected six enterprises to conduct an experiment in expanding enterprise autonomy and achieved good results. Later, the experiment in Sichuan Province was extended to one hundred SOEs. In July 1979, the State Council released a series of official documents, including *Provisions on Enlarging the Decision-Making Power for Operation and Management of State-Run Industrial Enterprises, Provisions on Implementing Profit Retention in State-Run Enterprises, Interim Provisions on Levying Fixed Assets Tax on State-Run Industrial Enterprises,* and *Interim Provisions on Implementing Full Loan Financing for Working Capital in State-Run Industrial Enterprises,* requesting all local governments and central departments to select some enterprises to conduct the experiment in expanding enterprise autonomy in line with these regulations. By the end of 1979, the number of experimental enterprises had reached 4,200 nationwide. In 1980, the experiment expanded to 6,600 large- and medium-sized SOEs, which accounted for 60 percent of the national budgeted industrial output and 70 percent of national industrial profits. During the first few months of the experiment, employees in experimental enterprises were strongly motivated to increase output and profit. However, similarly to Russia's Kosygin reform of 1965, the limitations of the reform soon became apparent.

The enterprises that were entitled to certain autonomy under the new system had neither the constraint of fair market competition nor the guidance of a price system reflecting the degree of commodity scarcity. Therefore, allowing enterprise enthusiasm to fully manifest itself was not always conducive to the efficient allocation of resources of the society. Besides, in those days, the growth target of industry was set too high, generating great pressure to increase investment and resulting in exploding aggregate demand, soaring fiscal deficits, and economic disorder. Meanwhile, reform in non-state sectors and off-plan parts of the economy was under constant exploration and emerged gradually as the mainstream of reform.

1.3.2 The Shift of the Focus of Reform from "Inside the System" to "Outside the System"

In the early 1980s, amid macroeconomic disorder and stagnant SOE reform, a debate over planned economy and market regulation arose among leaders on economic affairs and economists, mainly between two views.

One view advocated plan-oriented reform to improve the planning and keep its dominant position. The unsuccessful reform of expanding enterprise autonomy in SOEs strengthened the position of statesmen and theorists advocating planned economy as the mainstay. They believed that the difficulties occurring at the time were caused by overemphasis on the roles of market and money and advocated reversing the market orientation of reform, improving planning, and tightening up planning discipline.

Economists advocating reform held an opposing view. They believed that the difficulties were not caused by market-oriented reform itself, but by the inappropriate way it was carried out. In fact, people advocating market-oriented reform had been aware of the shortcomings of reform measures with power-delegating and profit-sharing being the main way and with market mechanism applied only partially. In 1980, Xue Muqiao (1904 -2005), who was then in charge of the System Reform Office of the State Council, pointed out explicitly the limitations of the reform of power delegating and profit sharing. He proposed to focus the reform effort on the reform of the price control system and the reform of circulation channels, to gradually abolish the administrative pricing system and establish a commodity market and a financial market. The essence of his proposal was to establish an economic system based on the market.[20]

At that time, the statesmen and theorists advocating planned economy as the mainstay won the upper hand, resulting in the political negation of the proposition that socialist economy is commodity economy and the establishment of the guideline of planned economy as the mainstay with market regulation as the supplement.[21] Under such circumstances, the SOE reform lost its direction. Although the contracting experiments were still carried out in several industrial and commercial enterprises like Capital Steel,[22] the issues of giving enterprises full management authority, letting them assume full responsibility for profits and losses, and establishing a system of commodity economy were seldom mentioned.

When the reform of expanding enterprise autonomy in the state sector fell into plight, the Chinese leaders headed by Deng Xiaoping shifted the focus of reform from the urban state sector to the rural non-state sectors. A major measure was lifting the ban on contracting output quota to each household.[23]

In September 1980, the CCCPC decided to allow peasants to carry out the household contracting system (jiating chengbao jingyingzhi) at their will.[24] Within only two years, the household contracting system,[25] or the family farm system, replaced the people's commune system of three-tier ownership with production team as the basic unit among the overwhelming majority of the rural population. The rural economy took on an entirely new look. Township and village enterprises, mainly collective-owned, were springing up vigorously under such favorable circumstances. From then on, China adopted a new strategy different from the strategy of the Soviet Union and Eastern European countries that emphasized the reform of existing SOEs. Instead of taking major reform measures in the state sector, China focused its reform effort on non-state sectors, aiming at establishing market-oriented enterprises so as to let them drive the growth of the economy. The new strategy was called the strategy of "outside the system" proceeding "inside the system," or the strategy of incremental reform.

1.3.3 The All-Round Implementation of Incremental Reform

After the initial success of incremental reform in agriculture, the Chinese government applied it to other industries to promote the growth of non-state sectors. In addition, the already implemented policy of opening to the outside world generated a number of joint ventures of mixed ownership with foreign investment in coastal regions. Gradually, these non-state enterprises became the main force in China's economic development.

The strategy of developing non-state sectors was carried out in the ways discussed in the following three sections.

1.3.3.1 Encouraging the Growth of Non-state Enterprises

Allowing the growth of nonpublic sectors has always been a politically sensitive issue in China. Even in the process of bringing order out of chaos after 1976, such dogmas as "the larger in size and the more public in ownership, the better" and "the task of the communist party is to extinguish capitalism" remained dominant in people's minds. Therefore, at the beginning of reform, nonpublic sectors had to develop in roundabout ways.[26] Not until the legalization of "contracting output quota to each household" based on household operation were such ideological shackles broken. Together with the effort by the government to eliminate ideological and policy impediments to the development of non-state sectors, collective-owned and individual-owned township and village enterprises (TVEs) sprang up like mushrooms. Within the ten years between 1979 and 1988, the number of peasants working in industrial and commercial TVEs reached 100 million. Private enterprises also started to develop after 1983.

Non-state sectors immediately displayed their advantages on their emergence and grew with each passing day. In the 1980s, the growth rate of industrial output of non-state sectors was about twice that of the state sector. In the mid-1980s, non-state sectors, including the collective sector, the individual business sector, and the private sector, came to occupy a decisive position in both industrial production and the whole national economy. Their share in industrial output amounted to more than one-third (see Table 1.1). Their share grew even more rapidly in retail sales (see Table 1.2).

Table 1.1 **Gross Value of Industrial Output by Ownership** (%)

Year	1978	1980	1985	1990
State sector	77.6	76.0	64.9	54.6
Collective sector	22.4	23.5	32.1	35.6
Nonpublic sector*	0.0	0.5	3.0	9.8

* Nonpublic sectors refer to the collection of all non-state and noncollective economic entities, such as individual businesses, private enterprises, and foreign-invested enterprises.

Source: The National Bureau of Statistics, *China Statistical Yearbook* (Zhongguo tongji nianjian), Beijing: China Statistics Press, various years.

Table 1.2 **Total Retail Sales by Ownership** (%)

Year	1978	1980	1985	1990
State sector	54.6	51.4	40.4	39.6
Collective sector	43.3	44.6	37.2	31.7
Nonpublic sector*	2.1	4.0	22.4	28.7

* Nonpublic sectors refer to the collection of all non-state and noncollective economic entities, such as individual businesses, private enterprises, and foreign-invested enterprises.

Source: The National Bureau of Statistics, *China Statistical Yearbook* (Zhongguo tongji nianjian), Beijing: China Statistics Press, various years.

Since the economic activities of non-state sectors were mainly market-oriented, as non-state sectors developed, markets of a limited scope gradually came into being, and market forces began to play an increasingly important role in resource allocation.

1.3.3.2 Integrating Parts of China into the International Market by Opening to the Outside World

The development of a domestic market is always a long process in the economic development of any country. Because Old China had a very weak commercial culture and tradition, and thirty years of practicing planned economy in the People's Republic of China almost completely wiped out market forces, it was even harder to develop a domestic market in China. Under such circumstances, the Chinese government adopted an ingenious policy- getting parts of China with proper conditions integrated into the international market by opening them to the outside world. By doing so, the so-called advantages of backwardness could be exploited, competitive forces could be introduced, and the formation and expansion of the market could be accelerated.

In 1979, special policies and flexible measures were adopted for Guangdong Province and Fujian Province so that they could take advantage of their geographical closeness to Hong Kong and Macao. In 1980, four special economic zones- Shenzhen, Zhuhai, Shantou, and Xiamen- were set up. In 1985, fourteen coastal port cities were opened up. An open belt of considerable width along the coast, along the border, and along the Yangtze River gradually took shape after China started to open to the outside world.

Coastal open areas made great contributions to the growth of exports and the introduction of foreign technology and capital. China's foreign trade dependence ratio increased continuously (see Table 1.3). Foreign loans and foreign direct investment (FDI) started to flood into China.

Table 1.3 **Degree of Openness of China's Economy** (%)

Year	1978	1985	1990
Ratio of total exports and imports to GNP	9.9	24.2	31.9
Ratio of total exports and imports to GNP	5.2	14.7	14.8
Ratio of total exports to GNP	4.7	9.5	17.1

Source: The National Bureau of Statistics, *China Statistical Yearbook* (Zhongguo tongji nianjian), Beijing: China Statistics Press, various years.

In the initial stage of the reform and opening up, loans from foreign countries accounted for a greater part of foreign capital than FDI. In the first seven years of reform (1979-1985), total FDI was only US$7.4 billion, but it rose to US$18.6 billion between 1986 and 1991. Since the 1990s, FDI has increased rapidly and become the major form of incoming foreign capital.

Opening to the outside world facilitated domestic economic reform. Participating in the fierce competition of the international market gave business managerial personnel in China both a good understanding of the international market and a great sense of urgency to improve product quality and reduce production costs. To survive competition, it was necessary for Chinese enterprises to operate with more autonomy and to improve operation and management. Participation in competitive import and export markets also brought the domestic price structure closer to the international norm, and thus accelerated the price reform.

1.3.3.3 Implementing Regional Advancement of the Reform and Opening Up by Establishing Experimental Areas

Because market-oriented reform could not be carried out throughout the country simultaneously, and the reform had to be systematically conducted, setting up experimental areas in some coastal regions, where both developed markets and suitable conditions were available, was a good choice. When such areas applied the two approaches of the reform and opening up (encouraging the growth of non-state enterprises and integrating into the international market) in combination, a regional "microclimate" was created in which the new economic system could run effectively to a certain degree. Such successful experiences would also provide examples for inland areas and drive reform there. Facts proved that this was another effective approach to reform- regional advancement.

Regional advancement helped raise living standards of people in those areas considerably. In his speech, "Make a Success of Special Economic Zones and Open More Cities to the Outside World", in 1984, Deng Xiaoping predicted that coastal regions would be the first to become wealthy. He said, "We are not in a position to adopt the suggestion to encourage high wages and high consumption as our policy nationwide. However, as we develop the coastal areas successfully, we shall be able to increase people's incomes, which accordingly will lead to higher consumption. This is in conformity with the laws of development."[27] After more than ten years of development, by the early 1990s, a vast area with a rudimentary market and a vigorous economy had emerged along the Chinese coastline from the Liaodong Peninsula to Guangxi Province. Even inland, some preliminarily invigorated areas emerged. These areas became powerful bases for promoting market-oriented reform, where market force was projecting its impact in all directions. Incremental reform over more than a decade brought fast growth to the Chinese economy. During the twelve-year period from 1978 to 1990, on average, GDP grew by 14.6 percent annually, and the per-capita disposable income of urban residents grew by 13.1 percent annually (see Table 1.4).

Table 1.4 **Economic Growth during 1978-1990**

Year	1978	1980	1985	1990
GDP (RMB billion)	362.41	451.78	896.44	1854.79
Total industrial output (RMB billion)	423.7	515.4	971.6	2392.4
Total exports and imports (RMB billion)	35.50	57.00	206.67	556.01
Total exports (RMB billion)	16.76	27.12	80.89	298.58
Total retail sales of consumer goods (RMB billion)	155.86	214.00	430.50	830.01
Per-capita disposable income of urban residents (RMB)	343.4	477.6	739.1	1510.2

Source: The National Bureau of Statistics, *China Statistical Yearbook* (Zhongguo tongji nianjian), Beijing: China Statistics Press, various years.

1.3.4. The Emergence of the Dual-Track System

To ensure the survival and development of non-state enterprises in an environment where the system of allocating resources by plan had not yet been changed, the Chinese government made a special institutional arrangement, namely, the dual-track system in price and other aspects that enabled non-state enterprises to obtain a supply of raw materials and sell their products via a market.

In a planned economy, the means of production were transferred among units in the state sector by the state and price was just a tool for accounting among these units. Furthermore, consumer goods were uniformly distributed by state commercial departments with their prices uniformly set by price control departments at various levels. Therefore, there was almost no real market except country fair trade (free market), which accounted for only a very tiny proportion of the goods sold. Moreover, compared with the Soviet Union and Eastern European socialist countries, China's planned economy had even stronger administrative control. During a long period before 1979, the rationing system for daily necessities was so pervasive as to give China a strong flavor of an economy in kind. Such conditions had to change after TVEs, individual businesses, and other non-state enterprises emerged in the early 1980s. Otherwise, they would not be able to survive because of the absence of regular channels of supply and marketing.

In the initial phase of the reform and opening up, to solve the problems of the channels of supply and marketing and the pricing of products for non-state enterprises, various nonstandard practices were adopted, such as bartering between enterprises[28] in the name of cooperation. *Provisions on Enlarging the Decision-Making Power for Operation and Management of State-Run Industrial Enterprises* adopted by the State Council in 1979 allowed enterprises to sell products exceeding the planned quotas and thus opened the second track (the market track) of commodity circulation.[29]

In the early 1980s, non-state sectors expanded rapidly. By 1984, non-state enterprises accounted for 31 percent of the gross value of industrial output of the nation. They would not be able to survive without free trading in the market. Meanwhile, the scope of off-plan production and trading of SOEs was also expanding. *The Circular on Lifting Control over the Prices of Overfulfilled and Producer-Marketed Industrial Means of Production* issued by the State Administration of Commodity Prices and the State Bureau of Materials and Equipment in January 1985, allowed enterprises to sell and buy off-plan products at market prices, thus officially introducing the dual-track system for the supply and pricing of the means of production. Those state-owned enterprises enjoying the right to get planned allocation of materials and equipment before 1983 could still get the same quantities of materials and equipment as they did in 1983 (namely the "83 base quotas") at allocation prices. The parts exceeding the "83 base quotas" could be purchased in the market at market prices.

The formal establishment of the dual-track system provided non-state sectors with the basic operation environment for their survival and development. Such an institutional arrangement was compatible with the strategy of developing non-state sectors and played a positive role in the rapid development of non-state sectors and the whole national economy in the early stage of the reform and opening up.

With the increasing share of non-state sectors in the national economy, the quantities of commodities circulating outside the plan was also increasing. Therefore, the scope of market pricing was gradually enlarged. Meanwhile, as foreign trade expanded, the international market prices exerted great influence on the domestic market prices, gradually closing the gaps between relative prices in the domestic market and those in the international market. Commodities priced by plan no longer held a dominant position in total domestic commodity turnovers by the early 1990s.

Economists expressed different opinions regarding the merits and demerits of the dual-track system created by partial liberalization. American economists Kevin Murphy, Andrei Shleifer, and Robert Vishny believed that resources would be misallocated unless controls over prices were lifted all at once.[30] But Lawrence Lau, Qian Yingyi, and Gérard Roland proved the Pareto-improving nature of dual-track liberalization of prices based on a general equilibrium analysis.[31] Moreover, the introduction of the dual-track system might make reform more acceptable for those officials who benefited from it. A majority of economists believed that the dual-track system broke the monopoly of plan in resource allocation and granted newly born non-state sectors with room and conditions for growth, and thus definitely had more merits than demerits in the early stage of transition. However, it would also enable some people with powerful connections to gain from rent-seeking activities and to form social groups to block further marketization reform. Moreover, these corrupt activities would arouse public resentment and thus cause social instability.[32] In particular, the dual-track system created inequity in operation conditions between SOEs that could obtain subsidies in disguised forms and non-state enterprises that could only obtain raw materials, equipment, and loans at market prices. As a result, the dual-track system became an obstacle to the further growth of non-state sectors as these sectors developed.[33]

Hungarian economist Janos Kornai[34] believes that there are two pure strategies in compact form for the transition to a market economy: Strategy A is called the strategy of organic development whose most important task is to create favorable conditions for bottom-up development of the private sector and Strategy B is called the strategy of accelerated privatization whose most important task is to eliminate state ownership as fast as possible. He believed that the transition experiences of former socialist countries showed that Strategy A, which promoted organic development of the private sector, was the correct choice. And Strategy A can also be used in the analysis of the transition of socialist countries from a planned economy to a market economy. Incremental reform created conditions for the birth of new non-state enterprises, trained a large contingent of entrepreneurs, and greatly strengthened market forces. In addition, incremental reform played a positive role in promoting SOE reform.

1.3.5 The Negative Outcomes of the Long-Time Practice of the Incremental Reform

The strategy of incremental reform played a positive role in promoting China's reform in the 1980s. In contrast, the Soviet Union and Eastern European socialist countries fixated on the reform of the state sector. Because noticeable success in the reform of the state sector would be hard to achieve in a short term, it would be difficult for the state sector to simultaneously undergo reform and support the economic life of the whole society as the dominant sector of the economy. That was why, after ten to twenty years of reform, all these countries were trapped in a predicament. By comparison, China's reform of "outside the system" preceding "inside the system" had the following three advantages: (1) the rapid development of a group of enterprises and regions with economic vigor could make people and cadres feel the effects of reform in terms of their immediate self-interest and realize that only reform would lead to vigorous development; (2) the increasingly vibrant non-state sectors could absorb the unavoidable reform-related economic turbulence and maintain economic prosperity and political stability; and (3) the demonstration effect of and the competition pressure from non-state sectors could promote the reform of the original state sector. In a word, the development of non-state sectors and the development of the state sector promoted each other and created such a situation that the only way out was to maintain economic prosperity by sticking to marketization reform.

The purpose of the incremental reform strategy in China was to reduce obstacles to reform, to accumulate forces of reform, and to shorten the duration of reform so as to eventually establish a unified system of a market economy. Therefore, the state sector was sure to be reformed, after all. When the outside-the-system reform had paved the way for the all-round establishment of the institutions of a market economy, an overall and coordinated reform had to be launched in the state sector, which controlled most of the important resources of the national economy. This process ensured the all-round transition from a planned economy to a market economy. However, in the mid-1980s, when most reformers did not have a clear theoretical understanding of market-oriented reform and were still accustomed to reform based on "crossing the river by groping for the stones," it was very difficult for most people to accept the necessity of switching the reform strategy.

Because the reform strategy failed to be switched in time, intense conflicts occurred between the invigorated outside-the-system sectors and the inside-the-system sectors that were still fettered by the traditional economic system, many loopholes existed in the economic system, and stable economic development was constantly threatened. As Masahiko Aoki (1938-) pointed out in *Comparative Institutional Analysis: A New Approach to Economic System,*[35] because various institutions in a system are strategically complementary, when one or more institutions change, other institutions either change accordingly or obstruct the functioning of the new institutions due to their incompatibility with the new institutions. Therefore, system change should be of overall advancement in nature although the change can be implemented in steps. Otherwise, the system will run only at enormous cost.

The negative effects of the sluggish reform of the state sector and the coexistence of the two tracks were mainly manifested in the following ways:

1. Financial conditions of SOEs deteriorated. Although non-state sectors had achieved considerable progress since 1979, the development of SOEs lagged far behind, mainly for two reasons. First, the state sector retained much of the enterprise system of the traditional planned economy, its improvement in efficiency was very limited, and its output growth was mainly supported by vast inputs of resources, especially investment. Second, the state sector carried out the reform of power-delegating and profit-sharing to expand enterprise autonomy, but did not establish effective constraints of ownership and market competition, which led to insider control[36] and further softened budget constraint over SOEs.[37] Thus, the state sector as the mainstay of the national economy became increasingly feeble.

2. The pressure of inflation always existed and hyperinflation broke out from time to time. Since 1979, the rapid growth of China's economy was always accompanied by wild economic fluctuations. The persistence of a huge fiscal deficit made hyperinflation a constant threat. The fiscal deficit was the result of deteriorating financial conditions of the state sector as the main source of fiscal revenue and the lack of a complete transformation of the state fiscal system and the heavy burden of fiscal expenditure. Meanwhile, because of the coexistence of a planned economy and a market economy, the effectiveness of planning control greatly decreased while macroeconomic control compatible with the market system was yet to be established. This situation meant that the monetary authorities were unable to achieve the monetary policy goals and to maintain macroeconomic stability. These factors caused lasting pressure of hyperinflation in China's dual-track economy. Once the economic growth rate reached double digits, hyperinflation would break out soon.

3. Rampant rent-seeking activities (accumulating personal wealth by abusing public power) and administrative corruption were widespread. The coexistence of a command economy and a market economy provided abundant opportunities for rent-seeking activities[38] and other forms of corruption. The crucial causes of the problem were that (1) as a result of the strategy of "outside the system" preceding "inside the system," the economy had been monetized to a large extent, but

administrative power that had a dominant position in the planned economy were still interfering with market transactions; (2) reform had created independent enterprises, but most resources, such as means of production, land, investment, and credit, were still under the control of the government and were still distributed by administrative means. Thus, the whole economy became a gigantic hotbed of rent-seeking activities.

4. The gap between the rich and the poor continued to widen. Since the beginning of the reform and opening up, the average income level of Chinese residents increased considerably, but the income gap among them widened rapidly as well. The main reasons were (1) the incremental reform strategy applied different policies to different regions, departments, and economic sectors, resulting in rapid widening of the income gap among different social groups; (2) the negative factors mentioned earlier, such as deteriorating financial conditions of SOEs, hyperinflation, and rampant corruption, widened the gap between the rich and the poor; and (3) huge waste and low efficiency resulting from the sluggish reform of urban industrial and commercial sectors made it impossible to create enough employment opportunities to absorb rural surplus laborers, which led to more and more agricultural laborers crowded on less and less arable land, unable to shake off poverty and attain prosperity.

In sum, sustainable and stable economic growth was threatened by the aforementioned contradictions, which, once intensified, might result in social and political upheavals.

1.4
Strategy of "Overall Advancement"
(1994 to Present)

Maintaining the dual-track system received praises from some people both at home and abroad[39] and was particularly supported by many local officials and SOE leaders who benefited from it. However, its limitation and negative effects became increasingly obvious. Initiated by Deng Xiaoping, an attempt at launching all-round reform was made in the mid-1980s.

1.4.1 The Attempt at Changing Reform Strategy and Launching All-Round Reform in 1984-1986

As an advocate of incremental reform, Deng Xiaoping did not rest on the early achievements in non-state sectors. When non-state sectors became strong enough to provide support to all-round reform, Deng Xiaoping proposed to shift the strategic focus of reform to the state sector.

When meeting guests from Japan in June 1984, Deng Xiaoping, as Chairman of the Military Commission of the CCCPC and Chairman of the Advisory Commission of the CCCPC, pointed out that after the success of reform in rural China, "the urban reform will include not only industry and commerce but science and technology, education, and all other fields of endeavor as well."[40] The Third Plenary Session of the 12th CCCPC, held in October 1984, discussed the implementation of this shift and adopted the *Decision of the CCCPC on Reform of the Economic System*. With this, the strategic focus of China's reform shifted from rural to urban areas.

The Decision of the CCCPC on Reform of the Economic System, made at the Third Plenary Session of the 12th CCCPC, declared the start of all-round reform focusing on urban areas and defined establishing and developing a socialist commodity economy as the goal of reform and thus was a landmark in the history of China's reform.

To carry out the *Decision*, the *Proposal for the Seventh Five-Year Plan* (1986-1990) (hereinafter the Proposal) was put forward at the National Conference of the CPC in 1985. The Proposal demanded reform in three interrelated aspects: (1) changing enterprises into business operators with full management authority and full responsibility for profits and losses; (2) improving the market system; and (3) establishing a macroeco-nomic control system functioning mainly by indirect means. The *Proposal* demanded that "effort should be made to lay the foundation for a vigorous socialist economic system in the following five or more years." The *Seventh Five-Year Plan* formulated according to the *Proposal* defined details of the aforementioned requirements.

At the beginning of 1986, Zhao Ziyang (1919-2005), then Premier of the State Council, put forward a tentative plan of coordinated reform that focused on price, taxation, and fiscal systems. He declared that the guideline for the State Council in

1986 was to improve macroeconomic management on the premise of continuously reinforcing and improving macro-control, to improve supply conditions on the premise of restraining demands, and to make preparation for achieving a decisive progress of reform in 1987.[41] Afterwards, Zhao delivered several important speeches on the reform situation and requirements during the earlier stage of the *Seventh Five-Year Plan*. He pointed out that it might be harmful to let the old and new systems coexist and conflict with each other for too long a time. Therefore, significant measures should be taken to establish the dominance of the new system in 1987 and 1988. With this aim, he argued that a big stride forward was needed to establish the market system and to practice indirect control to enable enterprises to really assume full responsibility for profits and losses and to compete on a more or less equal footing. "To be more specific, next year's reform may be designed and studied in the following three aspects: price, taxation, and government finance. They are interrelated... Reform of the price system is the key and other reforms should center on it."[42]

To implement the proposed coordinated reform, the State Council set up the Economic System Reform Program Design Office in April 1986. Under the direct leadership of the State Council and the CCCPC Financial and Economic Leading Group, the office drew up programs for coordinated reform during the earlier stage of the Seventh Five-Year Plan with a focus on price, taxation, government finance, banking, and foreign trade. The program for the price reform was to start with prices of the means of production in 1987. The specific measures of the price reform were similar to what Czechoslovakia adopted in the mid-1960s, which Ota Sik had introduced to his Chinese colleagues in 1981: "adjustment first and liberalization second."[43]

In other words, first, adjust prices in an all-round way based on calculation; then, spend one or two years to liberalize prices in an all-round way so as to merge the two tracks. The main measures taken in the fiscal system were to change the current revenue-sharing system into a tax-sharing system, and to introduce value-added tax.[44]

In August 1986, these programs were approved at the executive meeting of the State Council and endorsed by Deng Xiaoping, who, on September 13, 1986, spoke highly of them when hearing the report of the CCCPC Financial and Economic Leading Group and instructed officials to carry them out accordingly. However, Zhao Ziyang, the leader of the State Council, changed his mind in October that year. Instead of implementing coordinated reform in price, taxation, government finance, banking, and foreign trade, he changed direction to focus on the reform of SOEs and implemented the so-called "five contracting/responsibility systems"[45] in 1987 and 1988 and thus returned to the old practice of maintaining the coexistence of a market economy and a planned economy in the hope of improving the performance of the state sector with some trivial repairs. The loss of this golden opportunity to push reform forward resulted in the economic crisis of 1988, the political disturbances of 1989, and the ensuing resurgence of conservative thinking.[46]

1.4.2 The Third Plenary Session of the 14th CCCPC Started a New Era of Overall Advancement of Reform

After the economic crisis of 1988 and the political disturbances of 1989, some conservative statesmen and theorists blamed these upheavals on market-oriented reform. They branded "abolishing the planned economy and realizing marketization" as "changing the socialist system and implementing a capitalist system."[47] Accordingly, another resurgence of conservative thinking occurred. A new upsurge of the reform and opening up did not take place until the beginning of 1992, when Deng Xiaoping made his famous South China speeches[48] to promote the reform and opening up.

In October 1992, the 14th National Congress of the CPC set the reform target of establishing a socialist market economy. In November 1993, the *Decision on Issues Regarding the Establishment of a Socialist Market Economic System* was adopted at the Third Plenary Session of the 14th CCCPC, and important breakthroughs were made on the following issues.

First, a new reform strategy of "overall advancement with key breakthroughs" was explicitly put forward, demanding that the reform should not be confined to peripheral issues, but firmly carried out in the state sector and that a socialist market economic system should begin to take shape by the end of the twentieth century.

A Glimpse Into China's Long March Toward A Market Economy

Second, a blueprint was made for reforms in five key areas of the fiscal and taxation system, the banking system, the foreign exchange control system, the enterprise system, and the social security system.

Reform of fiscal system aims at transforming the existing fiscal responsibility system (also called the central-local fiscal responsibility system) into a "tax-sharing system" based on a rationalized division of power and responsibility between the central and local governments. And reform of tax system aims at standardizing the taxation system in accordance with the principle of unified tax law, equitable tax burden, simplified tax structure, and fair division of power so as to establish a taxation system that meets the requirement of a market economy in order to promote fair competition.

The main tasks of the reform of financial banking system are to establish a banking system in which state-owned commercial banks are kept as the mainstay, diverse forms of financial institutions are allowed to develop side by side, and policy-related banking is separated from commercial banking; also to establish a unified and open system of financial markets with orderly competition and strict regulation. And specific tasks include: (1) to establish a central bank system that can carry out monetary policy independently under the leadership of the central government; (2) to commercialize the operation of the existing state-owned specialized banks and diversify commercial banks; and (3) to set up policy banks such as the China Development Bank, the Export-Import Bank of China, and the Agricultural Development Bank of China so as to take over the policy-related business previously done by the specialized banks of raising funds at low interest rates for those projects of long construction cycle, low profitability, but significant externalities within a state-designated scope.

China's central government decided to take two steps in reforming the foreign exchange control system. First, to abolish the dual exchange rate system in domestic and foreign enterprises in sequence for merging the two exchange rates and achieving the managed convertibility of RMB under the current account. Second, to abolish control over capital flow and make RMB a fully convertible currency when the time is right.

As to the Reform of SOEs, The *Decision* pointed out that "the operation mechanism of SOEs must be further transformed and a modern enterprise system, which is characterized by clearly established property rights, well defined power and responsibility, separation of enterprise from government, and scientific management, must be established." Later, the *Company Law of the People's Republic of China* was passed by the National People's Congress according to the *Decision*.

As to the establishment of a new social security system, it was decided to set up a multi-layer social security system to include social insurance, social relief, social welfare, special care and placement, social mutual aid, and private saving security, in which a system combining social pooling funds with individual accounts was to be instituted for old-age pension and medical insurance for urban workers.

1.4.3 In-Depth Development of the Overall Advancement Strategy

By the mid-1990s, China's reform had made significant progress in establishing a macro-economic control system and adjusting the ownership structure. The fundamental indicator of the progress was that the state sector no longer monopolized the whole economy, and its share in the national economy was significantly reduced. However, the bottleneck to reform-the establishment of the ownership foundation of a market economy-had not been broken. As late as 1993, most scarce economic resources were still in the hands of the government and SOEs, despite the fact that the state sector accounted for less than half of GDP. One example was that the state sector consumed more than 70 percent of bank loans. In addition, the dominance of the government and SOEs in the national economy made it impossible to establish a sound banking system, a sound fiscal and taxation system, etc., which were compatible with a market economy.

The root cause of this situation was that the old state sector, or the State Syndicate as proposed in Lenin's *State and Revolution*, or the Party-State Inc. in modern language, is the core of the old system, and vested interests attached to it are deep-rooted. Some people, especially elites of the society, have high stakes in maintaining this system. If people with vested interests in the old system do not care about the interests of the entire society as much as they care about their own, they will use all kinds of excuses (including political excuses) to block the process of reform and restructuring of the state sector. Therefore, reform and restructuring will encounter a great deal of resistance.

Another historic breakthrough in reform of the state sector was made at the 15th National Congress of the CPC in 1997. At the congress, the Soviet viewpoint that "the higher the proportion of the state sector in the national economy, the better" was discarded; keeping public ownership as the mainstay of the economy and allowing diverse forms of ownership to develop side by side was stipulated as the basic economic system in the primary stage of socialism for at least one hundred years.

Accordingly, the third-generation leader Jiang Zemin called for adjustment and improvement of the ownership structure of the national economy and the establishment of a long-term basic economic system based on the *Three-Favorable Principle* (i.e., whether it promotes the growth of productive forces in a socialist society, increases the overall strength of the socialist state, and raises the people's living standards). The three items of adjustment were (1) to reduce the scope of the state sector and to withdraw state capital from industries nonessential to the national economy; (2) to seek various forms for materializing public ownership that can greatly promote the growth of the productive forces and to develop diverse forms of public ownership; and (3) to encourage the development of nonpublic sectors of the economy such as the individual business sector and the private sector and to make them important components of a socialist market economy.

In 1998, the aforementioned decision of the 15th National Congress of the CPC was incorporated into the Amendments to the Constitution of the People's Republic of China, specifically, "In the primary stage of socialism, the State upholds the basic economic system of keeping public ownership as the mainstay of the economy and allowing diverse forms of ownership to develop side by side... Nonpublic sectors of the economy, such as the individual business sector and the private sector, within the limits prescribed by law, are important components of a socialist market economy... The State protects the lawful rights and interests of the individual business sector and the private sector."

At the turn of twenty-first century, an outline for a market economy based on mixed ownership emerged (see Table 1.5).

Table 1.5 **GDP by Ownership (%)**[49]

Year	State sector	Collective sector	Nonpublic sector
1990	47.7	18.5	33.8
1995	42.1	20.2	37.7
1996	40.4	21.3	38.3
1997	38.4	22.1	39.5
1998	38.9	19.3	41.9
1999	37.4	18.4	44.2
2000	37.3	16.5	46.2
2001	37.9	14.6	47.5

** Nonpublic sectors refer to the collection of all non-state and noncollective economic entities.
Source: The National Bureau of Statistics, *China Statistical Yearbook* (Zhongguo tongji nianjian), Beijing: China Statistics Press, various years.

At this moment, the issue about how to ensure that the market economy established in China was a good market economy instead of a bad market economy was raised. In other words, social and political reforms in line with marketization reform were placed on the agenda.

Such demand has been echoed by the decisions of leading organs of the party and the government. In 1997, the 15th National Congress of the CPC called for "building a socialist country under the rule of law." In 2002, the 16th National Congress of the CPC put forward requirements to push political reform forward, to promote political civilization, to develop democratic politics, and to build a country under the rule of law.

The Decision on Issues Regarding the Improvement of the Socialist Market Economic System by the Third Plenary Session of the 16th CCCPC in September 2003 was a programmatic document for social and political reforms. It indicated that China's economic, social, and political reforms will continue to advance in an all-round way in the future.

Notes and References

1. During May to July 1951, Liu Shaoqi, according to Mao Zedong's opinion, expounded to the party's senior leaders the guiding principle of "preparation for three years and construction for ten years." See Liu Shaoqi, "Preparation for Three Years and Construction for Ten Years (San nian zhunbei, shi nian jianshe);" "Speech at Chun'ouzhai (Chun'ouzhai tanhua)," the Party Literature Research Center of the CCCPC (ed.), *Liu Shaoqi on Economic Construction in New China* (Liu Shaoqi lun xin Zhongguo jingji jianshe), Beijing: Central Party Literature Publishing House, 1993, pp. 178-210.

2. Totalism is a concept introduced by Professor Tang Tsou (1918 - 1999) of the University of Chicago. Different from the concept of "totalitarianism" in Western political science, it refers to a particular state that controls every part of social life with powerful political organizations so as to transform or rebuild the society. See Tang Tsou, *Twentieth Century Chinese Politics: From the Perspectives of Macro-history and Micromechanism Analysis* (Ershi shiji Zhongguo zhengzhi: Cong hongguan lishi yu weiguan xingdong jiaodu kan), Hong Kong: Oxford University Press, 1994.

3. Chen Yun, " New Issues after the Completion of Socialist Transformation in the Main (Shehuizhuyi gaizao jiben wancheng yihou de xin wenti) (1956)," *Selected Works of Chen Yun* (Chen Yun wenxuan) (1956-1985), Beijing: People's Publishing House, 1986, pp. 1-13.

4. Zhou Taihe et al., *Economic System Reform in Contemporary China* (Dangdai Zhongguo de jingji tizhi gaige), Beijing: China Social Sciences Press, 1984.

5. Under this system, after achieving its quotas of total output value, profit, and remittance of profit, each enterprise could draw an enterprise incentive fund not less than 4 percent of the total wage bill from the planned profit and above-quota profit in accordance with a department-specific proportion set by the state. However, the enterprise incentive fund should not exceed 10 percent of the total wage bill.

6. The profit retention proportion was first calculated for each department in charge. The future profit retention proportion is the total of the four items of expenditure during the First Five-Year Plan period (including enterprise incentive fund as well as technological upgrading and sporadic capital construction appropriated by the finance, etc.) and 40 percent of retained above-quota profit divided by total achieved profit of the same period. Once determined, the retention proportion remains unchanged for five years. Within the scope of the total retention, each department in charge could decide the retention proportion for each enterprise according to its specific conditions.

7. On November 18, 1957, Mao Zedong pointed out in his speech at the Moscow Meeting of Representatives of the Communist and Workers' Parties that "Comrade Khrushchev told us that the Soviet Union can surpass America within 15 years. So I suppose we can catch up with or surpass Britain within 15 years." (Mao Zedong, "Speech at the Moscow Meeting of Representatives of the Communist and Workers' Parties (Zai Mosike Gongchandang he Gongrendang Daibiao Huiyi shang de jianghua)," *Mao Zedong's Manuscripts since the*

Founding of the PRC (Jianguo yilai Mao Zedong wengao), Vol. 6, Beijing: Central Party Literature Publishing House, 1992, p. 635.) Afterwards, the supposed time period was shortened with the launch of the Great Leap Forward. In April 1958, Mao Zedong claimed that "It will not take as long as supposed before to catch up with capitalist countries in the industrial and agricultural production." "It will take ten years to catch up with Britain and ten more years to catch up with America." (Mao Zedong, "Introduction to a Cooperative (Jieshao yi ge hezuoshe)," *Mao Zedong's Manuscripts since the Founding of the PRC* (Jianguo yilai Mao Zedong wengao), Vol. 7, Beijing: Central Party Literature Publishing House, 1992, p. 177 - 179.) He declared at the enlarged meeting of the Military Commission of the CCCPC on June 21, 1958 that "We will surpass Britain in the main within 3 years and surpass America within 10 years. It is quite sure." (Bo Yibo, *Review of Some Important Decisions and Events* (Ruogan zhongda juece yu shijian de huigu), Vol. 2, Beijing: The Central Party School Publishing House, 1993, p. 702.)

8. According to Mao Zedong, two fundamental principles of the Great Leap Forward were "taking grain as the key link and ensuring an all-round development" and "taking steel as the key link to drive everything else forward." Impractical quotas were set for grain and steel production as a result. In 1958, the Fifteen-Year Program Compendium for Socialist Construction (Draft) (Shiwunian shehuizhuyi jianshe gangyao (chugao)), formulated by the CCCPC, required that by 1972, the yield of grain per mu (a Chinese unit of area equal to 1/15 of a hectare or 1/6 of an acre) nationwide should be 2,500 to 5,000 kg; the yield of cotton permu be 250 to 500 kg; and arable land nationwide be divided into three parts of one-third each: one-third for crops; one-third fallow or for green manure crops; and one-third for trees and grasses. In June 1958, Mao Zedong himself worked out a plan for steel production: to reach 11 million tons m 1958, more than twice the 5.35 million tons produced m 1957; to reach 25 milliontons m 1959, surpassing Britain; and to reach 60 million tons m 1962. (Bo Yibo, *Review of Some Important Decisions and Events* (Ruogan zhongda juece yu shijian de huigu), Vol. 2, Beijing: The Central Party School Publishing House, 1993, pp. 679-702.)

9. Zhou Taihe et al., *Economic System Reform in Contemporary China* (Dangdai Zhongguo de jingji tizhi gaige), Beijing: China Social Sciences Press, 1984, pp. 73-75.

10. Estimates by various scholars put the number of "abnormal deaths" nationwide caused by the Great Leap Forward and the People's Communes Campaign between fifteen and thirty million. See Sun Yefang, "Strengthen Statistics Work and Reform the Statistics System (Jiaqiang tongji gongzuo, gaige tongji tizhi), " *Journal of Economic Management*, 1981, No. 2. See also Basil Ashton et al., "Famine in China, 1958-1961," Population and Development Review, 1984, Vol. 10, No. 4; Denis Twitchett and John K. Fairbank, The Cambridge History of China: Volume 14, The People's Republic, Part 1, The Emergence of Revolutionary China, 1949-1965, Cambridge: Cambridge University Press, 1987.

11. Liu Shaoqi, "Report at the Enlarged Working Conference of the CCCPC (Zai Kuoda de Zhongyang

当代中国经济改革

文化中国

Gongzuo Huiyi shang de baogao) (January 1962)," *Selected Works of Liu Shaoqi* (Liu Shaoqi xuanji), Vol. 2, Beijing: The Central Party School Publishing House, 1985, p. 349.

12. Zhou Taihe and others summarized the actions and outcomes of this "big change in the economic system focusing on blind transfer to lower levels" as three parts: "First, blindly transferring enterprises to lower levels and intensifying the chaos m operation and management. Second, practicing the 'all-round responsibility system' in fiscal revenue and expenditure, materials and equipment allocation, and capital investment and achieving no expected results. Third, simplifying the taxation, credit, and labor-wage systems and weakening the role of economic levers." (See Zhou Taihe et al., *Economic System Reform in Contemporary China* (Dangdai Zhongguo de jingji tizhi gaige), Beijing: China Social Sciences Press, 1984, pp. 134-146.)

13. Wu Jinglian, "On Urban Economic Reform-Speech at the Cadres Conference in Shenyang on August 2, 1984 (Lun chengshi jingji gaige-1984 nian 8 yue 2 ri zai Shenyang Shi Ganbu Huiyi shang suozuo baogao)," *Research on Issues of Economic Reform* (Jingji gaige wenti tansuo), Beijing: China Outlook Press, 1987, pp. 218-227. See also Wu Jinglian, "The Key Issue in Urban Reform Is Invigorating Enterprises-Speech at the Weekly Forum of World Economic Herald in Shanghai on September 15, 1984 (Chengshi gaige de guanjian shi zengqiang qiye de huoli-1984 nian 9 yue 15 ri zai Shanghai Shijie Jingji Daobao Xingqi Jiangyanhui shang de baogao)," *World Economy Herald*, September 24, 1984 or *Selected Works of Wu Jinglian* (Wu Jinglian xuanji), Taiyuan: Shanxi People's Publishing House, 1989, pp. 389-413. See also Lou Jiwei, "Decentralization at Local Government Level Should Not Be Practiced Any More (Ying bimian jixu zou difang fenquan de daolu) (1985)," Wu Jinglian, Zhou Xiaochuan et al., *Overall Design of the Reform of China's Economic System* (Zhongguo jingji gaige de zhengti sheji), Beijing: China Outlook Press, 1988, pp. 204-216.

14. Wu Jinglian pointed out, "All genuine reforms in socialist countries are market-oriented." See Wu Jinglian, "The Postscript to 'Research on Issues of Economic Reform' (Jingji Gaige Wenti Tansuo houji) (June 17, 1986)," *Research on Issues of Economic Reform* (Jingji gaige wenti tansuo), Beijing: China Outlook Press, 1987, pp. 434-437.

15. As early as the 1960s and 1970s, the distinction between economic decentralization and administrative decentralization had been made by some Western scholars. For example, American scholar Herbert Franz Schurmann pointed out in 1966 that there were two types of decentralization in socialist economies. Decentralization I delegated decision-making power down to production units, whereas Decentralization II delegated power only to subordinate administrative units. He believed that when China started to think about system reform in 1956, the idea of Decentralization I dominated; the reform decided in 1957 was a mix of Decentralization I and Decentralization II; However, the reform actually carried out in 1958 was Decentralization II. This mode of decentralization led to chaos, and recentralization became necessary. See Herbert Franz Schurmann, *Ideology and Organization in Communist China*, Berkeley: University of Califormia Press, 1966. In 1977, American comparative

economist Morris Bornstein pointed out in his testimony to the U.S. Congress on economic reforms in Eastern Europe that there were two different concepts of decentralization: administrative decentralization and enonmic decentralization. The former aimed to improve the exising administrative measures to make them more effective, and the latter aimed to switch to a regulated market economy. See Morris Bornstein, "Economic Reform in Eastern Europe", *Eastern-European Economies Post-Helsinki*, Washington, D.C.: U.S. Government Publishing Office, 1977, pp. 102-134.

16. The negative consequences of administrative decentralization are thoroughly discussed in Wu Jinglian and Liu Jirui's book, *On Competitive Market System* (Lun jingzhengxing shichang tizhi), Beijing: China Financial and Economic Publishing House, 1991,pp. 154-168. Barriers between regions and market segmentation remained major obstacles to the formation of a unified national market until China's entry into the WTO in 2001. Supachai Panitchpakdi, Director-General of the WTO, showed the severity of the situation by the example of Shanghai and Wuhan municipal governments imposing extra license fee and sales tax on cars produced by each other to protect local producers. (Supachai Panitchpakdi and Mark L. Clifford, *China and the WTO: Changing China Changing World Trade.*)

17. Path dependence is originally a feature of system evolution discovered in the study of nonlinear systems. Douglass C. North generalized this concept to institutional change. He pointed out that "the present choice set is narrowed by choices made m the past." Once institutional change is on a certain path, its existing direction will reinforce itself m later development. Hence, economic and political institutions may improve along the right path, or go away from their goals by following a wrong path. Or even worse, they may be locked m an inefficient state. Once locked in, it will be extremely difficult to exit. North claimed that turning of existing direction usually needs external force, such as an exogenous variable, or a regime change. See Wu Jinglian. "Path Dependence and China's Reform-Comments on the Speech of Professor North (Lujing yilai yu Zhongguo gaige-dui Nuosi Jiaoshou jiangyan de pinglun)," *Where to Find Macro Wisdom.* (Hechu xunqiu dazhihui), Beijing: Joint Publishing, 1997, p. 351-358.

18. Xu Chenggang and Qian Yingyi clarified their viewpoints in their paper "Why Is China's Economic Reform Different from Others: M-Form Hierarchy and the Entry and Expansion of Non-state Sectors (Zhongguo jingji gaige weishenme yuzhongbu-tong-M xing de cengjizhi he feiguoyou bumen de jinru yu kuozhang) (1993)," Qian Yingyi, *Modern Economics and China's Reform* (Xiandai jingjixue yu Zhongguo jingji gaige), Beijing: China Renmin University Press, 2003. They claimed that, different from Eastern Europe and the Soviet Union that adopted a "U-form economic structure" organized on the basis of functional and specialized departments, China, since 1958, adopted an "M-form economic structure" based on geographical regions in a multi-tier and multi-region fashion. This was the main reason for the continuous entry and vigorous expansion of non-state sectors during China's reform.

19. "Communique of the Third Plenary Session of the 11th CCCPC (Zhongguo Gongchandang Di Shiyi Jie Zhongyang Weiyuanhui Di San Ci Quanti Huiyi gongbao) (December 22, 1978)," the Party Literature Research Center of the CCCPC (ed.), *A Selection of Important Documents since the Third Plenary Session* (Sanzhongquanhui yilai zhongyao wenxian xuanbian), Beijing: People's Publishing House, 1982.

20. Xue Muqiao, "Some Opinions on Economic System Reform (Guanyu jingji tizhi gaige de yixie yijian) (June 1980);" "Price Readjustment and Reform of the Price Control System (Tiaozheng wujia he wujia guanli tizhi de gaige) (July 1980)," *On China's Economic System Reform* (Lun Zhongguo jingji tizhi gaige), Tianjin: Tianjin People's Publishing House, 1990, pp. 211-218, 325-340.

21. See the interview between *Hundred Year Tide* magazine and Wu Jinglian: "About the Debate between Planned Economy and Market Economy (Guanyu jihua jingji yu shichang jingji de lunzheng)," Hundred Year Tide (Bai nian chao), 1998, No. 2, pp. 1-10. Under the circumstances, then, at the 12th National Congress of the CPC m September 1982, Hu Yaobang had to affirm in his report on behalf of the CCCPC that "a fundamental issue in economic system reform is to adhere to the principle of 'planned economy as the mainstay with market regulation as a supplement.'" When *Selected Works of Deng Xiaoping (1975 - 1982)* was published in 1983, the wording of "combining plan regulation and market regulation" in Deng Xiaoping's 1980 article of The Present Situation and the Tasks Before Us had to be changed to "letting market regulation play a supplementary role under the guidance of planned economy." The wording was not changed back until Deng Xiaoping himself reviewed the new edition of *Selected Works of Deng Xiaoping* in 1994.

22. In May 1979, six departments including the State Economic Commission and the Ministry of 2Finance selected eight SOEs including Capital Steel for the experiment of enterprise reform featured by profit retention in Beijing, Tianjin, Shanghai, etc. In 1981, Capital Steel started to experiment m the practice of "responsibility for progressive quota of turned-in profits," under which the enterprise would guarantee a turned-in profit with an annual growth rate of 7 percent and retain above-quota profit and the state would not provide investment to the enterprise by fiscal allocation any more. This practice was carried out until the mid-1990s.

23. According to the Decision of the CCCPC on Issues Regarding Accelerating the Development of Agriculture, which was discussed at the Third Plenary Session of the 11th CCCPC in December 1978 and adopted at the Fourth Plenary Session of the 11th CCCPC in September 1979, "distributing land for individual farming" and "contracting output quota to each household" in ordinary areas were explicitly prohibited. The Decision wrote: "Distributing land for individual farming shall not be allowed. Contracting output quota to each household shall not be practiced except for some special cases in sideline production and for some isolated households in remote mountainous areas."

24. In September 1980, the CCCPC transmitted with endorsement Some Issues Regarding Further Strengthening and Improving the Responsibility System for Agricultural Production (Summary of the Symposium of First Secretaries of Party Committees of Provinces, Municipalities, and Autonomous Regions on September 14 to 22, 1980), which pointed out that "In those remote mountainous areas and poverty-stricken backward regions and in those production teams that have been relying on state-resold grain for food, loans for production, and social relief for living for a long period of time, if the masses have lost their confidence m the collective and request contracting output quota to each household, such requests should be granted and either contracting output quota to each household or contracting responsibility to each household may be practiced and such arrangements are to be kept unchanged for a fairly long period of time." (See the Party Literature Research Center of the CCCPC (ed.), *A Selection of Important Documents since the Third Plenary Session* (Sanzhongquanhui yilai zhongyao wenxian xuanbian), Beijing: People's Publishing House, 1982, p. 507.)

25. In addition to its popular name of baochan daohu (contracting output quota to each household), jiating chengbao jingyingzhi (the household contracting system) has several other names in the Chinese language, a clear indication of the spontaneous, multi-origin and bottom-up nature of Chinese rural reform. See Chapter Four for more information.

26. For instance, in the late 1970s, argument for allowing private merchants to engage in long-distance transport of goods for sale was that it could serve as an expedient measure to solve the problem of unemployment. Argument for allowing private businesses to hire labor was a numerical example found in Chapter 9, Volume 1 of Karl Marx's *The Capital*, which demonstrates how to calculate the exploitation rate with assumed figures and shows that an employer with fewer than eight employees is not an exploiter but still an individual laborer. Using that numerical example, economists advocating reform succeeded in convincing the political leaders to loosen the restriction on hiring labor. Since 1980, the Chinese government drew a distinction between individual enterprises with fewer than eight employees and larger private enterprises, and called the former "individual business sector," as opposed to the then prohibited "private sector."

27. Deng Xiaoping, "Make a Success of Special Economic Zones and Open More Cities to the Outside World (Banhao jingji tequ, zengjia duiwai kaifang chengshi) (February 1984)," *Selected Works of Deng Xiaoping* (Deng Xiaoping wenxuan), Vol. 3, Beijing: People's Publishing House, p. 52.

28. Bartering between enterprises means that one enterprise exchanges its products for necessary equipment and raw materials with another enterprise.

29. In July 1979, *Provisions on Enlarging the Decision-Making Power for Operation and Management of State-Run Industrial Enterprises* (Guanyu kuoda guoying gongye qiye jingying guanli zizhuquan de ruogan guiding) granted enterprises limited power to sell and price their off-plan products.

Specifically, "Products made according to the supplementary plan are first to fill the orders from commercial, foreign trade, and materials and equipment departments. Enterprises can sell their products not purchased by commercial, foreign trade, and materials and equipment departments at the price set by the State, or let commercial, foreign trade, and material departments sell their products on a commission basis. If an enterprise has excess productive capacity, it may process supplied materials for other enterprises."

30. Kevin M. Murphy, Andrei Shleifer, and Robert W. Vishny, "The Transition to a Market Economy: Pitfalls of Partial Reform," *The Quarterly Journal of Economics*, August 1992, Vol. 107, No. 3, pp. 889-906.

31. Lawrence J. Lau, Qian Yingyi, and Gérard Roland, "Pareto-Improving Economic Reforms through Dual-Track Liberalization," *Economics Letter*, 1997, Vol. 55, No. 2, pp. 285-292; "Reform without Losers: An Interpretation of China's Dual-Track Ap-proach to Transition," *Journal of Political Economy*, February 2000, Vol. 108, No. 1, pp. 120-143. Using a model based on industrial organization theory, Zhang Jun explained the role of the dual-track system m the continuous growth of China's industrial output. He believed that the plan track ensured the full exploitation of the existing productive capacity of the state sector and the achievement of planned output while the market track increased output and gradually establish a competitive market structure by introducing non-state sectors to compete with the state sector. Therefore, "pitfalls of partial liberalization of prices" and recession caused by the "Shock Therapy" were avoided. See Zhang Jun, *Introduction to China's Transitional Economy* (Zhong-guo guodu jingji daolun), Shanghai: Lixin Accounting Press, 1996, pp. 59-78; *Economics of Dual-Track System: China's Economic Reform* (1978-1992) (Shuangguizhi jingjixue: Zhongguo de jingji gaige (1978-1992)), Shanghai: Shanghai Joint Publishing and Shanghai People's Publishing House, 1997, pp. 219-288.

32. There was a viewpoint claiming that the "monetization of power" brought about by the dual-track system was a correct approach to promote reform. A researcher of the Research Institute of the State Commission for Restructuring Economic Systems stated, "In a dual-track economy, there is a mechanism for administrative power to allocate resources (i.e., voucher). Under certain conditions, the monetization of voucher will lead to the monetization of power, i.e., the power to allocate voucher is in fact the power to allocate money. In other words, power itself can be measured by money."

33. Gérard Roland, *Transition and Economics: Politics, Markets and Firms*, Cambridge, Mass.: MIT Press, 2000.

34. Janos Kornai, "Ten Years after 'The Road to a Free Economy':The Author's Self-Evaluation," Boris Pleskovic and Nicholas Stern (eds.), Annual World Bank Conference on Development Economics 2000, Washington, D.C.: World Bank, 2001, pp. 49-66. See also Xiao Meng, "The Road of Hungary: An Interview with Professor Janos Kornai (Xiongyali daolu: zhuanfang Yanuoshi Ke'ernai Jiaoshou)," *Speculation on the Post-Socialist Transition* (Hou shehuizhuyi zhuangui de sisuo), Changchun: Jilin People's Publishing House, 2003, pp. 299-312.

35. Masahiko Aoki and Masahiro Okuno (eds.), *Comparative Institutional Analysis: A New Approach to Economic System* (Jingji tizhi de bijiao zhidu fenxi), Chinese edition, Beijing: China Development Press, 1999, pp. 30-31, 306-310.

36. A concept employed by Professor Masahiko Aoki of Stanford University m his analysis of modern corporate governance. See Masahiko Aoki, "Controlling Insider Control: Issues of Corporate Governance m Transition Economies (Dui neiburen kong-zhi de kongzhi: zhuangui jingji zhong gongsi zhili jiegou de ruogan wenti) (1994)," Masahiko Aoki and Qian Yingyi (eds.), *Corporate Governance in Transitional Economies: Insider Control and the Role of Banks* (Zhuangui jingji zhong de gongsi zhili jiegou: neiburen kongzhi he yinhang de zuoyong), Beijing: China Economic Press, 1995, pp. 15-36.

37. The concept of soft budget constraint of SOEs was put forward by Janos Kornai, a Hungarian economist, in his analysis of the Hungarian economy in transition. See Janos Kornai, *Economics of Shortage*, Amsterdam: North-Holland Publishing Company, 1980.

38. See Wu Jinglian, "Rent-Seeking Theory and Some Negative Phenomena in China's Economy (Xunzu lilun yu wo guo jingji zhong de mou xie xiaoji xianxiang) (1988)" and "The Preface to the Second Edition of 'Corruption: Exchange between Power and Money' (Fubai: Quanli yu Jinqian de Jiaohuan zaiban qianyan)," *Corruption: Exchange between Power and Money* (Fubai: quanli yu jinqian de jiaohuan), 2nd edition, Beijing: China Economic Publishing House, 1993, pp. 1-9.

39. John McMillan and Barry Naughton, "How to Reform a Planned Economy: Lessons from China," *Oxford Review of Economic Policy*, 1992, Vol. 8, No. 1, pp. 130-143.

40. Deng Xiaoping, "Building a Socialism with a Specifically Chinese Character (Jianshe you Zhongguo tese de shehuizhuyi) (June 1984)," *Selected Works of Deng Xiaoping* (Deng Xiaoping wenxuan), Vol. 3, Beijing: People's Publishing House, 1993, p. 6

41. Zhao Ziyang, "Speech at the National Conference on Economic Affairs (Zai Quanguo Jingji Gongzuo Huiyi shang de jianghua)," *People's Daily* (Renmin ribao), January 13, 1986.

42. Zhao Ziyang, "Speech at the Meeting of the CCCPC Fiancial and Economic Leading Group on March 13, 1986 (1986 nian 3 yue 13 ri zai Zhongguo Zhongyang Caijing Lingdao Xiaozu Huiyi shang de jianghua)" and "Speech at the Excutive Meeting of the State Council on March 15, 1986 (1986 nian 3 yue 15 ri zai Guowuyuan Changwu Huiyi shang de jianghua)", mimeograph.

43. Ota, Sik, "On the Mode of Socialist Economy (Lun shehuizhuyi jingji moshi)" (1981), the Academic Reference Room of the Economic Research Institute of the Chinese Academy of Social Sciences (ed.). *Socialist Economic System Reform* (Lun shehuizhuyi jingji tizhi gaige), Beijing: China Law Press, 1982. pp. 105-114.

44. Lou Jiwei, Xiao Jie, and Liu Liqun, "Some Thoughts on the Mode of Economic Operation and the Fiscal and Taxation Reform (Guanyu jingji yunxing moshi yu caizheng shuishou gaige de ruogan sikao) (1986);" Lou Jiwei and Liu Liqun, "Tentative Ideas on Reforming the Fiscal System and Solving the Deficit Problem (Gaige caizheng tizhi jiejue caizheng chizi wenti de

shexiang) (1986);" Wu Jinglian, Zhou Xiaochuan et al., *Overall Design of the Reform of China's Economic System* (Zhongguo jingji gaige de zhengti sheji), Beijing: China Outlook Press, 1988, pp. 111-151.

45. Namely, the enterprise contracting system, the department contracting system, the all-round fiscal responsibility system, the all-round foreign trade responsibility system, and the responsibility system of credit quota by region.

46. For an Explanation on this issue, see Wu Jinglian , "From Incremental Reform' to 'Overall Advancement'-Speech at the Third Seminar of the Central Party School for Chief Leaders at the Province/Ministry Level on April 13, 1994 (Cong zengliang gaige dao zhengti tuijin de gaige zhanlyue-1994 nian 4 yue 13 ri zai Zhongyang Dangxiao Di San Qi Shengbuji Zhuyao Ganbu Yantaoban shang de fayan)," *On Building the Infrastructure of a Market Economy* (Gouzhu shichang jingji de jichu jiegou), Beijing: China Economic Publishing House, 1997, pp. 44-56.

47. "Wang Renzhi" About Anti-Bourgeois Liberalization--Speech at the Symposium on Party Construction Theory on December 15, 1989 (Guanyu fandui zichanjieji ziyouhua-1989 nian 12 yue 15 ri zai Dangjian Lilun Yanjiuban de jianghua)," *Seeking Truth* (Qiushi), 1990, No. 4.

48. Deng Xiaoping, "Excerpts from Talks Given in Wuchang, Shenzhen, Zhuhai and Shanghai (Zai Wuchang, Shenzhen, Zhuhai, Shanghai dengdi de tanhua yaodian) (January-February 1992)," *Selected Works of Deng Xiaoping* (Deng Xiaoping wenxuan), Vol. 3, Beijing: People's Publishing House, 1993, pp. 370-383.

49. Quoted from Xu Xiaonian and Xiao Qian, "Another New Economy (Ling yi zhong xinjingji)," Report of the Research Department of China International Capital Corporation Limited (Zhongguo Guoji Jinrong Youxian Gongsi Yanjiubu baogao), 2003.

CHAPTER TWO

DEVELOPMENT OF PRIVATE SECTORS

In 1956, as the completion of socialist transformation, the Chinese economy became dominated by state ownership. And since 1978, market-oriented reform in China demanded the creation of private enterprises, which became the mainstay of Chinese economy. This is the most successful process in Chinese economic reform full of twists and turns.

2.1
Growth of Private Sector

According to the notion of socialist political economy of the Soviet Union, the dominance of the state sector and a planned economy based on state ownership are essential economic features of socialism. In the process of the reform and opening up, this traditional notion was gradually broken and private sectors gradually developed. The development of the situation led to objections from people self-labeled as "insisting on socialism" and a hot debate ensued regarding ownership structure during 1996 and 1997. The result of this debate was that it was widely accepted that private sectors are important components of a market economy and that diverse forms of ownership should be allowed to develop side by side. In 1997, the 15th National Congress of the CPC defined China's basic economic system as allowing diverse forms of ownership to develop side by side.

2.1.1 Disappearance of Private Sector in China

The Chinese economy before 1949 was dominated by the private sector. Private businesses accounted for two-thirds of total industrial output and more than 85 percent of total retail sales; moreover, the influence of private banks and old-style banking houses was significant.[1] The establishment of the dominance of the state sector by eliminating other economic sectors in 1955 and 1956 was the result of taking Russia as the model and accelerating the socialist transformation.[2] And after the completion of socialist transformation, the Chinese economy was then dominated by the state sector and the quasi-state, collective sector, while private sectors died out almost completely.

According to the dominant viewpoint of the time, the goal of socialism is complete state ownership. During the Great Leap Forward of 1958, Mao Zedong advocated people's communes, which meant not only turning cooperatives of collective ownership in name into units of state ownership, which were large in size and public in ownership, as well as integrating government administration and commune management, but also attempting to achieve communism in one single step. Only because of the huge losses of life and property resulting from the Great Leap Forward and People's Communes Campaign did Mao Zedong withdraw from his position of immediate transition to complete whole-people ownership of communism. Reversing himself, Mao declared at the Sixth Plenary Session of the Eighth CCCPC at the end of 1958 that people's communes were still economic organizations of collective ownership. However, one of the resolutions of the Sixth Plenary Session of the Eighth CCCPC still demanded that "the transition from socialist collective ownership to socialist whole-people ownership be gradually achieved in order to completely accomplish whole-people ownership," and the goal of making the state sector the only economic sector be achieved in "15 years, 20 years, or a longer period of time."

In the early stages of reform, any attempt to weaken the dominant position of state ownership met with vehement opposition from traditional ideologists. Therefore, leaders of China's reform, such as Deng Xiaoping, adopted the tactic of "don't argue" and a series of pragmatic and flexible policies to offer more business opportunities to people. On the second hand, as long as there were business opportunities, people would make the best use of them to engage in market transactions and start businesses. These activities were often carried out cautiously and in forms suitable to local policies and conditions. For example, to obtain legal status for their enterprises, some entrepreneurs even made them artificially affiliated to collective enterprises or state-owned enterprises so that they wore a "red cap." In this way, the private sector was introduced into Chinese economy again.

Roughly, the process of gradual introduction of private sectors occurred as follows.

2.1.2.1 The Lifting of the Ban on the Individual Business Sector

After the Great Cultural Revolution, it became urgent to find employment for a large number of educated urban youths who had been dispatched to work in rural areas and then returned to cities. Under the circumstances, some economists suggested that the unemployed should be allowed to engage in self-employed businesses and long-distance transport of goods for sale.[3] In February 1979, this suggestion was accepted in a report drafted by the State Administration for Industry and Commerce and transmitted with endorsement by the State Council. It pointed out that the industrial and commercial administration at various levels "may, according to the needs of local markets and with the approval of relevant departments, give permission to idle labor with permanent residence registration to undertake individual businesses in repair, service and handicraft industries, but hiring labor shall not be allowed." In August 1980, *Circular of the CCCPC on Transmitting the Documents of the National Conference on Labor and Employment* confirmed "the guideline of combining employment through labor administrations, employment through organizing cooperatives on a voluntary basis, and employment through establishing individual businesses." It required that "the development of the urban individual business sector be encouraged and fostered."

As might be expected, it soon became necessary to hire labor to expand operations when individual business owners could no longer make full use of market opportunities by themselves alone. At that time, however, hiring labor was considered exploitation and was strictly forbidden. Private sectors could not develop further if this rule remained in force. While drafting government documents, an economist[4] cited a numerical example in Marx's *The Capital* to assert that an individual business owner hiring fewer than eight laborers could still be considered an individual worker because the main source of his income was still his own labor. After this opinion was endorsed by political leaders, the State Council clearly stated in *Several Policies Regarding Urban Non-agricultural Individual Business Sector* of July 1981 that when necessary, an individual business owner "may hire one or two helpers; an individual business owner with high or special skills may have two, three, or no more than five apprentices." [5] From then on, fewer than eight hired workers became the borderline to distinguish individual businesses (geti qiye) from private enterprises (siying qiye).

2.1.2.2 The Rapid Development of Contracted Family Farms

From the autumn of 1980 to the end of 1982, the household contracting system had been universally adopted in rural China. The people's commune system characterized by a structure of three-level ownership with the production team as the basic accounting unit disintegrated, and peasants set up their own family farms on land collectively owned by villages and contracted (leased) to them. As to the nature of this sector, although the official documents still called it a cooperative sector of collective ownership,[6] it was in fact a sector of sole proprietorships. At the beginning of each of the five consecutive years from 1981 to 1985, the CCCPC publicized its "No. 1 Document" regarding the consolidation of the household contracting system. Later on, in the *Decision* of the Eighth Plenary Session of the 13th CCCPC in 1991 and *Decision* of the Third Plenary Session of the 14th CCCPC in 1993, it was clearly stipulated that the household contracting system must remain stable over a long period of time to further consolidate the family farm system.

2.1.2.3 The Rapid Development of Township and Village Enterprises (Xiangzhen Qiye)

As stated by Deng Xiaoping, "In the rural reform our greatest success-and it is one we had by no means anticipated-has been the emergence of a large number of enterprises run by villages and townships."[7] During the 1980s, township and village enterprises (TVEs) suddenly emerged as prominent players.[7] By the early 1990s, TVEs had become an important component of the Chinese economy and a vigorous driving force for its rapid growth. In 1992, the gross output value of TVEs was more than RMB 1,600 billion, almost equal to the national output value of 1985, of which the gross value of industrial output (GVIO) was more than RMB 1,200 billion, approximately 35 percent of the national total of GVIO of 1992 and almost equal to the national total of GVIO of 1986. Total employment in TVEs was more than 100 million, about the same as total employment in the state sector at that time; profits and taxes achieved was more than RMB 150 billion, of which taxes was approximately RMB 60 billion, with more than 30 percent of growth in taxes coming from TVEs.

TVEs of different regions had different characteristics and ownership structures. For quite a long time, the TVEs of the South Jiangsu area were highly praised as models. Their origins could be traced back to commune and brigade enterprises in the era of the Great Cultural Revolution. After the beginning of the reform and opening up, by virtue of their close relationships with Shanghai, these enterprises rapidly developed in technology and sales channels. TVEs in Wenzhou and Taizhou of Zhejiang Province were also highly developed, most of which were private enterprises grown from individual businesses. These various types of TVEs were generally categorized as the collective sector and thus received recognition and support.

2.1.2.4 The Development of Foreign-Invested Enterprises in the Opening Up Process

The Third Plenary Session of the 11th CCCPC in 1978 adopted the guiding principle of reform and opening up and adjusted foreign economic policies, requiring that state-owned enterprises in every region and every department "actively carry out equal and mutually beneficial economic cooperation with other countries in the world on the basis of self-reliance." *The Law of the PRC on Sino-Foreign Equity Joint Ventures* of 1979 marked China's transition from prohibiting to actively encouraging foreign direct investment. The main aim of this transition was to acquire the latest technology and advanced management skills from foreign countries. Foreign-invested enterprises were of three different forms: (1) equity joint ventures, (2) contractual joint ventures, and (3) wholly foreign-owned enterprises. During 1979 to 1988, because of the controversy surrounding foreign investment, the Chinese government set up five special economic zones and fourteen coastal open cities for opening to the outside world in the first instance. As people's opinions about foreign investment changed, other regions began to adopt competitive policies to attract foreign investment.

After the aforementioned reforms, the Chinese economy embraced foreign-invested enterprises and sole proprietorships with some limitations. Until the early 1980s, however, private capitalist industry and commerce were still strictly prohibited. *The Constitution of the People's Republic of China* adopted in December 1982 stipulated that "The basis of the social and economic systems of the People's Republic of China is socialist public ownership of the means of production, namely, ownership by the whole people and collective ownership by working people... The state sector is the sector of socialist whole-people ownership and the leading force in the national economy. The state ensures the consolidation and growth of the state sector... The individual business sector of urban and rural working people, operated within the limits prescribed by law, is a supplement to the socialist public sectors." The private sector was not mentioned at all.

2.1.2.5 The Legalization of the Private Sector

After the green light was given to hiring workers and long-distance transport of goods for sale, the private sector developed rapidly with many enterprises hiring eight or more employees. In early 1983, some statesmen and theorists, still holding on to the planned economic system, claimed that capitalism was occurring everywhere and should be cracked down. The answer they received was "No discussion for three years." As a result, the private sector continued to develop under the protection of the policy of "Don't argue; try bold experiments and blaze new trails."[9] The 13th National Congress of the CPC in 1987 explicitly advocated a policy of encouraging the development of the individual business sector and the private sector. In April 1988, the First Session of the Seventh National People's Congress passed an amendment to the Constitution of the

PRC, which stated in Article 11 that "The State permits the private sector to exist and develop within the limits prescribed by law. The private sector is a supplement to the socialist public sectors. The State protects the lawful rights and interests of the private sector, and exercises guidance, supervision, and control over the private sector."

By the ways mentioned above, the new, non-state sectors gradually developed in the original national economy in China. And the share of those non-state sectors in the national economy increased steadily and became the basis for the steady and speedy growth of the Chinese economy in the 1980s. In the late 1980s, private sectors play an equal role as state sectors in Chinese economy.

In sharp contrast to china, during their economic reform processes, the Soviet Union and Eastern European countries also tried to introduce the private sector without changing the leading position of the state sector but they ended in failure. As a result, after fundamental changes in their political systems, these countries had to simultaneously carry out marketization reform and large-scale privatization. How could China successfully introduce new ownership components without changing the leading position of the state sector? Economists Jeffery Sachs and Wing T. Woo held the viewpoint that the main reason for China's success in introducing the private sector into an economy of public ownership was that China was still in an elementary stage of social development, with plenty of surplus laborers available to private enterprises. The Soviet Union and Eastern European countries, which were more developed than China, did not have this labor surplus, and thus marketization reform forced them to adopt a strategy of shock therapy.[10] Xu Chenggang and Qian Yingyi offered an alternative explanation that the rapid development of Chinese TVEs resulted from the fact that the Chinese planning system was significantly different from the unified planning system of the former Soviet Union. After the decentralization reform advocated by Mao Zedong, the social structure of China was similar to an M-form enterprise organized under the principle of multiple divisions. Therefore, it became possible for markets to develop within and between different jurisdictions.[11]

2.2
The Strategic Readjustment of
the State Sector

The readjustment of ownership structure refers to the fact that the state sector needs to withdraw from ordinary competitive industries and concentrate on some strategic industries. This readjustment further enhances the position and effect of private factor.

2.2.1 The Guiding Principle for the Layout Readjustment of the State Sector

In contrast to the rapid development of non-state sectors, the situation of the state sector had been worse and worse since the commencement of the reform and opening up. This was the result of fundamental deficiencies in the enterprise system as well as the excessive scale and unreasonable layout of the state sector.

According to statistics from the former State Administration of State-Owned Assets, by the end of 1995, the total amount of operating state assets was approximately RMB 4,500 billion; the total amount of state assets in industry and commerce was approximately RMB 3,600 billion, excluding some specific sectors such as armies, post offices, and railways. Since 20 percent of all these assets in industry and commerce were nonproductive assets (such as housing, schools, hospitals, and so forth), the total amount of state assets used in production and business was less than RMB 3,000 billion. Yet these state assets were distributed among 291,000 enterprises in virtually all industrial and commercial fields, ranging from retail trade to long-range missiles. The average amount of state assets in each enterprise was just about RMB 10 million.

In view of the insufficient capital funds for SOEs, some people suggested that the state muster financial resources and inject a great quantity of capital through the state treasury into state-owned enterprises to expand their scale and enhance their competitiveness. However, according to estimates by the Development Research Center of the State Council in 1997, if the existing distribution of state assets across industries and enterprises remained unchanged, the state would have to invest at least RMB 2,000 to 2,500 billion to make state-owned enterprises competitive enough on the market. Of this investment, RMB 600 billion would be needed to relieve enterprises of their bad debts, and RMB 1,800 billion would be used to replenish insufficient capital funds and to upgrade outdated production facilities. In addition, funds in the order of RMB trillions would be needed to replenish the pension funds of older employees and finance some urgent projects that the state should have launched but did not for lack of resources. Such huge amounts of funds were completely unavailable under the existing economic conditions.[12]

Reality made people realize that to change this situation, the state sector must be strategically restructured. The state sector needed to withdraw from ordinary competitive industries and concentrate on some strategic industries that need to be controlled by the state sector. Currently, "strategic industries" mainly refer to industries related to national security, such as important military industries and the coinage industry; large infrastructure projects; and other projects of significant externalities, such as projects to control major rivers and projects of major forest belts as well as social welfare undertakings, which generate large social benefit for numerous beneficiaries but that non-state enterprises are unable or unwilling to carry out; large projects for nonrenewable resources (such as oil fields and coal mines) requiring huge investments with long payoff periods that are beyond the capacity of private capital but cannot be controlled by foreign capital and, thus, must be dominated by state capital; and the development of public domain high technologies that are of strategic significance to the long-term development of the nation.

There are two different approaches for restructuring the state sector. The first is by state planning. That is, the government proposes a plan, deciding which enterprises in which industries should be strengthened, which should be merged, and which should be closed down, and then carries out this plan by state investment or administrative allocation. In the past few decades, there have been many unsuccessful examples of piecing together giant enterprises such as trusts by the government in a vain attempt to avoid the institutional innovation of enterprises. It had been shown that restructuring state-owned enterprises by this approach of "arranged marriage" would not achieve the goal of optimizing the structure. On the contrary, because of strengthened administrative control and the process of economic reform, the conditions of the state sector might deteriorate. In the mid- and late 1990s, some departments and regions attempted to readjust industrial and enterprise structures under the leadership of the governments, with either the result that large-scale yet low-efficiency enterprises were created or the result that bad enterprises were not turned around while good enterprises were dragged down after mergers. Lessons should be learned from these failures.

The other approach is to improve the structures of industries and enterprises by restructuring state assets in an optimal way based on existing or emerging strong enterprises, relying on market mechanism and financial operations on the capital market. These financial operations include financing by share-issuance, selling shares to cash out, mergers and acquisitions, debt restructuring, and bankruptcy liquidation. Many cases have shown that such restructuring not only gives full play to the superiority of the state sector in specific industries but also makes full use of the strength of other economic sectors.

The restructuring of the state sector through the capital market depends on the autonomous actions of independent enterprises. Therefore, turning state-owned enterprises into real enterprises is a prerequisite for restructuring the state sector. The first step is to change the functions of government to separate government administration from enterprise management, that is, to split the government's economic administrative function from its function as the owner of state assets. Specific institutions that exercise owner's rights on behalf of the state should replace administrative institutions that combine government administration with enterprise management.

According to recent practice, the major difficulty in restructuring the state sector is caused by barriers between departments and regions that are mainly caused by combining government administration with enterprise management. Although administrative departments in charge are not the real owner, they have real control over enterprises. Their interests do not lie in increasing the value of assets, but rather in achieving other economic and non-economic goals by virtue of such control. Therefore, to make state assets flow freely, the state assets management has to be reformed. In addition, the existing fiscal, taxation, and financial regulations that impede the free flow of capital across industries and enterprises, such as collecting enterprise income tax by administrative affiliation and allotting credit quotas by region, need to be changed as well.

2.2.2 Letting Go of and Invigorating Small and Medium SOEs

Small and medium enterprises (SMEs) have always been on the periphery of state economic policies in China. That position made small and medium SOEs the first target of ownership reform. These enterprises also provide a practical proving ground for the policy of categorized guidance for the reform and restructuring of the state sector.

In the early stage of the reform and opening up in China, the most frequently used policy toward small and medium SOEs was to delegate power to their management or to handle them as contracting operations. Compared with the direct supervision of administrative institutions, this method was more likely to maximize the enterprise management's enthusiasm for increasing production and income. However, contracting often led to "insider control" and widespread short-term thinking on management's part. This behavior was popularly described as "distributing bonuses whenever money is available, borrowing a loan whenever money is not available and leaving repayment of the money to the next management." Some enterprise managers even used the enterprise capital to speculate in high-risk markets, such as the stock market, the futures market, and the real estate market. Other managers fabricated account books, reported false profits to hide true losses, and embezzled public property, turning the contracted responsibility system into ownership by factory director or ownership by factory director's family and relatives.[13]

TVEs were established under the direct leadership of township-level governments and above. Most of them were wholly owned by grassroots governments. Because of protection from grassroots governments and good financing conditions, TVEs used to be full of vigor in the early stages of reform. However, as reform deepened and TVEs grew larger, their weaknesses, which are similar to those of their SOE counterparts, became increasingly clear. By the 1990s, TVEs in many regions were experiencing slowdown in growth and deterioration in their financial conditions. The number of financially distressed firms grew rapidly, highlighting the urgent need for transformation.

The guiding principle of the reform of state-owned enterprises fundamentally changed around 1995. In essence, the primary objective of the reform was switched from invigorating every state-owned enterprise to making strategic readjustments in the layout of the state sector. The main concept was "grasping large enterprises and letting go of small enterprises." To be specific, "grasping large enterprises" meant concentrating effort on one thousand large and medium-sized SOEs that were essential to the national economy. "Letting go of small enterprises" meant releasing and invigorating small and medium SOEs by means of merger, leasing, contracting, offering for sale, or bankruptcy.

This new guiding principle generated a great deal of intense discussion among economists and political leaders, as might be expected. These people recommended that in implementing this principle, the focus should be on letting go of small enterprises; that is, transforming small and medium SOEs and enterprises affiliated to governments at the township level.

Letting go of small enterprises did not gain momentum until the second half of 1995. Based on information from various regions, methods of transforming small and medium SOEs were as follows:

1. Transferring part or all of the property rights to employees to create a cooperative enterprise or a joint stock cooperative enterprise.

2. Selling the enterprise in its entirety to nonpublic legal entities or individuals. The enterprise after the sale became a non-state enterprise, a joint venture, or a foreign-invested enterprise, either as an independent firm or subsidiary of other firms.

3. Transforming the enterprise into a limited liability company or a joint stock company in accordance with the procedures prescribed in the *Company Law of the PRC.* Some of the transformed companies retained state-owned shares; some companies' shares were mainly held by their employees; some belonged to Sino-foreign joint ventures; and in some others, shares were held by various owners.

4. By acquisition and merger, transforming the enterprise into part or a subsidiary of another large, state-owned enterprise.

5. Leasing all or part of the enterprise's assets to the management or employees of the enterprise or those of another enterprise. In most cases, only state-owned real estate such as land and buildings were leased to the new owner who then paid rental fees to the state and took full responsibility for the management of the enterprise.

However, some unhealthy practices occurred in the process of transforming SMEs that impaired the rights and benefits of relevant stakeholders. Therefore, some economists claimed that it was necessary to correctly deal with the rights and benefits of various parties in the process of letting go of small enterprises, especially in the evaluation of the enterprise's property and in handling the social security issues of employees to ensure social justice.

2.3
The Emergence of a Diverse Ownership Structure with Multiple Forms of Ownership Developing Side by Side

During the incremental reform, the private sectors, emerging from scratch, grew up to break down the monopoly of the state sector and laid the foundation for their further development. In the mid-1990s, private sectors received a further boost by the SOE reform policy of letting go of and invigorating small and medium enterprises. In 1997, the 15th National Congress of the CPC affirmed that "keeping public ownership as the mainstay of the economy and allowing diverse forms of ownership to develop side by side" was China's basic economic system, and private sectors were important components of China's socialist market economy. This removed ideological impediments and laid down the political foundation for the development of private sectors. The development of private sectors has accelerated since then.

2.3.1 The Rapid Development of Private Sectors

In early 1998, the reemployment of those laid-off SOE employees was a concern of the entire society. Because small and medium private enterprises were apparently the main sources of new jobs, the leaders of the State Council made prompt decisions to adopt a series of new measures to support the development of private enterprises. Since 1998, with the implementation of various policies, the share of private sectors in the national economy has grown rapidly. By the end of the twentieth century, private sectors had taken over the largest share of China's national economy and become the fundamental driving force in China's economic growth (see Table 2.1).

Table 2.1　**Investment and Employment by Ownership (%)**

Year		1997	1998	1999	2000	2001	2002
Investment in Fixed Assets	State sector	52.5	54.1	53.4	50.1	47.3	43.4
	Collective sector	15.4	14.8	14.5	14.6	14.2	13.8
	Private sector*	32.1	31.1	32.1	35.3	38.5	42.8
Urban Employment	State sector	53.1	41.9	38.2	35.0	31.9	28.9
	Collective sector	13.9	9.1	7.6	6.5	5.4	4.5
	Private sector	33.0	49.0	54.2	58.5	62.7	66.6

* Private sectors refer to the collection of all non-state and non-collective economic entities.

Source: The National Bureau of Statistics, *China Statistical Yearbook* (Zhongguo tongji nianjian), Beijing: China Statistics Press, 2003.

Figure 2.1　**Non-state Sectors Speeding Up Economic Growth (2000)**

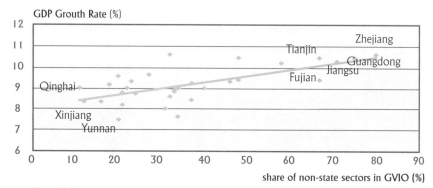

Note: GVIO here is the total GVIO of all state-owned industrial enterprises and non-state industrial enterprises with annual sales revenue of RMB 5 million or more.

Source: The National Bureau of Statistics, *China Statistical Yearbook* (Zhongguo tongji nianjian), Beijing: China Statistics Press, 2001; Data from China International Capital Corporation Limited (CICC).

Non-state sectors were not only huge in size but also superior in performance. This can be seen in Figure 2.1 from the relation between the share of non-state sectors in each region's economy and the GDP growth rate of each region: the larger the share of non-state sectors, the faster the growth of GDP.

2.3.2 The Emergence of Diverse Ownership Structures with Multiple Forms of Ownership Developing Side by Side in Some Regions

The greatest success from China's economic reform is that private sectors developed from supplementary components to major contributors of the whole national economy. These trends occurred mainly in China's southeast coastal regions, where the ownership structure had been improved and diverse forms of ownership developing side by side had become a reality. The enterprise system and business environment in these regions unleashed the entrepreneurial talent and enthusiasm in the Chinese people, resulting in rapid increase in social investment, unprecedented vigor of foreign trade, exceptional inflow of foreign direct investment, abundant employment opportunities, and stable social order. These regions have become the engines of the rapid development of the national economy.

Zhejiang Province was the first region to experience these trends. The main driving force of Zhejiang's economic development lay in the rapid growth of its small and medium private enterprises and the resulting swift transfer of rural surplus laborers to jobs in urban industry and commerce. Starting from household workshops and small enterprises of "shop at the front and factory at the back," private enterprises in Zhejiang evolved into enterprise clusters based on specialized markets, and their products were sold in markets throughout China and the world.

Before the reform and opening up, Zhejiang was only a moderately developed province. In 1980, its GVIO was only RMB 20.1 billion, and its private industry and commerce were underdeveloped. Between 1981 and 1985, small and medium private enterprises in Zhejiang expanded rapidly. In 1982, the number of rural and urban non-state enterprises was 79,000, and the total number of employees in these businesses was 80,000, approximately eight times those figures in 1980. In 1985, there were 264,000 rural individual businesses and joint household enterprises, implying that hundreds of thousands of peasants were employed in nonagricultural industries. Correspondingly, the annual growth rate of the net income of rural residents was as high as 20.1 percent between 1980 and 1985. In 1986, the net income per capita of Zhejiang rural residents was the highest of all Chinese provinces and autonomous regions, excluding those municipalities directly under the central government. Since then, small and medium non-state enterprises in Zhejiang have continued to grow rapidly. In 2000, the total industrial value added by urban and rural non-state enterprises accounted for 49 percent of that of the whole province.

In the twenty years from 1981 to 2000, rural surplus laborers in Zhejiang took jobs in urban nonagricultural industries in huge numbers. The share of the agricultural labor force in the total work force declined from 67.7 percent in 1980 to 37.2 percent in 2000, a reduction of 30.5 percentage points. In other words, close to half the people who worked in agriculture in 1981 no longer worked on farms in 2000. The urbanization level rose from 14.9 percent in 1980 to 48.7 percent in 2000, an increase of 33.8 percentage points, 12.5 percentage points higher than the national average. Zhejiang's per capita GNP and per capita income ranked first in all provinces, surpassed only by large cities, such as Shanghai and Beijing.[14]

Therefore, at the turn of the century, Zhejiang's economy could be characterized as having diverse forms of ownership developing side by side and rural and urban areas developing side by side (see Table 2.2).

Table 2.2 **Economic Growth in Zhejiang** (year-on-year growth, %)

Year	GDP	Value Added	Fixed Assets	Total Exports
2000	11.0	12	18.5	51.1
2001	10.5	11	22.1	18.2
2002	12.3	13.5	24.9	28.0

Source: Zhejiang Provincial Bureau of Statistics, *Statistical Yearbook of Zhejiang* (Zhejiang Tongji Nianjian), Beijing: China Statistics Press, various years.

In Jiangsu province, some fluctuations in economic development occurred. In the 1980s, TVEs in the South Jiangsu model were quite competitive compared with those governing state-owned enterprises. They were deemed the model for other rural areas in China. However, in the early 1990s, these semi-state-owned enterprises, even with their increased operating scales, began to show weaknesses similar to those of state-owned enterprises. Declining efficiency and slow growth resulted. In the past, Jiangsu had always been the first province to emerge from adversity and lead the national economy to recovery. However, in 1998 and 1999, economic performance in Jiangsu Province was worse than the national average. When the 15th National Congress of the CPC put forward "grasping large enterprises and letting go of small enterprises" in 1997, it was commonly accepted that enterprise system reform needed to be intensified with TVEs in the South Jiangsu model. Great efforts were taken in the South Jiangsu area to let go of small enterprises. However, two problems appeared immediately. First, authorized persons sold enterprises to relatives at extremely low prices. Second, when enterprises were transformed to the shareholding cooperative system, current employees not only could get no compensation for implicit liabilities of social security, but they were also forced to purchase stock in the enterprise or they would be fired. Such an unreasonable practice was strongly opposed by employees. The State Economic and Trade Commission promulgated notice to stop those deflections and, as a result, some localities stopped letting go of small enterprises.

TVEs in South Jiangsu started to learn from TVEs in Wenzhou and Taizhou of Zhejiang Province with great enthusiasm when they finally encountered serious financial crises. The former borrowed from the latter's enterprise systems and undertook restructuring of property rights. Most of the South Jiangsu enterprises have been transformed into sole proprietorships or companies.[15] South Jiangsu's economic situation changed a great deal after that: GDP increased significantly, industrial production revived, and investment escalated. Foreign trade increases were especially satisfactory (see Table 2.3).

Table 2.3 **Economic Growth in Jiangsu** (year-on-year growth, %)

Year	GDP	Value Added	Fixed Assets	Total Exports
2000	10.6	12.2	9.2	40.7
2001	10.2	11.5	10.3	12.1
2002	11.6	14.0	16.5	33.3

Source: Jiangsu Provincial Bureau of Statistics, *Statistical Yearbook of Jiangsu* (Jiangsu Tongji Nianjian), Beijing: China Statistics Press, various years.

The export-oriented economy of South Jiangsu area was better than Zhejiang. In recent years, the Suzhou Industrial Park, jointly constructed by China and Singapore, has utilized the administrative "software" (rules and regulations) of the Singaporean government. This software was later introduced to other Jiangsu development zones and contributed significantly to the improvement of the Jiangsu investment environment. Moreover, South Jiangsu area is close to Shanghai, the largest commercial and financial center of China. This helps further in attracting a large amount of foreign investment.

Guangdong is another region that experienced experimental reform early. Guangdong excels in export-oriented TVEs and has established an economy in which diverse forms of ownership have coexisted for a long time. However, around the turn of the century, as a result of its tardiness in reforming the state sector and improving the legal environment, Guangdong's economic performance, whether measured internally or externally, was not as satisfactory as the Yangtze River Delta in general and Zhejiang in particular. Currently, some areas in Guangdong have begun to catch up by improving the investment climate and accelerating the reform of state-owned enterprises (see Table 2.4). If Guangdong can take full advantage of the process of complementary economic integration with Hong Kong, its future economic performance should be assured.

Table 2.4 **Economic Growth in Guangdong** (year-on-year growth, %)

Year	GDP	Value Added	Fixed Assets	Total Exports
2000	10.5	12.8	7.9	18.3
2001	9.5	11.1	10.6	3.8
2002	10.8	13.3	12.5	24.2

Source: Guangdong Provincial Bureau of Statistics, *Statistical Yearbook of Guangdong* (Guangdong Tongji Nianjian), Beijing: China Statistics Press, various years.

2.4
Impediments to Further Development of Private Sectors

In recent years, private sectors in China have developed fast and contributed greatly to the national economy. However, there are still many problems in the business environment of private sectors including in organizational systems, management strategies, and incentive mechanism. Meantime, SMEs in private sectors have great competitive advantages that generate positive externalities of intensifying competition in the whole market, but they also have some innate disadvantages, and therefore need special support from the society.

2.4.1 Improving the Business Environment of Private Sectors

In China, as a result of the legacy of ownership discrimination in a planned economy and ultra-left ideology, private enterprises have both innate and acquired disadvantages. If the government had not removed impediments and provided the necessary support for private enterprises, it would have been very difficult for them to develop. Since the late 1990s, the situation has been gradually improving.

First, discriminatory regulations have been abolished, and national treatment has been applied to private enterprises. In the early stages of reform, many regions and departments divided enterprises into various grades and ranks in accordance with their ownership. The state sector received "upper-caste" treatment; the collective sector received "lower-caste" treatment; but nonpublic sectors were often treated as outcaste. Some private entrepreneurs subconsciously viewed themselves as second-class citizens. This mindset affected every aspect of the economic system and economic policy and became a huge impediment to the development of private sectors.

The decision of the 15th National Congress of the CPC established the political foundation for equal treatment for enterprises of various ownerships. China's accession to the WTO in 2001 further called for equal national treatment. Governments at various levels have promulgated rules and regulations to implement equal national treatment. For instance, according to *Opinions on Promoting and Guiding Domestic Private Investment and Opinions on Policies and Measures to Speed Up the Development of Service Industries during the Tenth Five-Year Plan Period*, promulgated by the State Planning Commission in December 2001, domestic private investment should be encouraged and permitted in all areas where foreign investment is encouraged and permitted. In investment areas with preferential policies, those policies shall apply equally to domestic private investment. The Third Plenary Session of the 16th CCCPC clearly restated that "laws and regulations that hinder the development of nonpublic sectors must be cleaned up and revised in order to eliminate the institutional impediment. The market should be open to nonpublic sectors and nonpublic capital should be allowed to enter industries and fields that are not prohibited by any laws and regulations, such as infrastructure and public utilities. Nonpublic enterprises should be treated in the same way as other enterprises in investment, financing, taxation, land use, foreign trade, etc."[16]

Second, the financing environment of Private enterprises has been improved to some degree. A most pressing issue is the lack of smooth financing channels for private enterprises. To solve the lack of credit guarantees for SMEs, every locality has set up credit guarantee institutions to share risks with banks. To further develop financing channels for private enterprises, experimental efforts have been made with various kinds of financial institutions, including private banks and cooperative financial organizations, which are flexible in operation. These institutions allow for the easy establishment of relationships of mutual trust with private enterprises and help them carry out credit transactions.

Third, the credit culture of the society has been improved, and a market environment of the rule of law has been developing. A good market economy has to be based on fair and transparent game rules; in other words, on the rule of law. This is also important for the healthy development of private enterprises. Currently, China's market order is still a mess, and bad business practices, such as bullying competitors and dominating the market; repudiating debts; and breach of promise are prevalent. As a result, people perceive business as a dangerous undertaking. The popular opinion in China that government should govern as little as possible is one-sided. The problem is that government governs when it should not while it fails to govern when it should. It is the inescapable responsibility of the government to establish market rules, to develop market infrastructure, and to enforce the law fairly and strictly. In 2001, under the auspices of some government agencies, the first credit information institution was established in Shanghai on a trial basis. Afterwards, private credit information organizations began to develop as well. In 2002, the establishment of a society-wide credit system was put on the agenda, and lawful and open administration became a key item of government reform.

Fourth, chambers of commerce (trade associations) and other business/social organizations (such as community productivity promoting centers) have started to play an important role. In China, trade associations organized in a top-down fashion are often called "intermediary organizations" and were granted administrative power in trade management. This practice evolved from the "drive gears" and "transmission belts" under Lenin's proletarian dictatorship system and is not appropriate now. Chambers of commerce should be organizations of entrepreneurs with the mission of protecting entrepreneurs' interests and should be self-educated, self-supervised, and self-disciplined.

2.4.2 Enhancing Support to Small and Medium Enterprises

China's private enterprises are mostly small and medium ones, which have some strengths, such as flexibility and competitiveness, but some weaknesses as well. For instance, a considerable number of SMEs have only limited capital and insufficient credit. It is hard for them to establish their own support departments such as market information and research and development. Moreover, their economic activities are characterized by positive externalities, and they raise competition in the whole market by the so-called catfish effect.[17] Therefore, if they received the support they needed from governments and social organizations, SMEs would overcome their weaknesses, fully exploit their advantages, and generate their positive externalities in the market. For that reason, major market economy countries consider supporting the development of SMEs as their basic national policy and provide systematic help to those enterprises.

Since 1998, the Chinese government has adopted the following measures to support the development of SMEs:

1. The Small and Medium Enterprise Department was established under the former State Economic and Trade Commission in 1998 to help SMEs solve problems encountered in their development. Many local governments have set up similar institutions to facilitate the development of SMEs.

2. Commercial banks have been required to set up small and medium enterprise credit departments to further improve credit service to SMEs. The range of lending interest rates for SMEs has been broadened to gradually liberalize the interestrate. Credit guarantee institutions for SMEs with a flavor of policy financing have been organized in each province and city. Reform of rural financing and building financial systems at the county and township levels have been listed as key items in ongoing financial reforms.

3. A series of preferential tax deductions and exemptions have been applied to SMEs by the Ministry of Finance and the State Administration of Taxation. For instance, the value-added tax rate for SMEs has been reduced from 6 to 4 percent.

4. The National People's Congress promulgated in June 2002 and began to implement on January 1, 2003, the Law of the PRC on Small and Medium Enterprises. Aiming to "improve the business environment of small and medium enterprises, facilitate the healthy development of small and medium enterprises, enlarge employment in both urban and rural areas, and maximize the significant effect of small and medium enterprises in the national economy and society development," this law established the legal position of SMEs; clarified the responsibilities of the government; and further confirmed the policy of facilitating the development of SMEs in legal forms. The implementation of this law and its supporting rules and regulations will create a good environment for the development of SMEs.

5. The service of the government and the society to SMEs has been improved. SMEs are in urgent need of information about management, technology, industrial development, supply and demand in the world market, and so on. It would cost too much for each individual enterprise to acquire such information independently. It would be much more efficient for the government or a social organization to provide the information. When the government provides services, it needs to change its traditional leading methods under a planned economy and semi-planned economy. The government needs to investigate what services it should provide and how to provide these services. It should not limit itself to some patchwork operation within the framework of the original mindset, but rather adapt to the new situation of a market economy. This is a new issue to be addressed by government institutions.

SMEs have been developing very fast since 1998. According to a joint survey by the Development Research Center of the State Council, China Entrepreneur Survey System (CESS), and other agencies,37 by the end of 2001, there were 29.3 million SMEs in China with a total employment of 174 million. In 2001, SMEs created 50.5 percent of China's GDP, created more than 75 percent of new jobs, and accounted for 43.2 percent of national tax revenue.

2.4.3 Private Enterprises Should Make Even Greater Endeavors

Private enterprises have met with enormous success in many areas. However, they will have to make additional sustained efforts as the main engines of China's economic growth in the context of globalization.

2.4.3.1 Improving the Enterprise System

Whether developed from individual businesses or transformed from small and medium SOEs or quasi-state-owned TVEs, most of China's private enterprises have similar weaknesses in this aspect. All effective enterprise systems have one common characteristic, that is, the boundary of property must be clearly defined. Enterprises with relatively large scales also require an effective governance structure based on clearly defined property rights. As a result, this issue has two aspects. One is that the owner should be present. The other is that the enterprise's governance structure should be sufficiently effective. This is relatively easy to achieve for a natural-person-owned enterprise, in which the owner manages the enterprise himself. In enterprise structures such as cooperatives or corporations, where managers are entrusted to run the enterprise and ownership and control are separate, the situation is beyond simple.

Private enterprises should pay special attention to the mistake about the multi-tier legal-person system. China is filled with small tenant peasants who are not accustomed to "legal person culture," that is, they are not accustomed to using hierarchical organizational forms with strict rules and regulations to organize large production operations. Instead, Chinese people are used to splitting property rights and distributing a share to every level to maintain relationships of economic cooperation. An effective way for private enterprises to expand is to acquire other enterprises during their development process. It is also appropriate to maintain the independent status of the acquired enterprises for a period of time, as it encourages the original owners and employees to remain with the enterprise. Therefore, most large and medium-sized private enterprises have adopted the organizational structure of enterprise groups that consist of closely affiliated layer enterprises (those not independent) and loosely affiliated layer enterprises (those maintaining the status of independent legal persons). However, those enterprise groups are not companies with centralized property rights. Moreover, they are different from the British-style group companies in which the parent company establishes a majority shareholding control over the subsidiary companies. Such a system inevitably leads to "independent kingdoms" within the enterprise and conflict of interest and should be gradually transformed according to the principles of the corporate system.

The issue of family enterprises needs specific attention in a discussion of enterprise systems. Generally, in Chinese society, where people treasure blood relationships, SMEs in the form of family enterprises have the advantages of intensifying internal cohesion and lowering transaction costs. However, when enterprises become large in scale, especially when the founders with strong management abilities have retired, and the enterprises need to be run by hired professional managers, it becomes an objective requirement to choose the modern corporate system with separation of property rights and managerial rights. Therefore, those family companies, while making full use of the advantages of family relationships, need to introduce professional managers and grant them power to use their management skills to improve the company and transition to a publicly owned corporation.

2.4.3.2 Formulating Appropriate Management Strategy

In their initial stages, private enterprises normally take advantage of gaps not covered by the state sector and adopt the strategy of providing low-priced commodities to markets. They did not have clear goals and strategies for development. This approach was suitable for newly established SMEs under conditions of seller's market dominated by the state sector. Since enterprises have become relatively large and buyer's market has become the norm, clear management and development strategies are needed to coordinate the efforts of employees, especially high- and middle-level managers, so that everyone strives to meet a common goal.

Currently, a habitual management strategy in private enterprises is to use price wars as a main competitive weapon. In the past, demand exceeded supply in almost all product markets, and SOEs enjoyed dominant status and did not need to do their utmost to satisfy market demand. As the saying goes, "A princess need not worry about her marriage." In such a situation, products of small and medium private enterprises were easily sold as long as their quality was not too bad and the price was low enough. As a result, many SMEs had a tradition of manufacturing in a rough way and selling low-quality products at low prices.

However, in China, the market situation has changed from seller's market, where demand exceeded supply, to buyer's market, where supply exceeds demand and competition is fierce. In such a situation, traditional price wars of cutthroat competition would lead to thinner and thinner profits until enterprises were forced to give up technological innovation or to use inferior materials and turn out substandard products to survive. As a result, the whole industry would be ruined.

As stated by Porter, there are three potentially successful generic strategic approaches to outperforming other firms in an industry: cost leadership, differentiation, and focus.[18] Price wars are implemented under the premise of overall cost leadership. However, as stated by Porter, this strategy requires continuous capital investment and improvement in process technology, strict supervision over workers, a low-cost distribution system, and other fundamental skills and resources.[19] Moreover, it requires basic organizational structures, clearly defined responsibilities, and strict control over costs. If these conditions cannot be satisfied, and a price war is launched by reducing profits and turning out low-quality products, then the enterprise is in fact committing suicide.

Just as management expert Shi Ziyi pointed out when criticizing the cut-throat competition among some Taiwanese enterprises, entrepreneurs do not always think of doing better than others in the market that has already been occupied; what is more important is to be more special than others.[20] Entrepreneurs exploit their core competencies to create products different from others', to offer new market segments for their products, and then to increase productivity, lower costs, and enhance competitiveness in those market segments. In other words, enterprises should apply the concept of "market segmentation," make every effort to avoid sharing the same market with other companies, adopt the customer-oriented strategy of differentiation, and explore new markets with specialized products designed for specific customers.

Another problem frequently seen in the management strategy of China's private enterprises is their excessive diversification. Many enterprises, after their initial development in one industry, enter other industries unrelated to their original industry, resulting in diverted financial, technological, and managerial resources and deviation from the strategy of differentiation. In contrast, enterprises do best in markets where they have competitive advantages. It is not wise for them to become involved in too many industries, and thus reduce their overall efficiency.

2.4.3.3 Associating with Government Officials Should Not Become the Basis for Establishing Businesses

Under the autocratic system of old China, the emperor and his officials held considerable power in resource allocation. Therefore, in the traditional Chinese business culture, associating with government officials and making deals between power and money were standard practice to ensure success. Since reform, because of the coexistence of the two economic systems, administrative power still plays an important role in resource allocation. Therefore, rent-seeking activities still occur throughout the country. In recent years, the overall social and economic environment of China has improved to some extent, yet this unhealthy business environment has not been eliminated. As a result, some entrepreneurs still hope to make their fortunes by making deals between power and money and employing tricks and skills often found in books telling stories of "merchants wearing high-ranking official hats," such as Hu Xue-yan.[21] These actions seriously impair the market order, degenerate commercial morals, and threaten the normal operation of markets. Moreover, it is the main source of the plague of crony capitalism. As anticorruption campaigns increase and orderly markets form, those upstart entrepreneurs who still rely on associating with corrupt officials to build their businesses will inevitably decline in number. The entrepreneurs should never surpass the law and the conscience or make abnormal relations with the official as their base of business.

Notes and References

1. Xue Muqiao, *Memoir of Xue Muqiao* (Xue Muqiao huiyilu), Tianjin: Tianjin People's Publishing House, 1996, p. 201.

2. "Taking Russia as the model" was originally proposed by Sun Zhongshan (Sun Yat-sen, 1866-1925). Mao Zedong came to the same conclusion m On the People's Democratic Dictatorship: "The October Revolution helped progressives m China, as throughout the world, to adopt the proletarian world outlook as the instrument for studying a nation's destiny and considering anew own problems. Follow the path of the Russians-that was their conclusion." See Mao Zedong, "On the People's Democratic Dictatorship (Lun renmm mmzhu zhuanzheng) (June 30, 1949)," *Selected Works of Mao Zedong* (Mao Zedong xuanji) (The Four-in-One Edition), Beijing: People's Publishing House, 1966, p. 1471.

3. For instance, in March 1979, at the National Forum on Reforming Wage System, and in July 1979, in his report at the CPC Central School, Xue Muqiao suggested that urban unemployed youth be encouraged and assisted to look for employment by allowing them to engage in individual businesses and long-distance transport of goods for sale. (Xue Muqiao, "Comments on the Issues of Labor and Wage (Tantan laodong gongzi wenti) (March 1979)" and "Comments on the Issue of Urban Employment (Guanyu chengzhen laodong jiuye wenti de jidian yijian) (July 1979)," *Selected Economics Papers of Xue Muqiao*.

4. This economist is Lin Zili, who was working in the Research Department of the Secretariat of the CCCPC at that time.

5. In Provisions of the CCCPC and the State Council Pertaining to Exploring All Possibilities, Invigorating the Economy and Solving the Urban Employment Problem (Zhonggong Zhongyang Guowuyuan guanyu guangkaimenlu, gaohuo jingji, jiejue chengzhen jiuye wenti de ruogan guiding) (October 17, 1981), this stipulation was formally stated as "As to individual businesses, the owners shall be permitted to hire no more than two assistants each; those having special skills may have no more than five apprentices each."

6. On September 1, 1982, at the 12th National Congress of the CPC, Hu Yaobang pointed out in his report entitled Create a New Situation of Socialist Modernization Drive in an All-Round Way (Quanmian kaichuang shehuizhuyi xiandaihua jianshe de xin jumian) that because of the rather low and very uneven standard of productivity development in China, it would be necessary for multiple economic sectors to coexist for a very long period of time. In the countryside, the main economic sector would be the cooperative sector of collective ownership by working people... No matter whether in the countryside or in cities, the individual business sector should be encouraged to adequately develop within the scope prescribed by the state and under the control of industrial and commercial administration, so as to serve as a necessary and beneficial supplement to public sectors.

7. Deng Xiaoping, "We Shall Speed up Reform (Gaige de buzi yao jiakuai) (June 12, 1987)," *Selected Works of Deng Xiaoping* (Deng Xiaoping wenxuan), Vol. 3, Beijing: People's Publishing

House, 1993, p. 238.

8. Chen Naixing et al., *Study on the Policy Guidance for the Development of Industry in Chinese Villages and Towns* (Zhongguo xiangzhen gongye fazhan de zhengce daoxiang yanjiu), Beijing: Economic Management Press, 1994, p. 262.

9. Deng Xiaoping mentioned later m his "South China Speeches" that "It was my idea to discourage contention, so as to have more time for action. Once disputes begin, they complicate matters and waste a lot of time. As a result, nothing is accomplished. Don't argue; try bold experiments and blaze new trails." See Deng Xiaoping, "Excerpts from Talks Given in Wuchang, Shenzhen, Zhuhai and Shanghai (Zai Wuchang, Shenzhen, Zhuhai, Shanghai dengdi de tanhua yaodian) (January-February 1992)," *Selected Works of Deng Xiaoping* (Deng Xiaoping wenxuan) Vol. 3, Beijing: People's Publishing House, 1993, p. 374.

10. Jeffrey Sachs and Wing Thye Woo, "Understanding the Reform Experiences of China, Eastern Europe and Russia," in Chung Lee and Helmut Reisen (eds.), *From Reform to Growth: China and Other Countries in Transition*, Paris: OECD, 1994; "Structural Factors in the Economic Reforms of China, Eastern Europe and Former Soviet Union," *Economic Policy*, April 1994, Issue 18, pp. 101-145.

11. Xu Chenggang and Qian Yingyi, "Why China's Economic Reform Is Different from Others (Zhongguo de jingji gaigeweishenme yuzhongbutong) (1993)" in Qian Yingyi, *Modern Economics and China's Reform* (Xiandai jingjixue yu Zhongguo jingji gaige), Beijing, China Renmin University Press, 2003, pp. 177-196.

12. Quoted from Wu Jinglian et al., *The Strategic Restructuring of the State Sector* (Guoyou jingji de zhanlyuexing gaizu), Beijing: China Development Press, 1998.

13. Yu Chengzhi, "A Great Pioneering Undertaking m the History of Socialist Reform: The Universal Significance of the Mixed Ownership System of Shunde Industry (Shehuizhuyi gaigeshi shang de yida chuangju: Shunde gongye hunhexing chanquan zhidu de pubian yiyi)," *SEZ and Hong Kong & Macau Economy* (Tequ yu Gang Ao jingji), 1995, No. 4.

14. As to Zhejiang's economic development, see Shi Jinchuan, Jin Xiangrong et al., *Institutional Change and Economic Development: Investigation on the Wenzhou Model* (Zhidu bianqian yu jingji fazhan: Wenzhou moshi yanjiu), Hangzhou: Zhejiang University Press, 2002.

15. As to the situation of Jiangsu TVEs in the late 1990s, see Xin Wang, "The Historical Ending of the South Jiangsu Model (Sunan moshi de lishi zhongjie)," *China Economic Times* (Zhongguo jingji shibao), December 30, 2000. This article recorded various controversies arising from the reform and restructuring of collective enterprises in the South Jiangsu area.

16. "Decision of the CCCPC on Issues Regarding the Improvement of the Socialist Market Economic System (Zhonggong Zhongyang guanyu wanshan shehuizhuyi shichang jingji tizhi ruogan wenti de jueding)" (approved by the Third Plenary Session of the 16th CCCPC on October 14, 2003), *People's Daily* (Renmin ribao), October 21, 2003, p. 1.

17. Catfish are ferocious fish. It is said that fishermen put catfish into the water trough to

stimulate other fish so that they take in oxygen by swimming at fast speed and thus do not die during transport.

18. Michael E. Porter, *Competition Strategy*(Jingzheng Zhanlue).,Beijing: Huaxia Publishing, 1997, p. 35.
19. Michael E. Porter, ibid., pp. 35-37, 45-46.
20. Shi Ziyi, "Transformation of the Century (Shiji biange) (1996)," *Niche Strategy-Successful Tips for Small and Medium Enterprises* (Liji celyue-zhongxiao qiye zhisheng zhidao), Beijing: Joint Publishing, 2002, pp. 3-132.
21. A book about the life of a Chinese business magnet (Hu Xueyan, 1823-1885) in the Qing Dynasty, who not only amassed huge wealth but also won the favor of the imperial court.

CHAPTER THREE
REFORM OF ENTERPRISES

An important part of the transitional process from a traditional centrally planned economy to a modern market economy is the transformation of the corporate sector, the basic economic unit, from a dependent unit in the State Syndicate to real enterprise. There are three basic approaches for this transformation: the first is to develop private enterprises; the second is to withdraw state-owned capital from ordinary competitive industries; and the third is to transform traditional state-owned units, turning them into modern enterprises compatible with a market economy. Coordinated action in these three approaches will gradually result in diverse forms of ownership developing side by side. From the discussion on transition strategy in Chapter 1, of these three approaches, the development of the private sector is the most fundamental. However, in terms of chronological order, the issue of state-owned enterprise (SOE) reform was the first one raised.

3.1
The Enterprise System of Traditional SOEs

China entered socialism "with drums beating and gongs clanging" in 1956. The Soviet-style state-owned and state-run enterprise system was soon established throughout the nation. The strangest thing of this system is that it is totally different from the essence of enterprise.

3.1.1 Basic Production Units of the "Immense Social Factory"

The traditional state sector was established according to the Lenin model of State Syndicate. After the residence registration system separated urban China from rural China, all nonagricultural industries in cities were organized into a gigantic enterprise and all urban laborers became employees of the government. In this Party-State Inc.,[1] the so-called "state-owned enterprise" was essentially a grassroots production unit for cost accounting. Attached to the party and government organs, an SOE had the basic task of carrying out all the instructions and directives from their superiors. In terms of economic activity, the primary task of an SOE was to accomplish the plan mandated by the government, rather than bringing into play its "vigor" and engaging in innovative activities. Government departments determined everything for an enterprise through planned directives: what to produce, how many to produce, how to produce, where to get raw and processed materials, and to whom the products would be sold. The role of the management of an enterprise was simply to carry out the instructions. SOEs had neither the motivation nor the capacity to make decisions for optimal allocation of resources based on their own interests and changes in market. Vertically, they were subordinate to the administrative organs that both held the ownership of enterprises and served as the regulator of society and economy.

3.1.2 Multiple Roles and Multiple Objectives

Under the highly integrated system of the party, the state, and the economy, SOEs were not only production units but also grassroots organizations of the party-state political system with extensive social functions.[2] Correspondingly, as the owner of SOEs, the state integrated its function as enterprise owner with its other political and social functions. As a result, the multiple objectives of SOEs conflicted with each other. The state regarded SOEs as instruments to achieve its political and economic objectives, such as to establish a strong military industry and to catch up with and surpass Western countries. Therefore, managers of SOEs were regarded as cadres of the party and were governed in the same way under the same system as staff of the party and government organs. Moreover, SOEs integrated the functions of employment, social security, and social relief, providing a full spectrum of social services from cradle to grave.

3.1.3 Dissevered Ownership

State ownership was exercised through an organizational system dissevered horizontally and vertically, without symmetry between power and responsibility. First, the tasks of running SOEs were shared by the central government and local governments at various levels. Based on administrative affiliation, SOEs were managed by governments at various levels. Second, at each level of government, the power to run SOEs was segmented into several government departments as well. Generally, the decision-making power regarding investment and production was held by administrative organs like the planning commission and the economic commission; the power to appoint, remove, assess, and supervise chief executives of enterprises belonged primarily to the organization department of the party and the personnel bureau of the government; under the financial system of unified control over revenues and expenditures, the government finance department acted as the financial department of SOEs, administering their cash flows, revenues, and expenditures and collecting taxes, fees, and profits; replacing the labor market with administrative measures, the labor department allocated labor forces for SOEs, and they set human resource policies involving employment, salaries, bonuses, etc. for SOEs. This was an ineffective institutional arrangement because it dissevered unified ownership and allowed departments of the party and the government to exercise their part of the ownership according to their own requirements and even their own interests. The performance of an enterprise depended on how each department exercised its power, but the departments each exercised their power without taking corresponding responsibility.

3.1.4. Highly Softened Budget Constraint

Due to the nonexistence of a product market and a production factors market, SOEs did not need to consider supply and demand of the market. Nor did they need to face market competition. The major work of the factory director was to deal with government organs. First, the system of management and mode of operation was to ensure the achievement of government objectives instead of meeting market demand. Second, they frequently had to negotiate with superior administrative organs to get more resource supplies and to get tasks that were more favorable and easier to accomplish. The most important characteristic of the relation between SOEs and the government is "soft budget constraint" as defined by Janos Kornai. Because key economic parameters such as prices of inputs and outputs and capital input and taxation-which would decide survival and development of enterprises-were all controlled by the state, enterprises could always change the constraints they faced through negotiation with the government. "If the firm is struck by financial difficulties, the state will bail it out with tax allowances, credits at preferential terms, financial grants, taking over the losses, or permitting price increases... If such interventions are quite frequent, the firm's behavioral norms are established in expectation of it."[3]

3.2
The Reform with the Main Theme of Power-Delegating and Profit-Sharing

From 1956 until 1993, when the Third Plenary Session of the 14th CCCPC proposed that the primary goal of SOE reform had been to have SOEs "run well and invigorated" on the premise that no change was to be made regarding the basic institutional framework of SOEs, either a decrease in losses or an increase in profits on the books. In spite of various reform measures in practice, the essence was to change the distribution of power, responsibility, and benefit between the government and the "insiders" of enterprises (i.e., the managers and workers), that is, to delegate power to and share profit with the insiders of enterprises.

3.2.1 Three Ways of "Power-delegating and Profit-sharing"
All reform measures with the main theme of "power-delegating and profit-sharing (fangquan rangli)" were based on a series of basic diagnoses of the problems

of SOEs. According to these diagnoses, the poor performance, low profitability, and inferior competitiveness of SOEs were not due to their basic institutional framework, but rather to the following factors: (1) decision-making power was excessively concentrated in the central government; (2) the government implemented administrative intervention in businesses; (3) the managers and workers of enterprises lacked initiative; (4) the party and government organs chose inappropriate persons to be factory directors (managers) or did not adequately supervise them; (5) the debt burdens of enterprises were too heavy, as were their social burdens; (6) enterprises lacked funds for technological upgrading; (7) enterprises had too many redundant workers; and so on. It was believed that all these problems could be solved through power-delegating and profit-sharing without changing the basic institutional framework of SOEs. There were three major forms of power-delegating and profit-sharing: "transferring enterprises to governments at lower levels (qiye xiafang)," "expanding enterprise autonomy (kuoda qiye zizhuquan)," and the "enterprise contracting system (qiye chengbao)."

3.2.1.1 Transferring Enterprises to Governments at Lower Levels

This was the primary measure for reforming SOEs in China from 1956 until 1978. The so-called "transferring enterprises to governments at lower levels" referred to transferring enterprises that had been directly under the central departments to local governments at the province, prefecture, or county level for administration. The logic was that the low efficiency of SOEs was caused by the excessive concentration of the control over SOEs in the hands of the central government so that administrative organs were far away from enterprises in location and unable to make correct and timely decisions. If enterprises were transferred to local governments closer in location and interests, the government control over enterprises and the performance of enterprises would improve.

The idea of "transferring enterprises to governments at lower levels" made its first appearance at the Eighth National Congress of the Communist Party of China (CPC) in September 1956. Out of a total of 9,300 enterprises and public institutions directly under the central departments, 8,100 were transferred to local governments in 1958. The share of enterprises directly under the central departments in national total of gross value of industrial output (GVIO) decreased from 39.7 percent in 1957 to 13.8 percent in 1958.[4] As discussed in Chapter 1, economic disorder resulting from the comprehensive delegation of administrative power together with the Great Leap Forward campaign forced the government to recentralize the control over SOEs. Between 1961 and 1963, many SOEs were gradually taken back by the central departments, and along with newly established ones, enterprises directly under the central departments in national total of GVIO rose to 42.2 percent in 1965.[5]

As the preexisting problems of SOEs emerged again after the recentralization of the control over SOEs, delegating power to local governments once again became the solution chosen by policy makers. In 1970, the State Council organized and implemented another round of transferring enterprises to governments at lower levels. After this round of decentralization, the number of enterprises in civilian industry directly under the central departments dropped to 142; the share of enterprises directly under the central departments in national total of GVIO declined once again to 8 percent.[6] The result of this round of decentralization was similar to that of 1958: it exacerbated the chaotic situation of the economy and ended up with recentralization.

The only change accomplished by administrative decentralization by transferring the control over SOEs from the central government to local governments was a change in the relationship between various levels of governments regarding the control over SOEs. It did not change the basic relationship between the government and the enterprise, let alone other aspects of the SOE system. Hence, it failed to improve the performance of SOEs. On the contrary, since resource allocation through administrative orders inherently requires a high degree of consistency in command and control by the government, administrative decentralization inevitably led to malfunction of the centrally planned system and to economic disorder.

3.2.1.2 Expanding Enterprise Autonomy

After Mao Zedong died in 1977, most enterprise leaders and economists were against reform of SOEs by "transferring enterprises to governments at lower levels." Generally agreeing with the viewpoint of Sun Yefang,[7] they believed that the lack of growth and efficiency of SOEs was caused by too much control and excessively tight control over them, and that the direction of reform should be delegating power to and sharing profit with enterprises. In the late 1970s, loosening control and delegating power as well as expanding autonomy and sharing profit became the mainstream belief of leading economic departments.[8]

Based on this new belief, the government of Sichuan Province chose six enterprises, including Chongqing Steel Factory, to experiment with expanding enterprise autonomy in October 1978. The so-called expanding enterprise autonomy is to relax the control by plan over enterprises by government departments and to permit the enterprise management to make the business decisions that had been made by the government in the past; that is, to transfer part of the control from the government to the enterprise management. As of 1980, the measures had been extended to 6,600 large and medium-sized SOEs that accounted for 60 percent of budgeted industrial output value and 70 percent of profits. Early in the reform of expanding enterprise autonomy, enterprises showed strong enthusiasm for increasing production and income. However, efficiency was not visibly improved, and before long, problems of chaotic economic order, skyrocketing fiscal deficit, and inflation emerged, bringing this reform into question by many. At the end of 1980, the Chinese government decided to readjust the national economy and SOEs shifted from the reform of expanding enterprise autonomy to the responsibility system for accomplishing the state plan.

Profit retention was the original form of profit-sharing. The definition of profit retention is that SOEs are permitted to retain a certain portion of profits and to use it for themselves instead of submitting profits in full to the state finance department as in the past. The State Council documents of 1979 divided retained profits into three parts (collectively known as the three funds): the production development fund, the employees' welfare fund, and the employees' bonus fund. The proportion of retained profits was the main parameter to adjust the relationship between the state and the insiders of enterprises in terms of economic benefit, and varied with time and location. The reform of substituting tax payment for profit delivery from 1983 to 1984 converted most profits, previously remitted to the state finance department by SOEs, to tax payments to the state finance department in the forms of enterprise income tax and "regulation tax." After the taxation system reform of 1994, SOEs basically did not need to remit profits to the state finance department, but rather, they paid enterprise income tax at a uniform rate.

3.2.1.3 The Enterprise Contracting System

There were various opinions why the reform of expanding enterprise autonomy had failed to achieve the expected success. The mainstream belief of the leading government department in charge of SOE reform attributed the failure to insufficient power-delegating and profit-sharing. Therefore, they proposed to introduce into industrial and commercial enterprises the contracting system that had been successful in rural reform.[9]

The contracted managerial responsibility system (chengbao jingying zerenzhi)[10] in enterprises is a special form of power-delegating and profit-sharing. Its unique feature is that a contract is established between relevant government organs and the management of the enterprise to specify the terms of power-delegating and profit-sharing, as well as the obligations of the insiders (managers and workers) of the enterprise.

In the early 1980s, the household contracted responsibility system with remuneration linked to output (the household contracting system in short) proved successful in the rural areas. Since a suitable way to reform SOEs was still not found then, the contracting system was introduced into SOE reform.

Under the contracting system, the party awarding the contract hands over its property to the party awarded the contract for management. The two parties reach an agreement that ensures the owner a fixed amount of profit; any profit exceeding this amount is then retained by the party awarded the contract or is shared by the two parties according to predetermined proportions. It is, in essence, a kind of hierarchical arrangement of property rights in which the owner in the lower hierarchy, under the condition of paying fixed rent or proportional rent, can get residual control from the owner in the upper hierarchy during the contract period and can enjoy residual claim to operation surplus after deduction of rent.

In early 1983, the leader of the Secretariat of the CCCPC put forth the slogan that "bring the contracting system to cities and all problems can be solved" and urged the introduction of the enterprise contracting system in all urban industrial and commercial enterprises. During a period of just two to three months, the system was implemented in all SOEs nationwide. But it led to chaotic economic order and rising prices, which forced the leader of the State Council (i.e., Zhao Ziyang) to urge the CCCPC to make a decision to stop implementing the contracting system and to hasten the reform of "substituting tax payment for profit delivery." In June 1983 and October 1984, there were two successive steps for the reform of substituting tax payment for profit delivery. Without necessary reforms in other aspects of the system, substituting tax payment for profit delivery alone still could not enable enterprises to have full managerial autonomy and full responsibility for profits and losses and to participate in fair competition.

At the end of 1986, the leader of the State Council stopped implementing the strategy of coordinated reform and shifted to a strategy with enterprise reform as the main theme. At that time, there was already some intention of using the corporate system (then called the shareholding system) as the main form for the new enterprise system. However, as people were quite unfamiliar with the corporate system, and both basic economic conditions and the legal environment required by the modern corporate system were not ready, people once again chose the contracting system, which was easy to accept. In December 1986, the State Council urged "implementation of diverse forms of the contracted managerial responsibility system and granting of sufficient managerial autonomy to managers." The second surge of enterprise contracting was in mid-1987. By the end of that year, 78 percent of all SOEs covered by the national budget (80 percent of them being large- and medium-sized enterprises) had implemented the contracting system.

The contracting system neither gave enterprises full managerial autonomy nor promoted the separation of government administration from enterprise management or fair competition among enterprises. At the same time, it solidified the existing system, obstructed the adjustment and optimization of the economic structure, impaired the improvement of economic efficiency, and further increased the difficulties for reform. Although people afterward proposed various correcting measures such as risk-deposit contracting, determining contract terms scientifically, and contracting through public bidding in an attempt to improve the contracting system, it was still impossible to achieve the goal of enabling enterprises to have full responsibility for profits and losses. The root cause of the problem was the innate defects in the institutional arrangement of the contracting system. After granting part of the residual control and residual claim to the party awarded the contract, the definition of the enterprise's property rights became more obscure, the conflict of interest between the two parties was intensified, and mutual infringements by both parties became more likely to occur. By the end of the 1980s and the beginning of the 1990s, except for a very few exceptions, people in all walks of life, including enterprise leaders, no longer thought that the contracting system was a good way to reform SOEs in China.

3.2.2 Achievements and Deficiencies of the Reform of Power-Delegating and Profit-Sharing

As part of the economic reform program in China, these reform measures, while maintaining social and political stability, gradually disengaged SOEs from a traditional planned economy and let them begin to participate in and adapt to market competition with non-state enterprises. In each key industry, a few high-performance SOEs emerged.

The reason for the reform of power-delegating and profit-sharing to achieve these positive results was that the division of ownership between the state and the insiders of enterprises improved the traditional SOE system in several important aspects. First, in terms of the incentive mechanism, as the management and workers of SOEs could actually share in the profits with the state, SOEs, which had been passive accessories of administrative organs and content with nothing more than the accomplishment of the state plan, were infused with the profit motive to varying degrees. For those enterprises with prospects of significantly improving profitability as long as the management and workers worked hard enough, this incentive was especially strong. The profit motive enabled enterprises to have the initiative and impulse of self-development. Second, in terms of the information mechanism and decision-making efficiency, in contrast to when government organs dominated everything, decision making was decentralized enormously because of the greatly expanded managerial autonomy of the management of enterprises and the greatly reduced administrative intervention of the government. The burden of information collecting and processing was shifted from the government to enterprises, enabling the decision making by enterprises to be more timely and effective than that by the government in the past.

However, the achievements of the reform of power-delegating and profit-sharing were quite limited. Meanwhile, attempts to improve the management performance of enterprises by dissevering the owner's rights between the state and the insiders also generated significant negative effects. First, the reform of power-delegating and profit-sharing did not change the basic institutional framework and ways for the state to exercise its ownership. It made reforms unavoidably fall into a dilemma. In order to overcome maladies of the traditional system of SOEs and to reduce administrative intervention of the government in operation of enterprises, the government had to delegate more managerial power to the insiders of enterprises, for it had to be either the government organs or the insiders of enterprises under this basic institutional framework. However, since the insiders of enterprises were not the real owner investing capital in the enterprises, power delegating to a certain extent would unavoidably lead to unchecked insider control. To keep insider control in check, the only system that could be relied upon was still government intervention, namely, strengthening the supervision and intervention by the party and government organs, which in turn would incur the perennial maladies of managing enterprises through administrative means by the government.

Second, the reform of power-delegating and profit-sharing did not change the basic institutional framework of SOEs. As business entities under the factory system, SOEs had a closed structure of ownership that would not admit multiple investment entities. Due to the lack of a modern corporate governance structure centered on a board of directors, enterprises under the factory system could rely only on the factory director responsibility system under the leadership of the party committee and had to rely on the party committee and workers and the superior party and government organs to supervise the factory directors. On one hand, this kind of governance structure often fell into a paralytic state due to the poorly defined division of power and responsibility between the factory director and the party committee; on the other hand, it often led to unchecked insider control and corruption.

Third, the reform of power-delegating and profit-sharing caused chaotic relationships of property rights and a serious problem of unchecked insider control due to the disseverance of ownership of SOEs between the state and the insiders. In the context of the reform of power-delegating and profit-sharing and following the philosophy of separation of ownership and control, the 1988 *Law of the PRC on Industrial Enterprises Owned by the Whole People* made a series of provisions that caused distortion of the enterprise property system. This distortion included defining factory directors as legal representatives of enterprises. Without a corporate governance mechanism like a board of directors, granting legal representatives a series of decision-making powers to run enterprises was essentially to grant them de facto partial ownership. This de facto partial ownership gave many legal representatives of enterprises a strong incentive to try to turn this ownership into de jure complete ownership. Maladies of this incentive mechanism are demonstrated in a series of corruption cases of legal representatives of SOEs.

3.3
Corporatization of Large SOEs

The Decision on Issues Regarding the Establishment of a Socialist Market Economic System, adopted at the Third Plenary Session of the 14th CCCPC in November 1993. The significance of the Decision of the Third Plenary Session of the 14th CCCPC was that it set corporatization as the direction of SOE reform in the form of the ruling party's document.

3.3.1. Progress in Corporatization of Large SOEs
On December 29, 1993, the National People's Congress passed the Company Law of the People's Republic of China, which went into effect on July 1, 1994. In November 1994, the State Council decided to convene the "National Working

Conference for Experiments in Establishing a Modern Enterprise System" and to select one hundred SOEs as pilot studies for corporatization. Due to the lack of emphasis on using diversification of share ownership to restructure existing SOEs into real enterprises, most enterprises involved in the experiment simply converted themselves to wholly state-owned companies that were similar to modern corporations only in form. Therefore, the prescheduled evaluation at the end of 1996 showed that almost no experimental enterprise had achieved the minimum standards of a modern corporation. It was not until the 15th National Congress of the CPC in 1997 and particularly until the Fourth Plenary Session of the 15th CCCPC in 1999, which reiterated the requirements for corporatization, that corporatization reform of large and medium-sized SOEs entered the period of establishing modern corporations according to internationally prevalent norms.

The Decision on Several Important Issues Regarding Reform and Development of State-Owned Enterprises, adopted at the Fourth Plenary Session of the 15th CCCPC in 1999, brought forth some new requirements for the corporatization of large and medium-sized SOEs. First, it emphasized corporate governance after corporatization by pointing out that "corporate governance structure, which can establish checks and balances between the owner and the manager, is the core of the corporate system" and required that all the corporatized SOEs establish effective corporate governance. Second, it required that, except for a minority of enterprises that could be monopolized by the state, the rest should "actively develop corporations with multiple equity-holding entities" and should introduce non-state equity investment. It mandated that large and medium-sized SOEs, especially well-performing ones suitable for the shareholding system, should be converted to shareholding enterprises by initial public offering (IPO), establishment of Sino-foreign joint ventures, and use of cross-shareholding among enterprises. These steps would develop a sector of mixed ownership, with the state holding a controlling interest in important enterprises.

Corporatization of large and medium-sized SOEs after 1998 basically included three successive steps: (1) separation of administrative function and enterprise function; (2) reorganization of monopoly enterprises into competitive enterprises; and (3) IPO on domestic and overseas securities markets after asset restructuring.

3 3.1.1 Separating Administrative Function and Enterprise Function

During the era of a planned economy, the government integrated its function as the administrator of society and economy with its function as the owner of state assets. Such being the case, economic units were both administrative organs and so-called "enterprises." To separate administrative function and enterprise function so they could be performed by different organizations, the new government that took office in 1998 took an important step. It transferred administrative function of ministry-level institutions ("national industry corporations" and "group corporations" that belonged to the central government and had both administrative and enterprise functions), to "state bureaus" under the State Economic and Trade Commission,[11] thus turning these national industry corporations and group corporations into enterprises without administrative function.

3.3.1.2 Breaking Up Monopolies

Under a planned economy, to maximize the scale of operation, usually only one enterprise was set up in one industry or one sub-industry. This enterprise held a monopoly status in its industry. After 1998, the state broke up monopolies to promote competition by splitting and restructuring those enterprises. Taking the petroleum industry as an example, before the reform and opening up, the state established the Ministry of the Petroleum Industry and the Ministry of the Petrochemical Industry to manage upstream businesses and downstream businesses, respectively. The Ministry of Petrochemical Industry, which managed the downstream businesses, was restructured into the China Petrochemical Corporation (SINOPEC) in 1983. Later, in 1988, the Ministry of the Petroleum Industry, which managed the upstream businesses, was restructured into the China National Petroleum Corporation (CNPC). SINOPEC and CNPC became two administrative corporations, holding both administrative and enterprise functions. In June 1998, after transferring the administrative function of both corporations to the State Bureau of Petroleum Industry under the State Economic and Trade Commission, the government decided to restructure them into comprehensive petroleum companies. The specific approach was to transfer downstream businesses such as oil refining and retail of SINOPEC in northern China to CNPC, to transfer the oil fields of CNPC in southern China to

SINOPEC, and to permit them to invest and operate in each other's territory. These two corporations, in addition to the China National Offshore Oil Corporation (CNOOC), which was originally engaged in offshore petroleum extraction, became the three comprehensive petroleum companies competing with each other in China. Similar approaches were employed to create a competitive situation in other industries. For some industries of natural monopoly, the government also adopted successful practices of other countries in reforming monopoly industries in the recent twenty years to limit monopoly operations within the most necessary scope and to subject these enterprises to strict supervision.

3.3.1.3 Restructuring for IPO

After the aforementioned reforms, SOEs generally still had bloated organizations, redundant personnel, heavy burdens of debt, and low-quality assets. One of two approaches could be used to convert them into real enterprises. The first approach was to spin off non-core assets by splitting and redundant personnel by early retirement and recommendation for reemployment, and to restructure core assets for IPO. The second approach was to carve out core assets from the original enterprise and restructure them for IPO, but to leave historical burdens such as non-core assets, non-performing financial claims, and redundant personnel to the original enterprise to improve the financial performance of the newly established enterprise to ensure the success of IPO. The first approach proved more effective but would take a longer time. The second approach took effect more quickly but it left more unsolved problems. China mainly employed the second approach. For example, in October 1999, CNPC carved out its core assets of extraction-refining-chemical-retailing and restructured them into PetroChina Company Limited (PetroChina) for IPO in Hong Kong and New York. Among the original 1.54 million employees of CNPC, 1.06 million were retained by the remaining enterprise, while the other 0.48 million were employed by PetroChina. PetroChina changed its wholly state-owned nature by introducing some public investors and strategic investors via IPO in March 2000 on stock markets in Hong Kong and New York in the form of H-share[12] and American Depositary Receipt (ADR), respectively.

Former large SOEs that listed in domestic and overseas stock markets, in order, included Qingdao Beer (1993 H-share of Hong Kong, A-share of Shanghai in the same year), China Mobile (1997 Red Chip Share of Hong Kong), PetroChina (2000 H-share of Hong Kong), China Unicom (2000 Red Chip Share of Hong Kong, 2002 A-share of Shanghai), SINOPEC (2000 H-share of Hong Kong), and Baoshan Iron & Steel Co., Ltd. (2000 A-share of Shanghai).

On the basis of diversification of share ownership, most transformed SOEs have built a basic framework of corporate governance according to the *Decision on Several Important Issues Regarding Reform and Development of State-Owned Enterprises*, adopted by the Fourth Plenary Session of the 15th CCCPC.

3.3.2 Governance Problems of Transformed Companies

The idea accepted by many people for reforming the state assets management system after the Third Plenary Session of the 14th CCCPC was a three-layer model. The first layer is the government, which set up a state assets management commission to perform the function of the state as the owner, to separate the function of the administrator of society and economy and the function of the owner of state assets, as described in the *Decision of the Third Plenary Session of the 14th CCCPC*. However, because there were too many SOEs under the jurisdiction of governments at various levels and the span of control of the state assets management commission was too wide, state assets management institutions (i.e., investment institutions authorized by the state,[13] as described in Article 64 of the *Company Law*) were designated as the second layer. The specific forms intended then included state investment companies, state holding companies, state assets management companies, group corporations of enterprise groups meeting certain requirements, and so on.[14] These institutions were to exercise shareholder rights in transformed companies at the third layer.

In later practice, the original intention to separate the government's function as the administrator of society and economy and its function as the owner of state assets by establishing the state assets management commissions at the first layer was not really implemented. The central government and most local governments did not set up this kind of institution. Although the state assets management commissions were set up quite early in localities such as Shanghai and Shenzhen, the separation of the two functions did not really materialize. These state assets management commissions were not entities, but "virtual" institutions composed of incumbent government leaders and leading officials of related functional departments. In practice, the planning commissions, the economic and trade commissions, the organization departments of party committees, and the finance departments still exercised the right to invest, the right to appoint senior executives, and the right to profits, respectively, and thus it was impossible for the state assets management commissions to be independent of the administrative function of the government.

Establishing authorized investment institutions as the second layer included the following situations. First, line ministries and bureaus of some industries were restructured into holding companies or assets management companies to perform the function of the state shareholder in enterprises that were originally affiliated with them. Second, existing administrative corporations, such as national industry corporations, were authorized to perform the function of the state shareholder in enterprises that were already under their control. Third, group corporations of some large enterprise groups were authorized to perform the function of the state shareholder in their affiliated enterprises. For example, one part of the experiment extended to 120 large enterprise groups in 1997 was to approve the group corporations of those enterprise groups that met certain requirements as investment institutions authorized by the state.

Some of these authorized investment institutions were created in the process called "first have a son, then have a father," that is, to first transform an SOE into a company and then create a "shell company" to act as the state shareholder of that company.

This institutional framework left transformed SOEs with some grave institutional defects.

3.3.2.1 Listed Companies Failed to Become Corporate Entities with Subsidiaries of Wholly State-Owned Authorized Investment Institutions, Rather than Fully Independent Corporate Entities

To maintain control by the government, corporatization usually left listed companies dominated by state-owned shares. Furthermore, shareholder's rights of these controlling shares were usually exercised by wholly state-owned authorized investment institutions (i.e., holding companies, group corporations, assets management companies, and so on). This led to two consequences. First, directors with the support of authorized investment institutions (usually their senior executives) dominated the boards of directors of listed companies. Meanwhile, although the China Securities Regulatory Commission required that there be "three separations (separation in personnel, assets, and accounts)" between listed companies and their parent companies, board chairmen of listed companies (usually CEOs of their parent companies) were exempted from this requirement. Furthermore, according to the provisions of the *Company Law* of 1993, the board chairman of a joint stock limited company is the legal representative of the company. As a result, even those listed companies that achieved diversification of share ownership were under the complete control of wholly state-owned authorized investment institutions and could not have independent operation as was required by a market economy. Second, using "remaining enterprises" that were built on the old system as authorized investment institutions on behalf of the state to control the listed companies built on the new market economic system was obviously detrimental to the goal of transforming the listed companies into businesses with market competitiveness.

3.3.2.2 "Remaining Enterprises" Controlled Listed Companies

The restructuring of SOEs in China was usually done by "carving out for IPO," in other words, state holding companies, state assets management companies, national industry corporations, and enterprise groups carved out their better-performing assets to set up joint stock limited companies for IPO financing. The assets and staff not carved out remained in the original enterprises, or authorized investment institutions, otherwise known as "remaining enterprises." Since remaining enterprises undertook the burden of assets, debts, staff, products, and other things not suitable to be carved out for IPO, many of them had the need to constantly obtain resources from their listed subsidiaries in order to survive. Since remaining enterprises were usually the controlling shareholders of their listed subsidiaries, they also had enough power to do so. Therefore, cases of parent companies grabbing money from the stock market through listed companies and cases of parent companies "hollowing out" listed companies mushroomed. Some group corporations, as authorized investment institutions, even adopted the practice of transferring high-quality assets to other enterprises or even to some individuals while leaving debts with the group corporations, which then filed for bankruptcy to default the debts. This practice posed a huge risk to the government and banks.

3.3.2.3 Ownership Was Exercised by the Insiders

Since the state shareholder was usually determined by authorization, shareholder rights of state-owned equity in most transformed companies were exercised by other wholly state-owned enterprises authorized by the state, such as state holding companies, state assets management companies, group corporations of enterprise groups, and "shell companies." In most cases, these authorized enterprises did not achieve the separation of ownership and control. They had just one unified "leading team" and leading team members were both representatives vested with full authority of the state-owned equity as well as executives employed by them. As a result, it was these leading team members that represented the interests of the state shareholder to supervise and motivate themselves as executives of transformed enterprises. The core of corporatization is the establishment of an effective corporate structure. However, in the process of corporatization in China, the most prominent problem was unchecked insider control,[15] which exists widely in enterprises that gained managerial autonomy in the reform, enterprises under the contracting system, and most of the pilot enterprises of the shareholding system.

3.3.2.4 Multi-Tier Legal Person System Was Prevalent

Backed by such policies as authorization and setting up enterprise groups, the long-existing phenomenon of the "multi-tier legal person system" in Chinese SOEs has further developed. There are subsidiaries ("daughter companies") under authorized enterprises, and there are "granddaughter companies" or even "great-granddaughter companies" under "daughter companies." All of these companies have independent legal person status, and the number of tiers can reach five, six, or even more. In many large groups, already the management of the enterprises authorized by the government to exercise state ownership cannot determine how many offspring their enterprises have in total. At most, they know only the number of second-tier enterprises directly under them and the total number of enterprises in the third tier. Furthermore, the influence of the state as the owner gradually weakens as the number of tiers increases.

This organizational form has many problems. First, the multi-tier legal person system is a concept conflicting with "legal person" in civil law. As we know, the so-called legal person refers to an organization that has the capacity for civil rights and conduct and that enjoys civil rights and undertakes civil obligations independently according to law. Meanwhile, a natural person refers to an independent individual who has inherent "natural power." In this respect, a legal person cannot be multi-tier. Under the multi-tier legal person system, second-tier and third-tier legal persons do not have completely independent rights. This is how it was in the days of a patriarchal society: even though a man was already an adult, as long as his father was still alive, the man was still subject to the patriarch and did not have complete independence.

The supposed advantage of the multi-tier legal person system is that it can mobilize enthusiasm of member enterprises by this kind of property arrangement. However, in fact, just as in the case of an extended family living under the same roof in old-time China, this practice that permitted each branch to set up its own private coffer and private savings often causes conflicts of interest among member enterprises (the so-called "incentive incompatibility" problem in economics). As we know, an effective incentive system must have incentive compatibility-it must mobilize the enthusiasm of lower-level organizations or individuals and at the same time ensure that the mobilized enthusiasm serves the objectives of the higher-level organization; otherwise, it would mobilize the enthusiasm of lower-level organizations to act against its objectives. From the perspective of enterprise organization, the institutional structure of the multi-tier legal person system violates the basic principle of incentive compatibility and causes conflict of interest among various parts of the enterprise. According to modern enterprise theory (incomplete contract theory), if the responsibilities of contracting parties can be clearly specified in a contract, all economic activities can be accomplished by fair trade among contracting enterprises. This way, the enthusiasm of contracting parties can be mobilized to the highest degree to accomplish complementary activities. As for matters that cannot be clearly specified in the contract, they are only suitable for transactions within an institution under the management of an administrative authority. Otherwise, problems may emerge, such as mutual infringement, mutual threats, endless disputes over minor issues, and friction among independent entities with conflicting interests, leading to a sharp rise in transaction costs. In some enterprise groups in China, there is this kind of friction among the core enterprise and member enterprises. For example, because many independent enterprises share one brand, member enterprises often seek private gain (of the member enterprise) at public expense (of the group company) by turning out low-quality products with shoddy work and inferior material, and they will refuse to mend their ways despite repeated admonition and education. This is very natural, as the root cause of the problem does not lie in the greed of a few individuals, but rather in an institutional arrangement with conflict of interest.

In the early stages of industrial development in various countries, after larger enterprises amalgamated smaller ones through mergers and acquisitions, they organized these smaller enterprises into a group in the form of a holding company. This was a common practice and represented progress. Nevertheless, to apply the multi-tier legal person system universally and to popularize it universally will make its negative aspect become more and more conspicuous.

3.4
Further Reform Measures to be Taken

3.4.1 Further Lowering the Proportion of State Equity Shares

To corporatize SOEs, diversification of share ownership must be achieved first. There are a number of ways to bring in new types of equity holders.

3.4.1.1 Debt-Equity Conversion

In the mid-1980s, the state finance department discontinued free fiscal appropriations to SOEs. Instead, funds were channeled to SOEs as bank loans with interest. After this reform, known as "substituting fiscal appropriations with bank loans," SOEs chronically relied on bank loans for financing. By the mid-1990s, the debt-to-asset ratio of all SOEs combined was as high as 85 percent or so, and 37 percent of nonfinancial SOEs were already in insolvency, even as calculated by book value.[16] The high volume of liability of SOEs included a huge amount of overdue loans, which were non-performing loans on the banks' balance sheets.

In view of this situation, many domestic and overseas economists suggested that the creditors (mainly state banks) apply debt-equity conversion to some of these liabilities. Doing this can create new types of owners for SOEs and hasten the processes of corporatization and diversification of share ownership in SOEs, while at the same time it can reduce non-performing loans in banks, thus mitigating financial risk.

At the end of 1998, the State Council decided to establish four asset management corporations (AMCs) to take over non-performing loans from four big state-owned commercial banks (the Big Four), respectively. In 1999, the four AMCs- Cinda, Huarong, Great Wall, and Orient- were established successively and took over non-performing loans of about RMB 1,400 billion at book value from the Big Four and the China Development Bank and immediately started debt-equity conversion for about 600 SOEs chosen by the State Economic and Trade Commission. The total amount of non-performing loans converted to equities was about RMB 460 billion. However, the debt-equity conversion by the four AMCs in 1999 was more of an administrative arrangement than a business operation. The debt-equity conversion was one of the "three super-weapons" for a scheme to get large and medium SOEs "out of the difficult position in three years."[17] Its main purpose was to convert interest payments of the debtor enterprises into profits on the books, therefore putting the loss-making enterprises in the black- in essence, government subsidied to these enterprises. The enterprises for debt-equity conversion were also decided by the State Economic and Trade Commission; AMCs were not allowed to choose these on their own. After the debt-equity conversion, although AMCs became shareholders or even controlling shareholders, they did not in fact perform the function of shareholders due to various limitations. By the end of 2002, most equities held by AMCs in the debt-equity conversion were still not cashed out. As a result, the AMCs' efforts to dispose of non-performing loans still have not made a significant impact on the structure of share ownership of SOEs.

However, as AMCs continue to cash out the debts and equities they hold to overseas and domestic non-state investors, the structure of share ownership of relevant SOEs will be further changed.

3.4.1.2 Inviting Private Investors to Become Shareholders

The debt-equity conversion deals with only the existing capital stock of SOEs. SOEs also need to increase capital by equity financing for further development and the capital increment created this way also brings new types of owners. In the reforms after 1992, there were two channels for domestic private investors to become shareholders of SOEs.

First, employees of SOEs invested to become shareholders. As early as the mid-1980s, the government launched some pilot projects of establishing shareholding companies by issuing new shares to employees. Most newly established enterprises of the shareholding system then issued shares mainly to their own employees because there was basically no other way to get non-state equity investment. This situation did not change much until the early 1990s. At the end of 1991, there were 3,200 pilot enterprises of the shareholding system of various kinds all over the nation and 2,751 of them had their own employees as shareholders.[18] After 1994, during the experiments to establish the modern enterprise system, issuing new shares to employees was also the most convenient and commonly used way to achieve diversification of share ownership and to establish limited liability companies instead of wholly state-owned companies.

Second, stocks were issued to public investors on the stock market. One characteristic of the modern corporate system is the transferability of rights and interests of investors, which allowed the corporate system to raise funds from public investors at a fast pace and on a large scale. Therefore, after SOEs were transformed into companies, new types of owners could be created when raising funds by issuing shares, thus achieving diversification of share ownership. In the reform of SOEs in China, however, the potential of equity financing on the stock market to change the ownership structure of SOEs was not fully realized. At the end of December 2002, the number of all classes of listed companies was 1,224 in China and the shares traded in the stock market accounted for only 34.7 percent of the total.[19]

There are two major reasons for the failure of the equity financing on the stock market to effectively drive diversification of share ownership of SOEs. First, in order to retain the state control over these companies, the government set a ceiling for the portion of shares that could be issued to the public by dividing the shares of these companies into tradable and non-tradable shares, thus making equity financing on the stock market less likely to affect the ownership structure of these enterprises in a fundamental way, and even less likely to change the control of these companies. Second, because of the inadequate protection of public shareholder rights, for the insiders and sponsor shareholders (usually shell companies as the state shareholder) of these companies, equity financing on the stock market did not impose a burden of repayment of principal and interest, as was the case for bank loan financing. Nor did it mean a cost in terms of loss of control over these companies. Therefore, it became a financing channel with the softest constraint. The drive for gain at such a huge magnitude made the corporatization transformation degenerate into a procedure of IPO for "grabbing money" rather than a reform of the management mechanism of enterprises.

3.4.1.3 Developing Institutional Investors

In developed market economies, especially Anglo-American economies, institutional investors hold prominent status in the shareholding structure of companies. In the United States in 1994, 46.2 percent of total equities of all companies were held by various institutional investors, of which two major types of institutional investors- pension funds and mutual funds- accounted for 25.9 percent and 11.9 percent, respectively.[20] In the corporatization transformation of SOEs in China, institutional investors are also a potentially important type of owner. Among them, pension funds have the greatest potential because a large part of the existing state equity is in fact financed by past contributions of workers for the purpose of social security. It has come hand in hand with the state's social security commitment to older workers, which is an implicit debt of the state. Many economists have been advocating "cutting a chunk" from the existing state assets and transferring it to social security funds as compensation for liability to older workers of SOEs in the pension system reform. If these measures are carried out, they could effectively kill two birds with one stone, namely improving the social security function by resolving the historical legacy in the pension system reform while also creating new institutional investors outside the government.

3.4.2 Strengthening the Internal Control Systems of Large Enterprises

For large enterprises, one important aspect of establishing good corporate governance is the establishment of an effective internal control system as per the requirements of market competition. At present, most large Chinese enterprises have adopted the multi-tier legal person system. Even private enterprises have imitated SOEs by restructuring themselves into enterprise groups of the multi-tier legal person system once they have developed to a certain size.

In the historical development process of industrial and commercial enterprises, there was once an organizational form of enterprises similar to China's multi-tier legal person system. This was the holding company structure (abbreviated as "H-form").[21] H-form mostly appeared in enterprises formed by horizontal mergers and acquisitions. After amalgamation, each subsidiary in this structure retained its status as a legal person so that it had significant independence from the headquarters. This structure was once widely used in Europe. In the UK, for example, the holding company structure was the most popular structure to control subsidiaries. In the United States, H-form gradually lost its popularity and had been replaced by the multidivisional structure (M-form) since twentieth century. On the eve of World War I, virtually no one in big industrial companies in the United States managed business in H-form.

The so-called multidivisional structure is an enterprise organizational form in which several divisions are set up under the headquarters. These divisions have considerable decision-making power for daily management and operation and are just "profit centers" without independent balance sheets. The divisions adopt the strategy of separation of revenue and expenditure and simply monitor the business profitability, with no right to dispose of profits. The basic units in this structure are semi-independent profit centers established by trademarks of products or regions; each profit center is organized in accordance with U-form. Above the profit centers is the headquarters, composed of senior executives and in charge of resource allocation for the entire company and the supervision and coordination of subsidiary units. Thus, the separation of policy making and operational management is achieved and the division of decision-making work is improved. Senior executives are able to free themselves of the work of daily management and operation and concentrate on strategic decisions. Because of centralized and unified accounting, the decentralization of decision-making power for production and investment will not result in loss of control, corruption, or waste. Therefore, the multi-divisional structure has become the basic organizational form of large non-financial corporations in various countries.[22]

3.4.3 Overcoming Defects of Insider Control

In order to achieve this goal, we must solve the problems discussed in the following five sections.

3.4.3.1 Making Sure That the Owner Is Present

The general meeting of shareholders is the supreme organ of power of a company, holding the final control (residual control). This guarantees fundamentally the effective functioning of corporate governance structure. To achieve this in Chinese enterprises, the erroneous ideas and legal provisions of excluding the owner from the enterprise formed in the reform of power-delegating and profit-sharing must be changed and the problem of "absence" of the owner must be solved to ensure that the owner holds final control over the enterprise. Of course, to solve the problem of absence of the owner, we should carry out diversification of share ownership and diversification of the forms of public ownership.

3.4.3.2 Making Sure That the Board of Directors Fulfills Its Fiduciary Duties in the Interest of Shareholders

In China, the insiders dominate the boards of directors in a great number of newly established companies and there is a tradition of paternalism and personal despotism. Therefore, the practice currently adopted in many localities of management by the so-called legal representatives authorized by the state has several problems: (1) the scope of authorization is not clear; (2) the party being awarded the authorization is not a collective but an individual; (3) there are some conflicts of interest between the party being awarded the authorization (the insiders) and the party awarding the authorization (the owner); and (4) the party being awarded the authorization does not have completely clear legal responsibility. These problems must be solved.

3.4.3.3 Making Sure that the Board of Directors Carries Out Supervision Over Senior Executives

In the modern corporation, the international practice of setting up a corporate governance structure is that the general meeting of shareholders elects the directors to constitute the board of directors, and then the board of directors appoints the company's senior executives who are responsible for the company's daily management. However, this common practice of the corporate system is incompatible with China's current system of the party's organization department and the government's personnel department appointing the officers of enterprises. Although many large- and medium-sized enterprises have corporatized themselves, their high-level managers and even middle-level managers are still appointed by the organization departments of higher-level authorities. The board chairman and the board of directors do not always perform their fiduciary duties conscientiously for the shareholders, and it is also very hard for the general meeting of shareholders to demand that they act in accordance with the investors' goal of making a profit. If the general manager and the executive team are not appointed by the board of directors, the board of directors will not have independent fiduciary duties, and their incentive to carry out supervision over senior executives on behalf of the shareholders will be weakened. This practice simply must be changed. In order to prevent criminals and other unqualified people from occupying important positions of publicly held companies, the party organization department and the government personnel department can carry out qualification checks on candidates for the board of directors and the general manager according to the actual situation in China and the international practice of criminal record checks on candidates for the board of directors of public companies. However, this qualification check should not become a direct appointment.

3.4.3.4 Letting the Securities Market Play a Role in Strengthening Corporate Governance

In the Anglo-American model of corporate governance, the securities market, especially the secondary market, makes a great contribution to the effective functioning of the corporate governance structure. It provides very strong incentives and constraints on senior executives through the operations in the securities market such as "voting with feet" (disgruntled investors pulling out their money), hostile takeover, and stock options for CEOs. At present, the securities market in China is greatly distorted and it really need to make great efforts on that aspect.

3.4.3.5 Providing Adequate Incentive to Executives

To ensure that they make great effort to achieve shareholders' goal, executives should not only be strictly supervised but also strongly motivated; otherwise, incidents damaging the interests of enterprises, such as the "phenomenon of age 58"[23] will occur. Incentives for executives can be in the form of promotion, on-the-job consumption, bonus, subsidized share ownership, stock options, etc. Each form has its own pros and cons and the incentives can be used in combination. When choosing the forms of incentives, attention should be paid to the compatibility of the executives' incentives with the achievement of the owners' goal. In developed market economies, stock options are the most frequently used form of incentive for executives. In an efficient securities market, since the stock price reflects the expected profitability of the company, to give executives stock options not only achieves good compatibility with shareholders' goals but also provides strong incentive. If the employed manager does not run the company well, he cannot get a penny from stock options; if he runs it well, he can earn a large reward. However, this method needs highly effective corporate governance and highly effective supervision of the securities market, and great effort is required to create these two conditions.

3.4.4 Bringing the SASAC into Play to Exercise Shareholder Rights in Accordance with the Law

According to the decision of the 16th National Congress of the CPC in 2002, the National People's Congress passed a resolution to create the State-Owned Assets Supervision and Administration Commission (SASAC). The creation of the SASAC ensures that the SOE reform in China will be led by an authoritative institution committed to upholding shareholder rights with full authority. The essential function of the SASAC is to further advance the readjustment of the layout of the state sector; to carry out the corporatization transformation of SOEs that have not corporatized; to exercise owners' rights on behalf of the state in the companies that have already been transformed (including wholly state-owned companies, state-controlled companies, and companies with non-controlling state participation); and to set up a mechanism of checks and balances between the owners and the managers to make these companies' corporate governance become more effective.

3.4.4.1 Further Advancing the Strategic Readjustment of the Layout of the State Sector

The SASAC should continue to carry out the guiding policy of the 15th National Congress of the CPC, planning as a whole and implementing step by step, to make the state sector withdraw in an orderly fashion from industries where it does not have an advantage. Resources thus freed can be used to improve the public service of the government and to strengthen pivotal industries and key fields as well as fields that non-state sectors are unwilling to enter. This will enable the state sector and non-state sectors to put their own advantages to full use.

At the same time, during the period when state capital is being withdrawn from some industries, effective measures should be taken to refrain and correct phenomena caused by a few people that damage social justice and erode public property. The SASAC should set criteria to regulate the change in state property rights and mobilize every part of the society to carry out the supervision in order to guarantee justice of procedures in aspects such as pricing and applying for purchase.

3.4.4.2 Expediting the Corporatization Transformation of SOES

After the creation of the SASAC, the "authorized investment" mode of state assets management should step down from the historical stage as quickly as possible. Under the jurisdiction of the SASAC, the first-tier enterprises can either maintain their status as authorized investment institutions or be transformed into corporations so that they become bigger and stronger on the basis of the modern corporate system. Units maintaining their status as authorized investment institutions will no longer be enterprises, but agencies of the SASAC for the reform of the state sector, and they should be led by civil servants appointed by the SASAC. These authorized investment institutions can take charge of the restructuring and corporatization transformation of their SOE subsidiaries by themselves or let domestic or overseas assets management companies do the same. After accomplishing the corporatization transformation, the original authorized investment institutions and their subsidiaries can become operational companies specializing in production operation, or they can become holding companies specializing in capital operation. In either case, once the corporatization transformation is accomplished, the enterprise should be set free and be managed directly by the SASAC as an equity owner in accordance with the *Company Law*. Even a wholly state-owned company should appoint a board of directors according to the *Company Law*, and the state shareholder should exercise its rights within the framework of the *Company Law*.

3.4.4.3 The SASAC Exercising Shareholder Rights in Accordance with Law in Transformed Enterprises

The Company Law is a basic law that regulates the behavior of corporations. The SASAC exercises the rights to supervise people, operate businesses, and manage assets of corporations transformed from SOEs on behalf of the state shareholder, but these should be done within the framework of the Company Law. The current phenomena that state assets management institutions overstep their authority or do not fully exercise their power should be rectified firmly.

For government administration departments to continue to carry out their administrative approval of the corporatization transformation of SOEs, especially approval of investment projects, is a special measure adopted to prevent investment risk and strengthen financial budget constraint when the owner is absent. The practice indicates that this is not a scientific or effective method. Once the SASAC had been founded and the investor (i.e., the owner) was present, the SASAC started performing the function of the owner, such as setting up effective corporate governance, transforming the financial constraint mechanism to impose an endogenous hard financial budget constraint, and undertaking business risk. Correspondingly, the duty of the government should be shifted from playing the role of the investor to providing administrative scrutiny on such issues as environmental protection to safeguard public interests. The SASAC also should not bypass the general meeting of shareholders and the board of directors, intervening directly in the investment and management of the enterprise. If it does so, the SASAC plus the preexisting government agencies will certainly restrict the enterprise to death. This is what the enterprise concerns most.

3.4.5 Learning from International Experience and Strengthening Corporate Governance

Improving corporate governance and dealing appropriately with the conflict between the "insiders" and the "outsiders" is an ongoing task to ensure the smooth functioning of the modern corporate system. In the 1970s, the conflict was revealed in different forms in companies of the Anglo-American model and the German model, respectively. The problem of the Anglo-American model was that, due to the highly dispersed ownership, most small shareholders would rather be free-riders, leading to inadequate owners' control and supervision over managers. The problem of the German model was that the corporate governance was excessively biased toward workers' interests. Both tendencies damaged the shareholders' interests and hurt the competitiveness of companies.

In the early 1990s, in order to solve this problem, countries using the Anglo-American model started the "corporate governance movement" to enhance the shareholders' value and strengthen the control of the company. One important feature distinguishing the corporate governance movement from other reforms of corporate and securities laws was that various non-government organizations issued self-disciplining and guiding codes of conduct to urge enterprises to improve their corporate governance procedure, and then the state institutions acknowledged these codes as administrative regulations. Corporate governance reform is often driven by crises and scandals. In the 1990s, the corporate governance reform in the United Kingdom, the United States, and other countries was triggered by waves of scandals of insider control in the context of highly dispersed ownership. In 2002, a series of corporate governance scandals- most notably the Enron case and the WorldCom Company case- inspired new deliberations and new reform efforts for corporate governance.

China can draw on the experiences of other countries- including Anglo-American corporate and continental European countries on this issue. In China, the Shanghai Stock Exchange issued the first guidance of this kind in 2000. In January 2002, on the government side, the China Securities Regulatory Commission and the State Economic and Trade Commission issued a compulsory Code of Corporate Governance for Listed Companies in China.

Notes and References

1. Due to the absolute dominance of the ruling party in the state organization of the Stalin model, Hungarian economist Maria Csanadi called this kind of state sector "Party-State Economy," or "Party-State Inc." (Maria Csanadi, *Party-States and Their Legacies in Post-Communist Transformation*, Cheltenham, U.K.: Edward Elgar Publishing, 1997.)

2. These functions of SOEs were pushed to the utmost m the era of the Great Cultural Revolution. The slogan at that time was, "Enterprises are fortresses of proletarian dictatorship."

3. Janos Kornai, *Economics of Shortage*, Amsterdam: North-Holland Publishing Company, 1980.

4. Zhou Taihe et al., *Economic System Reform in Contemporary China* (Dangdai Zhongguo de jingji tizhi gaige), Beijing: China Social Sciences Press, 1984, p. 70.

5. Ibid., p. 100

6. Ibid, 1984, p. 137.

7. See Chapter 1 for Sun Yefang's criticism on transferring enterprises to governments at lower levels.

8. Yuan Baohua, an important leader of China's SOE reform, expounded m an interview on the process of decision making on the guiding principle of expanding autonomy and sharing profit. See He Yaomin, "Expanding Autonomy and Sharing Profit: the Breakthrough Point in SOE Reform-An Interview with Yuan Baohua (Kuoquan rangli: guoyou qiye gaige de tupokou- fang Yuan Baohua tongzhi)," *Hundred Year Tide* (Bainian chao), 2003, No. 8.

9. For example, the leader of the State Economic Commission commented on expanding enterprise autonomy of 1978 to 1980 by saying that "the five documents were called documents of autonomy-expanding and profit-sharing, but both autonomy-expanding and profit-sharing were really limited m practice." See He Yaomin, ibid.

10. The official name for the enterprise contracting system.

11. Administrative function in foreign trade and telecommunication were not performed by state bureaus under the State Economic and Trade Commission; instead, they were performed by the Ministry of Foreign Trade and Economic Cooperation (MOFTEC) and the Ministry of Information Industry (MII), respectively.

12. H-shares are shares issued by companies incorporated in Chinese mainland but listed on the Stock Exchange of Hong Kong. A-shares are issued by companies incorporated in Chinese mainland and traded in RMB in domestic stock exchanges. "Red Chips" are shares issued by companies incorporated in Hong Kong and listed on the Stock Exchange of Hong Kong but owned (directly or indirectly) in significant proportions by the Chinese government or a Chinese SOE.

13. Tian Yanmiao (the Economic Law Section of the Commission of Legislative Affairs of the NPC Standing Committee) et al. (eds.), *Provision Interpretation and Legal Application of Company Law of the People's Republic of China* (Zhonghua Renmin Gongheguo Gongsifa tiaowen jieshi ji falyue shiyong), Beijing: China Democracy and Legal System Press, 2000, p. 122.

14. Hong Hu, "Explanation to 'Program of Selecting a Group of Large- and Medium-Sized SOEs for Experiments m Modern Enterprise System (draft)' (Guanyu Xuanze Yi Pi Guoyou

Dazhongxing Qiye). Economic and Trade Commission of the PRC (ed.), *A Collection of Documents of the National Working Conference for Experiments in Establishing Modern Enterprise System* (Quanguo Jianli Xiandai Qiye Zhidu Shidian Gongzuo Huiyi Wenjian Huibian), Beijing: Reform Press, 1995, p. 85.

15. "Unchecked insider control" is a defect that is likely to exist m the governance structure of modern corporations. When shareholders of a modern corporation lose residual control of the corporation due to overdiversification of share ownership or other reasons, the problem of a mismatch between residual control and claim to residual income emerges. Companies controlled by insiders often make decisions against shareholders' interests and embark on a road to decline and demise. In recent years, there was an extensive literature in management in western countries on how to prevent this problem from happening, illustrating its harmfulness to the management of enterprises.

16. Wu Jinglian et al., *The Strategic Restructuring of the State Sector* (Guoyou Jingji de Zhanlyuexing Gaizu), Beijing: China Development Press, 1998, p. 26.

17. On July 18 to July 24, 1997, Premier Zhu Rongji inspected ten large-sized SOEs-including Anshan Iron and Steel Group Corporation, Liaoyang Petrochemical Company, and Fushun Aluminum Factory-and held informal discussions with more than thirty leaders from enterprises m trouble and enterprises performing well, respectively, to assess the situation of reform and development of SOEs and to discuss how to eliminate losses and how to do a good job of running SOEs. During this inspection, Zhu Rongji pledged to get large- and medium-sized SOEs that were in the red out of trouble in about three years. See *People's Daily* (Renmin ribao), July 31, 1997.

18. Wu Jinglian, *Modern Corporation and Enterprise Reform* (Xiandai Gongsi Yu qiye Gaige), Tianjin: Tianjin People's Publishing House, 1994, pp. 222-223.

19. <http://www.csrc.gov.cn/CSRCSite/tongjiku/199911/default.html>.

20. Margaret Blair, *Ownership and Control*, Washington, D.C.: The Brookings Institute, 1995, p. 46.

21. In the developmental process of industrial and commercial enterprises over nearly a century, enterprises adopted three hierar chical organizational forms successively. The first one was centralized unitary structure (U-form); the second was holding company (H-form); and the third was a multidivisional structure (M-form). For an analysis of the three hierarchical organizational forms, see Alfred Dupont Chandler, Jr., *Strategy and Structure: Chapters in the History of the American Industrial Enterprise*, Cambridge, Mass.: MIT Press, 1962. See also Oliver E. Williamson, *The Economic Institutions of Capitalism*. New York: The Free Press, 1985.

22. Alfred Dupont Chandler, Jr., *Strategy and Structure: Chapters in the History of the American Industrial Enterprise*, Cambridge, Mass.: MIT Press, 1962.

23. "Phenomenon of age 58" refers to the phenomenon that frequently occurred in SOEs in recent years, in which some senior executives started to accumulate wealth by embezzling public funds and exchanging their enterprises' intellectual property for personal gains when they approached age 60 because they would lose all their power when they retired at age 60.

CHAPTER FOUR

RURAL REFORM

From the mid-1950s to the end of the 1970s, the focus of China's reform was placed on state-owned industry and commerce with no breakthrough being made. The new situation of "an enchanting sight in spring time" for China's economy appeared only in the autumn of 1980 when the household contracting system (jiating chengbao jingyingzhi) was implemented on a large scale in rural China. Therefore, rural reform was the genuine starting point and the driving force of China's economic reform.

4.1
The Collective Agriculture Under
The System Of People's Communes

People's Communes, which is the foundational form under the control of planning economic system, is unable to suit the nature of the agricultural economy. Thus low efficiency is common phenomena.

4.1.1 From Cooperatives to People's Communes

Mao Zedong launched a socialist upsurge of the cooperative transformation of agriculture (i.e., the Cooperative Transformation Campaign) in 1955. It took only about one year to abrogate the family farm system in agriculture and achieve the "advanced cooperative transformation."

At the end of 1955, there were only five hundred advanced cooperatives nationwide with member households accounting for 3.45 percent of the total number of rural households. By the end of 1956, one year after launching the Cooperative Transformation Campaign, 540,000 advanced cooperatives existed with member households accounting for 88 percent of the total number of rural households. Advanced cooperative transformation was fully achieved by the winter of 1957, and 120 million rural households nationwide were organized into 753,000 advanced cooperatives.[1]

Agricultural cooperatives, originally as a mutual aid and cooperative organization of laborers, provide the condition that cooperative members could freely join and withdraw. However, the Cooperative Transformation Campaign, launched in 1955, changed the nature of cooperatives from elementary ones with voluntary participation to quasi-state-owned "advanced cooperatives (gaojishe)" organized under social coercion. In "advanced agricultural producers' cooperatives" (i.e., advanced cooperatives), the property of the individual farmers were merged into indivisible collective property. Under conditions where members were not allowed to freely withdraw and cooperatives were managed by cadres, cooperatives were no longer different from state-owned enterprises, except that the state was not responsible for paying out wages.

Nevertheless, the scale of these advanced cooperatives was relatively small, with each cooperative comprised of only one hundred to two hundred households, and they were established separately from the grassroots governments. For the "convenience for exercising leadership," the CCCPC issued a directive on March 30, 1958, requesting that small cooperatives be consolidated into larger ones. Liu Shaoqi named these larger cooperatives "communes." In July 1958, Mao Zedong formally called for merging advanced cooperatives into "people's communes" that were "large in size and public in ownership" and "integrating government administration with commune management." Hence, a campaign of "organizing people's communes on a big scale" (i.e., the People's Communes Campaign) was launched nationwide. By the autumn of 1958, the entire rural China had been switched over to people's communes.

At the beginning, the people's commune implemented "one-level accounting," that is, pure commune ownership, and land and other means of production previously owned by advanced cooperatives were transferred to the commune and allocated by the commune in a unified way; the labor force of the entire commune was organized according to military establishment and allocated by the commune in a unified way. Based on this property rights system, unified management, unified distribution, and unified responsibility for profits and losses of the commune were thus implemented.

During the "three-year period of hardships" (1960-1962) following the Great Leap Forward and the People's Communes Campaign, the Chinese government adjusted its agricultural operation system and rural policies several times. In February 1962, the CCCPC issued the Directive on the Issue of Altering the Basic Accounting Unit of People's Communes in Rural Areas, designating the production team as the basic accounting unit. This system of "three-level ownership with the production team as the basic accounting unit" continued as the basic economic system in rural China until the end of the Decade of Turmoil (i.e., the Great Cultural Revolution of 1966-1976).

4.1.2 The Economical Effects Of The Collective Agriculture

After the Cooperative Transformation Campaign and the People's Communes Campaign, farmers lost control over the agricultural economy and claim to the surplus of their labor, and the system of integrating government administration with commune management (including the residence registration system, the grain coupon system, and the grain rationing system) restricted farmers' freedom of mobility so that their human capital had no way of being fully utilized. All in all, farmers lost the right to dispose of their own property. What to produce, how much to produce, and where to get the means of production were all to be decided by government departments at various levels; the production plan was made known to each of the levels below, and each level pressed for its implementation in seasons of planting and harvesting; once the plan was made by higher-level government departments according to leaders' preference, farmers were supposed to passively accept it. Because of the long cycles, the strong seasonality, and the wide spatial distribution of agricultural production, the measurement of effort was extremely difficult and supervision cost very high.In the collective production of people's communes, with commune members "showing up for work in big groups and making as much sound and fury but as little effort as possible," the consequence of such supervision and incentive was that "it is all the same whether you do more or less and whether you do better or worse." The state implemented unified purchase and marketing of major agricultural products, such as grain, cotton, and rapeseed, which were monopolized by state-owned commercial enterprises and quasi-state-owned "supply and marketing cooperatives (gongxiao hezuoshe)," allowed only limited rural fair trading, and forbade long-distance transport of goods for sale.

Farmers toiled all year round, and yet the yields were extremely low. Quite often, they could not even ensure that there would be enough food and clothing for their families, and basically they had no savings to speak of. In 1957, the average annual net income of each farmer was RMB 73.37. The figure was RMB 133.57 in 1978,[2] an increase of only RMB 60.20 in twenty-one years.[3] Moreover, about 250 million farmers did not have enough food and clothing.[4]

4.1.3 The Three Ups and Downs of "Contracting Output Quota to Each Household" before 1976[5]

After the cooperative transformation, land ownership was transferred to the collective. However, farmers generally had a spontaneous tendency of hoping to lease the collective land to build their own family farms. In 1956 (following the establishment of advanced cooperatives), in 1959 (following the founding of the people's commune system), and in 1962 (following the havoc of the second go-communism craze in 1960-1961), the tendency to resort to output-quota contracting had three upsurges, but all were ruthlessly suppressed.

As early as the autumn of 1956, just one year after advanced cooperatives were established across the nation, some localities spontaneously started the practice of paying farmers according to their agricultural output. This practice of "contracting output quota to each household" originated in Wenzhou Prefecture in Zhejiang Province, Wuhu Prefecture in Anhui Province, and Chengdu Prefecture in Sichuan Province. The CCCPC launched the campaign of "mass debates between socialist and capitalist roads." In this campaign of mass debates (i.e., campaign of criticism), "contracting output quota to each household" was labeled "marching along the capitalist road."

The second upsurge of "contracting output quota to each household" took place in 1959. During and after the People's Communes Campaign, all these did great harm to farmers. Seeing that agricultural production and the minimum living standard of farmers could scarcely be maintained and trying to save themselves, some localities started to practice "contracting output quota to each household" when they made the production team the basic accounting unit. Unfortunately, their attempt was regarded as a major manifestation of "Right Opportunism", even as "Capitalist Restoration" and was criticized.

Again from 1960 to 1961, for the third time, "contracting output quota to each household" was demanded by farmers. At that time, farmers in many localities were suffering from hunger and cold and were dying "abnormal death" (euphemism for death from malnutrition-related causes) in large numbers, and collective economic organizations could no longer maintain the minimum living standard of commune members. Under these circumstances, Anhui Province was the first to adopt the practice of "fixing output quota for each plot and designating responsibility for each person,"[6] hoping to preserve lives and restore agricultural production by doing so. Mao Zedong himself put forward the slogans that "class struggle and proletarian dictatorship should never be forgotten" and "grasp class struggle and all problems can be solved," and the decision that a large-scale socialist education campaign should be launched in the countryside across the nation. The Socialist Education Campaign (1963-1966) turned out to be the prelude to the decade of the Great Cultural Revolution.

4. 2
To establish the Household Contracting System throughout the country

4.2.1 Quick Spread of the Household Contracting System

After the decade of the Great Cultural Revolution, confronted with the devastation of the rural economy everywhere, the party and government leaders in some localities anxiously searched for a way out of their plight. When farmers in these localities once again demanded "contracting output quota to each household," they received support from these open-minded cadres. At that time, the responsibility system for agricultural production (nongye shengchan zerenzhi)[7] adopted in various localities could be categorized in three major ways- job contracting, output-quota contracting, and responsibility contracting- and in three major forms- contracting job to each work group, contracting output quota to each household, and contracting responsibility to each household (also called the all-round responsibility system).[8] Nowadays, people often refer to "contracting responsibility to each household" as "contracting output quota to each household" although the two concepts were different originally. This implies fundamental changes in agricultural production from collective operation to household operation on contracted land.

The basic method is that the collective (generally represented by the villagers' committee), as the land owner, contracts plots to farmers to operate according to the number of persons in the family or both the number of persons in the family and the number of laborers in the family; farmers fulfill their responsibilities to the state in terms of taxation and compulsory or contracted purchase as well as their responsibilities to the collective with contributions to a public accumulation fund and a public welfare fund; and all the remaining produce belongs to the farmers and is at their disposal. The biggest difference between "contracting responsibility to each household" and "contracting output quota to each household" is that the unified operation and distribution by the production team has been abrogated in the former. Essentially, "after handing in a sufficient amount to the state and contributing a sufficient amount to the collective, each household keeps all remaining harvest" is the farmers' description of "contracting responsibility to each household."

The wave of "contracting output quota to each household," with the "all-round responsibility system" as its main form, first sprang up in Anhui Province. By the end of 1978, the number of production teams practicing "contracting output quota to each household" in Anhui Province reached 1,200. In 1979, this number increased to 38,000, accounting for about 10 percent of the production teams in the province. In other localities in Sichuan, Guizhou, Gansu, Inner Mongolia, and Henan, "contracting output quota to each household" also expanded in a considerable scale. However, the CCCPC at that time still embraced the tenet of the "Two What-evers."[9] Therefore, only a few provincial committees of the CPC, such as those of Anhui and Sichuan, expressly committed to supporting "contracting output quota to each household."

In the year of 1980, Deng Xiaoping took over control of the leadership. He pointed out emphatically "The existence of multiple patterns of operation, multiple forms of labor organization, and multiple methods of remuneration should be permitted... Do not stick to one model or impose uniformity in all cases... In those remote mountainous areas and poverty-stricken backward regions and in those production teams that have been relying on state-resold grain for food, loans for production, and social relief for living for a long period of time, if the masses have lost their confidence in the collective and request contracting output quota to each household, such requests should be granted and either contracting output quota to each household or contracting responsibility to each household may be practiced and such arrangements are to be kept unchanged for a fairly long period of time." There was not an official policy basis for "responsibility contracting" until January 1982. In June 1982, production teams implementing "two contractings" nationwide accounted for 86.7 percent of the total, and this number further increased to 93 percent by the beginning of 1983. The majority of these were "contracting responsibility to each household."[10] By this time, the two concepts of "contracting output quota to each household" and "contracting responsibility to each household" had already been integrated into one. "Contracting responsibility to each household" became the mainstream of the household contracted responsibility system with remuneration linked to output (jiating lianchan chengbao zerenzhi),[11] signifying the completion of the transition of China's agricultural operation system from the collective economic system of people's communes to the system of family farms built by farmers on the "contracted" land.

The two main reasons why the operation system in rural China could be changed in an extremely short period of time were as follows.

1. The "contracting system" was a relatively familiar institutional arrangement to farmers and the most acceptable system to them, as well. Under the condition that

the system of collective land ownership is maintained, it is the most convenient option for farmers to "contract (lease)" land owned by the collective for long periods of time and build their family farms on this contracted or leased land. "Contracting output quota to each household" was exactly this kind of agricultural operation.

2. There was no serious social obstacle for the transition to the contracting system. During transition, as farmers had gains without losses and no harm was done to the interests of the other social groups, this reform was easily accepted by the public. Under the planned economic system, farmers were different from workers in that they could not receive welfare and security as urban workers did. Farmers would always have to assume risks by themselves and be responsible for their own livelihoods. There was no "big-pot meal" for them to eat. Therefore, with the transition, they had something to gain but nothing to lose. Furthermore, the fact that the catastrophe of the Great Cultural Revolution brought the Chinese economy to the verge of collapse made some practical-minded rural cadres also believe that they should support farmers in their institutional innovation of "contracting output quota to each household." In the meantime, "contracting output quota to each household" would not cost these cadres much in terms of power and interests; on the contrary, it would benefit their families and themselves. Therefore, in the transition to the household contracting system, many cadres played positive roles.

4.2.2 The Family Farm System Is The Operation System Best Suited For Agricultural Production

Experiences in the agricultural development of various countries show that the family farm system is the operation system best suited for agricultural production. This mode of operation works best for agriculture because of some specific features of agricultural production. As pointed out by economist Chen Xiwen, agricultural production is characterized by two salient features. First, agricultural production processes are integrated with the life processes of animals and plants; the production processes of agriculture in its narrow sense (crop cultivation) are integrated with the life processes of plants whereas the production processes of agriculture beyond its narrow sense (animal husbandry and fishery) are integrated with the life processes of animals. This requires that the producer constantly and carefully look after the life and growth of animals and plants as the object of his labor and make appropriate intervention in accordance with their growth conditions. Second, agricultural production is greatly affected by climate and other natural processes, such as sunshine, temperature, precipitation, and air currents, all of which are beyond human control and ever changing. These features pose special requirements for agricultural producers in contrast to their industrial counterparts. The conditions of animals and plants and information about natural changes in sunshine, temperature, precipitation, and air currents must be closely monitored in real time, and decisions must be correspondingly made in a timely fashion. As such, for agricultural producers (laborers) to possess total control, including specific control and residual control, is the most effective institutional arrangement.[12]

Of course, it may be feasible and efficient to have an institutional arrangement in which the owner mainly engages in management while direct production activities are conducted mainly by employed laborers. However, the issue of effective incentive is difficult to resolve when agricultural production activities are conducted mainly by employed laborers. In agricultural production, since the life processes of animals and plants are continuous, only the total effort made by the laborer can manifest itself as the final output of those animals and plants. This situation differs from manufacturing where the quantity and quality of the effort by each laborer in each phase of the production process can be measured. If the measurement of agricultural laborers' efforts is made without reference to the final output, that is, without each laborer working on the entire lifecycle of those living things, it is impossible to accurately measure each laborer's effort. The issue is further complicated because agricultural production jobs vary a great deal according to line of business, location, and season. However, if agricultural production activities are conducted on a household basis, the incentive issue is very easy to solve. As a family is a close-knit entity with common economic interests, the differences in objectives and conflicts of interest among family members are minimal, and they rarely give thought to the effort and income of individual family members, transaction costs are significantly reduced.

Specifically, household operation has several advantages.

1. It results in the optimal labor combination. Household coordination hardly has any transaction costs because family members share common objectives and have harmony of interests.

2. It has a very low decision-making cost. Most family decisions are collectively made by key members with sufficient information. Family decision making has the advantages of being quick, flexible, convenient, and authoritative, and is easily adaptable to changes in circumstances.

3. It has a strong capacity to bear risks. The blood ties among family members result in very strong cohesion, and the calculation of return on investment in the family farm is usually adequate.

4. It simplifies distribution of income within the family, which not only saves distribution cost but also avoids the costs of measurement, calculation, division, and supervision.

5. It has low management cost, low labor organizing cost, and low opportunity-taking cost.

All in all, since the family is the basic economic cell of society, which integrates production, consumption, education, and fostering of children and has enduring stability, the natural division of labor within the family reduces decision-making costs and minimizes measurement, supervision, and other transaction costs. All these have given household operation unparalleled superiority over other modes of operation in agricultural production. Thus, as stated by economist Justin Y. Lin and his colleagues, "Because agriculture does not display many characteristics of a scale economy, and because supervising and measuring agricultural work is difficult, agriculture is suitable for household operations."[13]

In socialist countries, the argument that collective agriculture is superior to household agriculture used to be prevalent. Even those who maintained a relatively open attitude toward the farmer issue and opposed the practice of "cooperative transformation first and mechanization second" were motivated by the belief that because productive forces determine relations of production, collectivization is the inevitable result of mechanization, and what they opposed was not collectivization per se, but the change in relations of production running ahead of the development of productive forces. After the household contracting system was implemented in rural China, many people still believed that this system was a measure of expediency adopted only when agricultural productivity was low. Agriculture would certainly "go collective" again when agricultural productivity improved and agricultural production mechanized. All these views shared a common theoretical basis in an assertion made by Karl Marx based on conditions in the United Kingdom that large-scale production was superior to small-scale production in agriculture, and therefore nationwide agricultural operation would generate greater momentum to production. In fact, as early as the end of the nineteenth century, a debate over whether large-scale production was superior to small-scale production in agriculture occurred in the socialist movement. At that time, such leading figures in the Social Democratic Party as Edward David (1863-1930) and Edward Bernstein (1850-1932) raised doubts about Karl Marx's assertion and said that peasant economy with the family as the unit had the potential for further development. Karl Kautsky (1854-1938) pointed out in his book, *The Agrarian Question*, that large-scale production can be necessarily superior to small-scale production in agriculture only when other conditions are the same. Lenin expressed his assent to Kautsky's view in his book, *Development of Capitalism in Russia*.[14] The development of agriculture in developed countries in the twentieth century indicates that even when agriculture is mechanized and highly socialized, the family farm system still has superiority and vitality. The UK, where the corporate farm system with wage labor was once implemented, has now returned to the family farm system, which is a powerful testimony that household operation is superior in agricultural production.

4.3
Economic Results of the Household Contracting System

The spread of "Contracting output quota to each household" influenced Chinese economy in different aspects.

Toward A Market Economy

A Glimpse Into China's Long March

當代中國經濟改革

文化中國

4.3.1 Influence of "Contracting output quota to each household" On Agriculture

The household contracting system, implemented during the late 1970s and the early 1980s, brought about tremendous changes to Chinese agriculture. Implementation of the contracting system in rural China greatly promoted agricultural development. According to calculations by Justin Y. Lin, the total contribution of various measures of rural reform to rural output growth from 1978 to 1984 was 48.64 percent, of which the contribution of the contracting system was 46.89 percent. One of the most direct economic effects was that agricultural output increased by a great margin. Between 1978 and 1984, agricultural production in China had experienced unprecedented changes since the founding of the PRC. In 1984, total national grain output reached a record high of 407.31 million tons, up by 33.6 percent as compared with 1978, with an average annual growth rate of 4.95 percent; total output of cotton measured 6.258 million tons, 1.89 times higher than that of 1978; output of oilseeds totaled 11.9[15] million tons, 1.28 times higher than that of 1978; total output of sugar crops was 47.8 million tons, 1.01 times higher than that of 1978.[16]

Also, both animal husbandry and fishery experienced tremendous growth. In 1988, the national output of pork, beef, and mutton combined was 21.936 million tons, increased by 1.56 times as compared with 1978, with an average annual growth rate of 9.9 percent- equivalent to 2.75 times the average annual growth rate during the twenty-six years prior to 1978; the national output of dairy products was 4.189 million tons, 3.3 times higher than that of 1978, with an average annual growth rate of 15.7 percent. In 1988, the national output of aquatic products was 10.61 million tons, 1.28 times higher than that of 1978, with an average annual growth rate of 8.6 percent.[17] The increase in agricultural, animal husbandry, and fishery products greatly improved people's standard of living. In 1988, grain per capita nationwide was 363 kilograms; cotton 3.8 kilograms; oilseeds 12.1 kilograms; pork, beef, and mutton combined 20.2 kilograms; and aquatic products 9.7 kilograms. They respectively increased by 13.5, 65.2, 120, 124, and 98 percent as compared with 1978.[18]

During and after the 1980s, agricultural production in China continued to grow in the 1990s (see Table 4.1).

Table 4.1   **Gross Output Value of Farming, Forestry, Animal Husbandry, and Fishery** (RMB billion)

Year	Total of Farming, Forestry, Animal Husbandry, and Fishery	Farming	Forestry	Animal Husbandry	Fishery
1978	139.7	111.8	4.8	20.9	2.2
1980	192.3	145.4	8.1	35.4	3.3
1985	361.9	250.6	18.9	79.8	12.6
1990	766.2	495.4	33.0	196.7	41.1
1995	2,034.1	1,188.5	71.0	604.5	170.1
2000	2,491.6	1,387.4	93.7	739.3	271.3

Source: The National Bureau of Statistics, *China Statistical Yearbook* (Zhongguo tongji nianjian), Beijing: China Statistics Press, various years.

With such increases in agricultural production, the rural industrial structure in China was rationalized each passing day; the proportions of forestry, animal husbandry, side-line production, and fishery increased considerably. First, in crop cultivation, the share of cash crops in 1988 reached 18.4 percent, an increase of 6.5 percentage points over 1978; the output value of grain crops fell to 58.2 percent.[19] Second, the share of the gross output value of agriculture in the gross rural output value dropped from 68.6 percent in 1978 to 46.8 percent in 1988; the share of rural industry increased from 19.4 percent to 38.1 percent; the share of rural construction increased from 6.6 percent to 7.1 percent; the share of rural transport service increased from 1.7 to 3.5 percent; and the share of rural commerce increased from 3.7 to 4.5 percent.[20]

In addition, specialized households engaging in rural industry, rural construction, rural transport service, and rural commerce had rapidly developed. In 1981, specialized households were still rare in rural China. But they numbered 15.61 million in 1982, 24.84 million in 1983, and 25.6 million in 1984. Driven by the contracting system, industrial enterprises in rural China adopted multiple forms of organization and operation, with four types predominating: township enterprises, village enterprises, joint household enterprises, and individual enterprises. By 1988, there were 386,900 joint entities in rural China engaging in industry, construction, transport, commerce, catering, service, and other sectors with 3.85 million employees, original value of fixed assets of RMB 7.154 billion, and net income of RMB 780 million.[21]

Along with the growth of agriculture, the income of Chinese farmers increased substantially. In 1980, rural per capita net income obtained from the basic accounting units of the collective economic organizations (i.e., production teams) was only RMB 85.9; rural per capita net income was RMB 191 when side-line production income was added.

Table 4.2 **Per Capita Annual Total Income and Annual Net Income of Rural Households** (RMB)

Year	1978	1980	1985	1990	1995	2001
Total Income	152	216	547	990	2,338	307
Net Income	134	191	398	686	1,578	2,366

Source: The National Bureau of Statistics, China Statistical Yearbook (Zhongguo tongji nianjian), Beijing: China Statistics Press, various years.

By 1985, the per capita net income of farmers increased to RMB 398,[22] doubling in five years.

4.3.2 Reform of Property Rights by the Contracting System

The effect on productivity of the contracting system was only one aspect of the issue. The contracting system also had great impacts on the economic system and even the political system. Among all these impacts, however, the foremost was that Chinese farmers acquired property rights.

Before rural reform, farmers hardly had any property of their own except their houses. In 1978, about a quarter of the production teams in the country had an annual per capita income of less than RMB 50. The estimated worth of each household property was no more than RMB 500. Even collective property was skimpy. In 1978, the total value of fixed assets of the collective sector in rural

China was RMB 72 billion, less than RMB 240 per laborer, which was equivalent to only 2.56 percent of RMB 9,400 - the average value of fixed assets per laborer of state-owned industry.[23] Because the government had control over the production, distribution, and pricing of agricultural products, the state had been obtaining a great deal of revenue from agriculture through the price scissors and other means since the 1950s. According to the calculation of some relevant departments, from 1951 to 1978, agriculture, through accumulation, provided RMB 434 billion for industrialization, which equals RMB 98 billion of tax revenue plus RMB 512 billion of the price scissors between industrial and agricultural products minus RMB 176 billion of state investment in agriculture. During the seventeen years from 1962 to 1978, only in five years was grain production profitable, with average profits per *mu* ranging from RMB 2 to 5; all the other years saw losses. Therefore, even the simple reproduction of agriculture could hardly sustain. During the twenty-one years from 1957 to 1978, the annual net income per capita of farmers increased only from RMB 73.37 to RMB 133.57, an average increase of less than RMB 3 per year. Taking the increases in commodity prices into account, the actual annual increase in rural per capita net income was RMB 1.[24] However, about half the central government's revenues were from agriculture either directly or indirectly. From 1952 to 1978, exports of agricultural and side-line products and their processed goods accounted for 62.6 to 90.6 percent of China's exports.[25] Therefore, most of the income created by farmers was contributed to the state.[26]

After the reform of the household contracting system, assets owned by Chinese farmers grew tremendously. As of 1992, total assets in rural China amounted to RMB 9,519.6 billion, of which, 22.71 percent were private household property and 77.29 percent were collective land properties and enterprise assets. Over 95 percent of the total collective assets had been contracted to rural households and individuals for operation on a long-term basis; less than 4 percent were operated collectively.[27] After the reform, Chinese farmers acquired three forms of property ownership. The first was personal property, mainly consisting of bank savings,[28] private houses, private means of production, and means of livelihood. The second was land-use right. Land was owned by the collective, but farmers had the right to use. Moreover, land had been contracted to farmers on a long-term basis, so they now enjoyed an unprecedented usufruct. The third was the growth of farmers' human capital. Farmers, now able to manage their activities themselves, greatly changed their mindset and attitudes and improved their abilities in the process of traveling and seeking employment.

4.3.3 Impact on the Development of TVEs

The predecessors of township and village enterprises (TVEs) were "commune and brigade enterprises" under the system of people's communes. There was a major difference between the two systems. "Commune and brigade enterprises" must adhere to the "three-locally principle," namely, obtaining raw materials locally, processing locally, and marketing products locally. In other words, they were not supposed to develop market-oriented processing, but rather to confine their operation within the scope of a self-contained economy. Therefore, at least by the original intention of the leadership, "commune and brigade enterprises" should belong to the so-called "traditional natural economy" in development economics.[29] By contrast, TVEs originated and developed when the household contracting system was already implemented in agriculture. So, TVEs were in sync with the development of a market economy.

During the Great Leap Forward of 1958 and the decentralization of 1970, the people's communes in various localities had all set up some machining and repair enterprises mainly related to agricultural machinery. To prevent rural industry from generating pressure on urban industry, the authorities had adopted various political and economic measures to limit the development of commune and brigade enterprises strictly within the scope of a self-contained rural economy.[30]

All this changed with the introduction of the household contracting system. First, the new system caused rural surplus laborers to emerge from their original concealment under the people's commune system and lawfully gain the freedom to seek employment in non-agricultural industries. This provided adequate labor supply for the development of TVEs and it also enabled all sorts of "able men" in rural China to bring into play their spirit of innovation, or "entrepreneurship" as described by Joseph Alois Schumpeter (1883-1950). Second, the introduction of the household contracting system also released the rural productive force that had long been fettered under the people's commune system, enabling agricultural production to yield a considerable surplus that could be turned into investment in the development of rural industry. Third, after the implementation of the household contracting system, farmers' increasing demand for consumable goods because of their rising living standard and the intensifying exchange of goods between urban and rural areas opened up markets for TVE products. After the 1980s, TVEs in China in general, and TVEs in such coastal regions as Middle Zhejiang, the Yangtze River Delta, the Pearl River Delta, and the Jiaodong Peninsula in particular, made considerable progress. Since the mid-1990s, rural industry has accounted for about one-third of industrial production in China. A number of TVEs have grown rapidly, despite market competition, to become leaders in their respective industries.

Table 4.3 **Number of TVEs and TVE Employment** (thousand unit/thousand people)

Year	1978	1980	1985	1990	1995	2000
Number of TVEs	1524	1425	12225	18504	22027	20847
Number of TVE employees	28266	29997	69790	92648	128621	128196

Source: The National Bureau of Statistics, *China Statistical Yearbook* (Zhongguo tongji nianjian), Beijing: China Statistics Press, various years; the TVE Bureau of the Ministry of Agriculture, *Annual Statistical Bulletin and Financial Statements of TVEs Nationwide* (Quanguo xi-angzhen qiye tongji nianbao ji caiwu juesuan ziliao), 2000.

4.4
Further Steps of Rural Reform

With continuous upward adjustment of purchase prices of agricultural products since 1993, the relationship between supply of and demand for domestic agricultural products took a new turn around the mid-1990s when agricultural products started to produce structural and regional surpluses as opposed to the overall shortages in the past. With these kinds of surpluses, prices of agricultural products such as grain, cotton, oil, and sugar in the domestic market have fallen for several consecutive years since 1998. Falling agricultural prices led to decelerating growth of farmers' incomes and a widening income disparity between urban and rural residents. As a result, the "three rural problems"- stagnant rural economy, poor rural residents, and backward rural society- have become an issue of wide concern. Further rural reforms need to be solved urgently.

4.4.1 Reforming the Purchasing and Marketing System of Agricultural Products

The CCCPC and the State Council announced in their No. 1 Document of 1985 the decision to reform the unified and quota purchase system of agricultural products. It proposed to expand the role of market regulation under the guidance of state planning and to implement the dual-track system of planned price for quota purchase and market price for non-quota purchase. At the beginning of 1992, the government leadership proposed to reform the purchasing, marketing, and pricing system of grain in the form of "different decisions for different regions and different implementations for different provinces." As a result, various localities lifted control over grain retail markets. By the end of 1993, control over grain selling prices had been lifted in more than 98 percent of all counties and cities across the nation.

However, owing to a sudden rise in grain prices and panic purchasing in some localities at the end of 1993, the situation changed dramatically. To ensure grain supply, the central government implemented in May 1994 a provincial governor (municipality mayor) responsibility system for regional balancing of grain and successively adopted the following measures:

1. raising the government purchasing price of quota grain by 46.6 percent in 1994, 29.0 percent in 1995, and 5.8 percent in 1996;[31]

2. requiring that state grain departments amass a bigger pool of grain;

3. allowing local governments to grant allowances on top of the purchasing price of quota grain when necessary;

4. stipulating that state-owned grain stores sell certain kinds of grain at government-prescribed prices.

These measures were effective in stabilizing the quantity of purchase and ensuring the grain ration supply to low-income urban residents. Notwithstanding, state grain departments in some localities breached the State Council's regulation of fixing the purchasing price according to market change. They lowered the purchasing price and purchased grain from farmers by imposing arbitrary quotas and then resold grain at higher prices to make profits. After two years of bumper harvests in 1995 and 1996, grain prices fell again[32] and farmers had difficulty selling grain. To ensure that farmers would continue to produce grain, in August 1997, the State Council issued the *Circular Concerning Unrestricted Purchase of Non-Quota Grain at Protective Price*, requiring that all localities promptly set up grain protective price: the price for quota grain could be no lower than that of the previous year, while the price for non-quota grain should be the base price for quota grain. On completion of the quota grain purchase assignment, all localities should resolutely purchase without restriction surplus grain from farmers at protective price. After promulgation of this policy, all local grain departments quickly changed their purchasing practices from purchasing non-quota grain at price fixed according to market change to purchasing non-quota grain without restriction at protective price. Accordingly, the quantity of grain purchased increased considerably, and grain depots in various localities were all filled to their capacities. Along with the continuous increase in grain stock, grain operation losses and unpaid bank credit also increased. By 1997, accumulated losses in the form of unpaid bank credit by state-owned grain trading enterprises for the past years reached RMB 100 billion, or over RMB 30,000 per employee for the state grain system of three million employees. As of March 1998, the balance of grain loans nationwide was as high as RMB 543 billion, indicating grain operation losses of RMB 214 billion by deducting the gross value of grain stock, or RMB 70,000 per employee of the state grain system.[33] Although various localities carried out the regulations of the State Council on unrestricted purchase of non-quota grain at protective price, as the overall grain supply exceeded demand, market price still fell for three consecutive years-1996, 1997, and 1998- and so did farmers' income from agriculture.

In response to problems of mismanagement by state-owned grain purchasing and marketing enterprises, the State Council issued the *Decision on Further Deepening Reform of the Grain Circulation System* in May 1998. In the *Decision*, it was pointed out that the basic principle of the reform of the grain circulation system was "four separations and one improvement:" separation of government administration from enterprise management, separation of reserve from distribution, separation of central government responsibilities from local government responsibilities, separation of new financial accounts from old financial accounts, and improvement of the grain pricing mechanism (i.e., gradual achievement of marketization).

On June 3, 1998, the national video working conference on grain purchase and marketing, convened by the State Council, further proposed that grain purchase and marketing reform should focus on the implementation of three policies. The so-called "three policies" were that (1) grain enterprises should purchase without restriction surplus grain from farmers at government-prescribed protective price; (2) grain purchasing and storage enterprises should implement "selling at mark-up price," i.e., selling at purchasing price plus minimum mark-up; and (3) purchasing funds lent by the Agricultural Development Bank of China to grain trading enterprises should "flow within a closed loop" according to the rules of "loan being linked to stock and money following grain." To ensure the implementation of the three policies, in November 1998, the State Council issued the *Opinion on Current Promotion of Reform of the Grain Circulation System*, requiring strengthening of the control over the grain purchasing market so that grain dealers, distributors, and grain processing enterprises were not allowed to purchase grain from farmers directly in grain-producing regions or from the fair trade market, except from the state-owned grain purchasing and storage enterprises. However, this set of policies could hardly be implemented. In some regions, the policy for grain purchasing and storage enterprises to purchase without restriction surplus grain from farmers at protective price could hardly be fully implemented; under a market economy, the order prohibiting private grain dealers from purchasing and marketing grain could hardly be enforced; and with a continuously declining grain market price, it would be very difficult for state-owned grain enterprises to realize selling at mark-up price. What actually happened was a sharply rising subsidy burden on the state finance system, an excessively high level of grain stock, and heavy losses incurred by grain purchasing and storage enterprises. To many experts, the reform of the grain purchasing and marketing system that was needed was to let market forces play their fundamental role by gradual marketization.

The *Opinion on Further Deepening Reform of the Grain Circulation System* issued by the State Council in July 2001 pushed the grain circulation system closer to marketization and liberalized the grain retail markets of eight provinces and municipalities of major consuming regions, including Zhejiang, Shanghai, Fujian, Guangdong, Hainan, Jiangsu, Beijing, and Tianjin. Similar reform experiments were also carried out in 2002 in selected localities in Hunan, Hubei, Jilin, Henan, and Zhejiang provinces. The direct subsidy reform primarily consisted of "two liberalizations and one adjustment," that is, liberalization of grain purchasing price, liberalization of grain retail markets, and adjustment to replace the indirect subsidy of state purchase without restriction at protective price with a direct subsidy in the form of state payments to farmers covering the price difference between the protective price and the market price. The *Decision of the CCCPC on Issues Regarding the Improvement of the Socialist Market Economic System* (hereafter the *Decision*) approved by the Third Plenary Session of the 16th CCCPC in October 2003 clarified the requirements of "improving the market system for agricultural products, liberalizing the grain purchasing market, and practically protecting the interests of grain farmers by carrying out direct subsidies to farmers instead of indirect subsidy through circulation."

In a similar manner, the reform of the cotton purchasing and marketing system also experienced twists and turns over its implementation. These reforms played a very important role in establishing a cotton purchase and marketing system compatible with a market economy. Notwithstanding, the problem of establishing cotton circulation enterprises with international market competitiveness, as well as an orderly market system, remains to be solved by further reforms.

4.4.2 Improving the Land System

The essence of the household contracting system is to separate land ownership from land-use right to a certain extent, and grant farmers land-use right during the contract period without changing land ownership. This land system innovation enabled farmers to build up their family farms on the "contracted" land, and this played a decisive role in promoting rapid growth in agricultural production. Nevertheless, the contracting system still had its limitations, as reflected in the following several aspects.

First, the land-use right obtained by farmers through contract was still imperfect. As the household awarded the contract did not possess a legal and permanent land-use right, the household felt great uncertainty, and therefore lacked incentive to make investment in the land. For this reason, most farmers' income was used on non-agricultural production investment. From 1978 to 1988, the net income of farmers increased about three times, but during the same period, the amount of investment in residential construction increased by about twenty times. In 1984, agricultural investment of collectives and individuals in rural areas accounted for 15.5 percent of the total rural investment, but this figure dropped to 11.9 percent in 1987. In contrast, non-agricultural investment rose from 84.5 to 88.[34] percent.l Dwindling investment in land by farmers year after year led to a decline in land productivity. To overcome these defects, the central government twice extended the period of farmland contracts. In 1985, various localities throughout the nation signed a fifteen-year contract. In 1993, the CCCPC proposed to further ex-tend the land contract period for another thirty years. Although the decision was warmly welcomed by farmers, contract period extension by no means fully resolved the issue of property rights. So, farmers still had misgivings about land investment and this also caused some difficulties for promoting new agricultural technologies.

Second, without clearly defined property rights, free transfer of the land-use right could not occur, and therefore larger scale agricultural operations could not proceed on the basis of land property optimization and reorganization, but only through administrative orders.

Third, land was transferred to non-agricultural uses in the process of accelerated industrialization and urbanization, but farmers had no legal claim to adequate compensation for the loss of their land-use right. Huge earnings from large amounts of land transferred from agriculture to non-agriculture were held back and swallowed up by various levels of government as well as industrial and commercial enterprises. According to estimates by economist Chen Xiwen, low-priced farmland requisition caused at least RMB 2,000 billion worth of losses to farmers since the commencement of the reform and opening up.[35] Moreover, farmers whose land had been occupied with no or inadequate compensation and who could not transfer themselves to non-agricultural industries, lost their means of making a living, which usually resulted in major social problems.

In view of these problems in the land system, the central government, in addition to stressing that the land contract period would remain stable for thirty years, also formulated laws to guarantee that farmers can fully exercise their rights of contractual operations within the contract period. In August 2002, the National People's Congress passed the *Law of the PRC on Land Contracts in Rural Areas* (hereafter the *Land Contract Law*). It expressly stipulated that:

1. the state protects the long-term stability of rural land contract relations according to law;

2. the state protects the rights of the party awarded the contract to transfer contractual operations with compensation, of their own will, and according to law;

3. the party awarded the contract has the right to use the land, to keep the income from the land, and to transfer the land-use contract, and that party is entitled to compensation for lawful requisition and appropriation of the contracted land according to law;

4. land circulation proceeds are owned by the party awarded the contract according to law.

Nevertheless, even after the promulgation of the *Land Contract Law*, there were still problems to be solved. First, rural collectives owned rural land, and yet the law failed to clearly define how the rural collective is formed and how farmers, as members of the collective, exercise their rights and functions. As land is the last line of defense for farmers' survival, if there were institutional defects in this line of defense, troubles would be bred in rural areas, and even the entire society. Second, as the use right of contracted land was limited by the contract period, the property rights of farmers were limited as well. For instance, farmers had no adequate legal means to resist acts of administrative authorities to requisition land for commercial purposes without adequate compensation. In short, the land property rights system required further improvement and reform in the future; procedures for farmers to exercise their rights as the owner of the village collective needed to be clarified; a permanent use right of contracted land (i.e., "field surface right") should be granted; and "field surface right" transfer, lease, and succession should be explicitly defined so as to better represent and protect farmers' rights and interests.

4.4.3 Alleviating Burden on Farmers

The Chinese government had issued orders and instructions many times to rigidly stipulate that the burden of "three retention fees and five contribution fees" on farmers should not exceed 5 percent of the per capita net income of the rural family in the previous year.[36] However, these policy measures hardly had any effect. In 2000, the government resolved to reform the rural tax and fee system.

In March 2000, an experiment in rural tax and fee reform was first launched in Anhui Province. In February 2001, the experimental reform scheme was introduced in 107 counties of more than 20 provinces. In March 2002, the State Council decided to further expand the experiment in 16 provinces and autonomous regions. By the end of 2002, more than 20 provinces and municipalities conducted rural tax and fee reform on a large scale, involving a rural population of 700 million. The fundamental ideas for this reform were to abolish administrative fees such as township contribution fees and government funds such as rural education pooling fund, collected solely from farmers; to abolish uniformly prescribed accumulation labor service and compulsory labor service; to abolish slaughter tax and reduce agricultural tax and agricultural specialties tax; to collect village retention fees as agricultural surtax in a unified way, with a maximum of 20 percent of agricultural tax. The village retention fees would be controlled at the township level and used at the village level.[37] Results achieved throughout the country indicated that rural tax and fee reform could alleviate the burden on farmers by about 30percent.[38]

In 2003, the State Council extended this reform to all rural China. At the same time, the Ministry of Finance and the State Administration of Taxation decided to gradually eliminate agricultural specialties tax, except for some special products such as tobacco leaves. In October 2003, the *Decision* of the Third Plenary Session of the 16th CCCPC said that agricultural tax would be further reduced in the future to alleviate the burden on farmers.

Although rural tax and fee reform has indeed alleviated the burden on farmers, it has by no means fundamentally solved the problem. The root causes of the problem are the bloated organizations and redundant personnel of governments at the grassroots level. After reform, revenues of townships and villages were reduced while their expenditures remained rigid, and transfer payments from central government finance were not enough to fill the gaps. Under the pressures of fund shortages, new taxes and fees began to be imposed on farmers in a few rural areas where tax and fee reform had been implemented; in some rural areas, the standard tuition fees and miscellaneous fees for primary and junior high schools have been raised without authorization, which has once again aggravated the burden on farmers. If fundamental measures are not taken, the specter of the so-called "Huang Zongxi Law" may haunt China again.[39]

It follows that to completely solve the problem of the overburden on farmers, the rural social and political organization in China must be changed. Taking the bloated organization and redundant personnel of local governments in rural China as an example, the root cause of this situation is that the administrative organization at the grassroots level is the extension of the "big government," and its cadres have been in charge of too many things. Therefore, the policy of better staff and simpler administration should be implemented. Meanwhile, rural democratic reform at the grassroots level should also be accelerated. Villagers' self-government should be improved according to the *Organic Law of Villagers' Committees of the PRC* of 1998. At the same time, direct election of grassroots governments should be expanded and mass supervision over township/town and county cadres should be strengthened. Only by doing so can the arbitrary imposition of miscellaneous fees by cadres be stopped, along with corruption and extravagance in various forms.

4.4.4 Solving Contradictions between Small Farmers and Big Markets

At present, one of the most serious problems to be solved in rural China is to overcome the contradictions between farmers engaged in small-scale operations and big markets. Agricultural production is scattered in space and seasonal in time. In contrast, the consumption of agricultural products is concentrated in space and continuous in time. In particular, the current scale of agricultural operations in China is small; the quantity of any agricultural product supplied to the market by any individual farmer is very limited. Therefore, there is a major contradiction between small farmers' supply and big markets' demand. The solution to this contradiction between small farmers and big markets has become an important issue in promoting the rural economy and improving the farmers' position in market transactions.

A common practice for connecting scattered individual farmers with markets is the so-called "company + farmer" model. Under this model, "flagship companies" engaging in industrial and commercial businesses and possessing strong advantages in capital, technology, and market information, establish relatively stable economic contact and benefit-sharing mechanism with numerous farmers. Farmers provide the companies with agricultural products as raw materials or primary products for processing and marketing according to conditions stipulated in contracts for purchase in advance. These companies usually provide assistance to farmers in the form of seeds/seedlings, technology, and funds.

At present, there are already some successful "company + farmer" economic groups in China. They have played a positive role in invigorating the rural economy and raising farmers' incomes. However, two problems often occur in the practice, harming the interests of either the farmers or the companies. One problem is that the companies take advantage of their powerful connections or private information about the market, while farmers may find themselves in a weak position, dominated by the flagship companies. As a result, the farmers share little in the value-added downstream processing of primary products. The other problem is that, compared to scattered farmers who have the power to make decisions, companies often found themselves in a weak position when collecting and mastering information about production. In particular, damages to companies' interests, such as low rates of contract performance on the part of farmers, always occur when companies have no powerful connections. According to experiences in market economy countries, one of the most effective approaches to link individual farmers with markets is for farmers to set up their own cooperative economic organizations to provide various preproduction and post-production services. These cooperative economic organizations are communities of interest for their members. They are not profit-oriented, and their purpose is to serve the members. In developed market economy countries, cooperatives in the realm of circulation play very important roles not only in providing an interface between small farmers and big markets, but also an important way for farmers to avoid market risks and protect their own interests.

During the Cooperative Transformation Campaign of the mid-1950s, a great number of agricultural producers' cooperatives known as "collective economic organizations" were set up in China. However, these cooperatives were in fact controlled by the state in much the same way as state-owned enterprises. Later, with agricultural producers' cooperatives as the model, even the original supply and marketing cooperatives and credit cooperatives organized on a voluntary basis were transformed into quasi-state-owned organizations, characterized by vertical integration and a strong flavor of government-run units. After the beginning of the reform and opening up, the Chinese government restored supply and marketing cooperatives and credit cooperatives that had been officially absorbed into the state sector during the Great Cultural Revolution. However, these cooperatives failed to recover their original nature as cooperative organizations formed by members on a voluntary basis and managed by members.[40] In contrast, some new cooperative economic organizations were spontaneously set up by farmers and other operators, such as various types of professional cooperatives, professional and technical associations, and agricultural service centers. As they are market-oriented and organized entirely according to the principle of voluntary participation, joint operation, democratic management, and return of benefits, they were therefore warmly welcomed by farmers. The *Decision* of the Third Plenary Session of the 16th CCCPC demanded that "support should be given to farmers, according to the principle of voluntary participation and democratic management, to develop various rural professional cooperative organizations."

To continue developing rural cooperative economic organizations in the future, the following problems must be solved. First, improvement of the cooperative legislation should be done as quickly as possible. To support the development of cooperatives, many countries confirmed their legal status by legislation. For instance, the United Kingdom passed the first *Cooperative Act* in the world in 1852, Germany promulgated a unified *Cooperative Law* in May 1889, the United States adopted the *Capper-Volstead Act* in 1922, and other countries also formulated laws pertaining to cooperative organizations.[41] Currently, China has not enacted any cooperative-related legislation. Many cooperatives or professional associations have been registered at the administrative bureau for industry and commerce, the civil administrative bureau, the agricultural bureau, or the association of science and technology. But some are not allowed to register anywhere.

Second, the original supply and marketing cooperatives, credit cooperatives, and other cooperative organizations should undergo thorough marketization reform to overcome their inclination to avoid practicing democratic management or serving members but rather maintaining cadres as masters of everything. These old cooperatives need to be transformed into genuine cooperative economic organizations, run according to the principle of the cooperative system.

Third, cooperative economic organizations should gradually expand their scale of operation across regions by implementing operation and management standardization, specialization, and professionalism. What needs to be stressed more, however, is that administrative measures to "go collective" should never be involved in these organizations' operations. Cooperative economic organizations should rely on market forces to develop and expand on their own according to the principles of voluntary participation, democratic management, and mutual benefit.

4.4.5 The Issue of the Transfer of Rural Surplus Laborers

The most deep-rooted cause of the "three rural problems" in China lies in the strong contradiction between an excessive rural population and scarce agricultural resources. Because each farming household has only about 8 *mu* (i.e., 1.33 acre) of farmland on average, if the huge quantity of surplus laborers cannot be transferred, the income level of farmers cannot increase significantly, nor can their production and living conditions improve no matter what measures the government adopts, such as increasing prices of agricultural products. Therefore, to solve the "three rural problems," the fundamental approach is to transfer rural surplus laborers to non-agricultural industries.

A comprehensive review of the history of more than two decades of the reform and opening up in China indicates that the transfer of rural surplus laborers to non-agricultural industries was gradually accelerating during the first decade, but the process obviously slowed down in the second decade.

The fundamental reason for the acceleration in the first decade was because China adopted a strategy to vigorously develop non-state sectors, particularly, township and village enterprises (TVEs). This brought about the following consequences:

1. Rapid growth of agricultural production and universal prosperity triggered an increase in rural accumulation, an essential condition for the transfer of rural surplus laborers;

2. On that basis, TVEs sprang up like mushrooms after rain, creating a great number of new jobs for rural surplus laborers;

3. The urban sector and the export sector of the economy made great progress and also took in a portion of rural surplus laborers to work in cities.

By the mid-1980s, the transfer of rural surplus laborers had reached a historical high. But, in the late 1980s, the transfer slowed down considerably not only because of TVEs' poor accumulation ability, decelerating quantitative expansion, and reduced capacity of unit capital to absorb laborers as a result of their increasing organic composition of capital, but also because of the state sector's stagnant reform, declining efficiency, and increased number of laid-off workers. The symptoms of "SOE disease" displayed by some TVEs owned by township/town governments also reduced their vitality and growth rate and slowed down the transfer. From 1984 to 1988, TVEs alone had absorbed on average about twelve million farmers annually to work in non-agricultural industries. After 1989, however, this figure dropped to five to six million.

After the 15th National Congress of the CPC in 1997, non-state small and medium enterprises rapidly developed. Correspondingly, the transfer of rural surplus laborers to non-agricultural sectors also sped up. To facilitate the transfer of rural surplus laborers to non-agricultural industries, vigorous development must be achieved in small and medium enterprises to provide more working opportunities for rural surplus laborers.

In addition to developing non-state small and medium enterprises, however, the urbanization issue is also related to the transfer of rural surplus laborers.

Over the past two and half decades, TVEs have developed in two different ways. One was to adopt the "three-locally principle," in which TVEs were scattered in rural areas with their employees "leaving the farmland but not the village home, entering the factory but not the city." This approach was generally adopted by TVEs in the inland regions. The other type of TVEs adopted the market-oriented guideline, in which TVEs were built near cities, in administrative towns, or small non-administrative towns. In those cases, these small towns where TVEs concentrate usually develop into new cities. TVEs in the coastal regions usually adopt this approach to development.

With these two different development models for TVEs as a backdrop, two different views appeared in the economic circles in China. One opinion supports the first approach, believing that under conditions in China, the capacity of cities and towns to absorb rural laborers is limited, whereas non-agricultural industries in rural areas play a decisive role in absorbing these surplus laborers. Therefore, relying on cities and towns to expand non-agricultural industries is neither advisable nor practical. This opinion argues that people must fully appreciate the uniqueness of China and take a critical view in adopting theories and policies pertaining to the "dual economy" to base rural development and rural labor transfer on the development of rural industry, which will also promote the development of the whole national economy. Some other economists hold the opposite view, however, believing that these kinds of enterprises scattered in rural areas have serious weaknesses. In addition to resulting in widespread sources of pollution and, therefore, difficulties in control and prevention, these kinds of scattered enterprises are usually low in efficiency as they can neither generate the agglomeration effects necessary for industrial development nor make use of what urban enterprises can, such as urban public service facilities, public support systems, cooperation based on division of labor among enterprises, and the convenience of a hub of communication.[42]

The development of the two types of TVEs over the past dozen years seems to have supported the second view. One important reason why some TVEs have failed to successfully develop in the inland regions is because they are scattered in rural areas, incurring high costs with low efficiency. Based on these experiences, it appears that the transfer of rural surplus laborers should be combined with the urbanization process.

Small towns,[43] because they are close to the countryside, with relatively low thresholds for entry, are comparatively more suitable for rural surplus laborers with relatively little accumulation of material capital and human capital. Since the inception of the reform and opening up, small towns have developed very fast and absorbed a great number of rural surplus laborers. At the end of 1978, there were only 2,173 administrative towns across the nation. However, by the end of 1998, administrative towns had increased to 19,216, with a total town population of 170 million. By the end of 2002, administrative towns numbered 19,811, nine times the number in 1978, accounting for more than 50 percent of the total number of townships and towns (39,240). The total town population had grown to 220 million, while the total population of the areas under their jurisdictions had reached over 640 million.

Small towns are only a fraction of the urban system. Comprehensive advance of urbanization requires coordinated development of large, medium, and small cities and small towns. Before the reform and opening up, the urbanization process in China was very slow. In 1951, the urbanization level was 11.8 percent; in 1978, it was only 17.9 percent. Since the commencement of the reform and opening up, the urbanization process in China has accelerated. Administrative cities increased from 223 in 1980 to 660 in 2002. The urbanization level increased from 17.9 percent in 1978 to 39.1 percent in 2002.

Statistics from the *World Development Report 1997* of the World Bank reveals that GNP per capita in China in 1995 was US$620, and the urbanization level was 30 percent. The average urbanization level in the same year of the eleven countries with GNP per capita between US$500 and 730 was 42.5 percent. This gap in urbanization level means that China urbanized about 150 million less rural population than it should have. Calculated according to purchasing power parity (PPP) by the World Bank, China's GNP per capita in 1996 was US$2,920. The average urbanization level of the nineteen countries with GNP per capita between US$2,000-3,800 (PPP) was 50.8 percent. So, according to this measurement, China urbanized about 250 million less rural population than it should have. In 1996, the average urbanization level of the world reached 45.5 percent, that of developed countries was generally more than 70 percent, and that of developing countries was on average over 40 percent. The urbanization levels of some developing countries with similar levels of economic development to China and of some newly industrialized countries were also considerably higher than that of China. For instance, the urbanization level of Brazil was 78 percent; Argentina, 88.4 percent; Australia, 84.7 percent; New Zealand, 86.1 percent; South Korea, 82.3 percent; North Korea, 61.5 percent; and the Philippines, 54.9 percent. The urbanization level of China was only 29.4 percent during the same period of time, grossly lagging behind.

Therefore, to vigorously develop small and medium enterprises, to increase urbanization in an orderly fashion, to abolish restrictions on farmers seeking employment in urban areas, to create more employment opportunities for farmers, to improve the environment for the transfer of rural surplus laborers, and to accelerate the employment of rural surplus laborers in non-agricultural industries are all arduous tasks for China to undertake for many years to come.

In October 2003, the 16th National Congress of the CPC put forward the requirement to "improve the environment for the transfer of rural surplus laborers," which included establishing and improving the training mechanism for rural laborers, promoting the reform and adjustment of TVEs, developing regional economies at the county level, enlarging the scope of rural employment, and abolishing restrictions on farmers seeking employment in urban areas to create more employment opportunities for farmers. Additional requirements were implemented to unify urban and rural labor markets step by step by providing better guidance and management, formulate the system of equal employment in both urban and rural areas, deepen the reform of the residence registration system, and improve the management of the transient population to direct the rural surplus laborers to transfer in a steady and orderly way. To accelerate urbanization, the rural population with stable jobs and residences in urban areas may be allowed, according to local rules, to have residence registration in their places of employment or residence and thus enjoy the same rights and undertake the same obligations as the local people. The implementation of these measures can significantly accelerate China's transfer of rural surplus laborers to urban non-agricultural industries.

Notes and References

1. Justin Y. Lin, *Institution, Technology and Agricultural Development in China* (Zhidu, jishu yu Zhongguo nongye fazhan), Shanghai: Shanghai People's Publishing House and Shanghai Joint Publishing, 1994, pp. 19-21.

2. The Agricultural Statistics Department of the National Bureau of Statistics, *Tremendous Changes in the Living Conditions of Chinese Farmers* (Wo guo nongmin shenghuo de juda bianhua), Beijing: China Statistics Press, 1985, p. 9.

3. Ibid., pp. 5-7.

4. The Agriculture Research Team of the National Bureau of Statistics, *Monitoring Report on Poverty in Rural China-2000* (Zhongguo nongcun pinkun jiance baogao-2000), Beijing: China Statistics Press, 2000, Table 2 of the Preface.

5. For a detailed description of this process, see Chen Xiwen, *Rural Reform in China: Retrospect and Prospect* (Zhongguo nongcun gaige: huigu yu zhanwang), Tianjin: Tianjin People's Publishing House, 1993, pp. 39-49. This section is to a great extent based on his description.

6. "Responsibility plots" in short, one of the many forms of "contracting output quota to each household."

7. An official and inclusive name for virtually all kinds of "contracting systems" and "responsibility systems" practiced in rural China since the late 1970s.

8. Zhou Taihe et al., *Economic System Reform in Contemporary China* (Dangdai Zhongguo de jingji tizhi gaige), Beijing: China Social Sciences Press 1984, pp. 269-270.

9. The "Two Whatevers" refers to the slogan that "whatever decision Chairman Mao made should be safeguarded firmly; whatever instructions he gave should be followed unswervingly."

10. The Rural Development Research Institute of the Chinese Academy of Social Sciences, "Reform of Rural Economic System in China (Zhongguo nongcun jingji tizhi de gaige)," the State Commission for Restructuring Economic Systems, *A Decade of Economic System Reform in China* (Zhongguo jingji tizhi gaige shi nian), Beijing: Economic Management Press and Reform Press, 1988.

11. Another, and more formal, name for "the household contracting system."

12. Chen Xiwen, *Rural Reform in China: Retrospect and Prospect* (Zhongguo nongcun gaige: huigu yu zhanwang), Tianjin: Tianjin People's Publishing House, 1993, pp. 57-60. Specific control and residual control can be separately owned, as in the case of a modern corporation where ownership (residual claim and residual control) and control (specific control) are held by shareholders and executives respectively.

13. Justin Y. Lin, Cai Fang, and Li Zhou, *The China Miracle: Development Strategy and Economic Reform*, Revised edition, Hong Kong: The Chinese University Press, 2003, p. 143.

14. Vladimir Lenin, "Preface to 'Development of Capitalism m Russia' ('Eguo zibenzhuyi de fazhan' xuyan) (1908)," *Complete Works of Lenin* (Liening quanji), Chinese edition, Vol. 3, Beijing: People's Publishing House, 1959. Conversation between Mao Zedong, Deng Zihui, and Du Runsheng in November 1952. See Du Runsheng, "My Recollection of Several Meetings between Mao Zedong and Me in the 1950s (Yi wushi niandai wo yu Mao Zedong de jici huimian)," *Collected Works of Du Runsheng* (Du Runsheng wenji), Taiyuan: Shanxi People's Publishing House, 1998, p. 784.

15. Justin Y. Lin, Institution, *Technology and Agricultural Development in China* (Zhidu, jishu yu Zhongguo nongye fazhan), Shanghai: Shanghai People's Publishing House and Shanghai Joint Publishing, 1994, p. 95.

16. Zhu Rong et al. (eds.), *Agriculture in Contemporary China* (Dangdai Zhongguo de nongye), Beijing: Contemporary China Press,1992, p. 375.

17. Ibid., p. 369.

18. Ibid., p. 369.

19. The National Bureau of Statistics, *Four Decades of Advance in Great Strides* (Fenjin de sishi nian), Beijing: China Statistics Press,1989, p. 23.

20. Ibid., p. 366.

21. The National Bureau of Statistics, *China Statistical Yearbook* (Zhongguo tongji nianjian) (1989), Beijing: China Statistics Press, 1989.

22. The National Bureau of Statistics, *China Statistical Yearbook* (Zhongguo tongji nianjian) (1981) and (1985), Beijing: China Statistics Press, 1981 and 1985.

23. *Investigation and Study* (Diaocha yu yanjiu), 1978, No. 12.

24. Chen Jiyuan (ed.), *Social and Economic Changes in Rural China* (Zhongguo nongcun shehui jingji bianqian), Taiyuan: Shanxi Economy Press, 1993, pp. 585-586.

25. Zhou Rili, "Evaluation of Achievements in a Decade of Reform and Ideas for Development in Rural Areas (Nongcun shi nian gaige de chengguo pingjia yu fazhan silu)," *Anhui Daily* (Anhui ribao), December 30, 1989.

26. According to research, gross accumulation by agriculture in 1980 was RMB 36.074 billion; deducting the portion used for the countryside by the state, the net capital outflow of agriculture was RMB 27.862 billion. See Feng Haifa and Li Wei, "Quantitative Study on Chinese Industrial Capital Accumulation Provided by Agriculture (Wo guo nongye wei gongye tigong zijin jilei de shuliang yanjiu)," *Economic Research Journal* (Jingji yanjiu), 1993, No. 9.

27. The National Bureau of Statistics, *China Statistical Yearbook* (Zhongguo tongji nianjian) (1993), Beijing: China Statistics Press, 1993.

28. Savings in rural credit cooperatives by farmers in 1992 amounted to RMB 210.78 billion. See ibid, 1993, p. 664.

29. Jahn Fei and Gustav Ranis, *Development of the Labor Surplus Economy: Theory and Policy*, Homewood, Ill.: R. D. Irwin, 1964.

30. Chen Xiwen, *Rural Reform in China: Retrospect and Prospect* (Zhongguo nongcun gaige: huigu yu zhanwang), Tianjin: Tianjin People's Publishing House, 1993, pp. 76-77.

31. The National Bureau of Statistics, *China Statistical Yearbook* (Zhongguo tongji nianjian) (2001), Beijing: China Statistics Press, 2001, p. 294.

32. On a year-to-year basis, grain purchasing price dropped by 9.8 percent in 1997, 3.3 percent in 1998, and 12.9 percent in 1999. Ibid.

33. Zhang Chi, Wang Shuo, and Li Yong, "RMB 214 Billion, What a Huge Grain Fund Deficit (2140 yi, hao da ge liangkuan ku-long)," *End-of-Month Issue of Securities Market Weekly: Finance and Economy* (Zhengquan shichang zhoukan yuemo ban: caijing) October 1998.

34. Chen Jiyuan (ed.), *Social and Economic Changes in Rural China* (Zhongguo nongcun shehui jingji bianqian), Taiyuan: Shanxi Economy Press, 1993, p. 534.

35. Chen Xiwen, "Speech at the Chang-An Forum m February 2003 (2003 nian 2 yue zai Chang'an Luntan shang de jianghua)," *21st Century Business Herald* (21 shiji jingji baodao), February 13, 2003.

36. "Three retention fees and five contribution fees" were three fees for the public accumulation fund, the public welfare fund, and administrative expenses as well as five fees for school establishment at the township and village levels, family planning, special care to disabled servicemen and families of martyrs and servicemen, militia training, and repair and construction of rural roadways that farmers turned in to township governments. See the State Council, "Regulations on the Control of Expenses and Labor Service Shouldered by Farmers (Nongmin chengdan feiyong he laowu guanli tiaoli)," *People's Daily* (Renmin ribao), December 13, 1991.

37. Ma Xiaohe et al., *A Study on Rural Tax and Fee Reform in China* (Nongcun shuifei gaige yanjiu), Beijing: China Planning Press, 2002, p. 156.

38. Ibid., p. 49.

39. The so-called "Huang Zongxi Law" was the recapitulation by Professor Qin Hui of Tsinghua University of the analysis made by the thinker Huang Zongxi (1610-1695) in the Ming and Qing dynasties, that m Chinese history every tax system reform led to an aggravation of tax. (Qin Hui, "The Reform of Integrating Fees into Taxes and the Huang Zongxi Law (Bingshuizhi gaige yu Huang Zongxi dinglyu)," *Farmers in China: Historical Retrospection and Practical Choices* (Nongmin Zhongguo: lishi fansi yu xianshi xuanze), Zhengzhou: Henan People's Publishing House, 2003, pp. 17-23.) Huang Zongxi pointed out that, in Chinese history, reform of integrating fees into taxes had occurred several times, including the "double tax law" in the Tang Dynasty, the "one lash law" in the Ming Dynasty, and "integrating poll tax into land tax" in the Qing Dynasty. After each tax reform, as a portion of non-tax miscellaneous impositions had been abrogated, the burden on farmers had been alleviated to some degree. However, as there was no way to stop local authorities from establishing new miscellaneous impositions on top of the already augmented

regular taxes, after a time, the burden on farmers would rise to a higher level than that before the reform. Huang Zongxi called this phenomenon the "evil of aggravation without alleviation." Vice Premier Wen Jiabao solemnly declared, when participating in discussions of Hubei delegation of the National People's Congress on March 6, 2003, "Communists are entirely to work for the people's benefits. We can certainly downsize township/town governments, lay off excessive staff, and get out of the vicious cycle of 'Huang Zongxi Law.'"

40. In China, as of the end of 2000, there were more than 28,000 grassroots supply and marketing cooperatives, with employees of the entire system numbering 3.62 million. Rural grassroots credit cooperatives numbered approximately 40,000, with principal capital of RMB 72 billion. In addition, there were also 2.234 million community cooperative economic organizations transferred from the people's communes, of which, 37,000 were at the township/town level and 2.197 million at the village level and below. Although community cooperative economic organizations were called cooperatives, most of them nevertheless affiliated to township/town governments and villagers' committees. In addition, they usually performed the economic administration functions of grassroots governments. Therefore, some people called township/town agriculture-industry-commerce corporations "representatives of the government, playing the role of the secondary township/town governments." See Zhang Xiaoshan et al., *Connecting the Farmer and the Market-An Exploratory Study on Farmers' Intermediaries in China* (Lianjie nonghu yu shichang-Zhongguo nongmin zhongjie zuzhi tanjiu), Beijing: China Social Sciences Press, 2002, pp. 14, 91-92.

41 Zhang Xiaoshan and Yuan Peng, *Theories and Practice of Cooperative Economy-A Comparative Study between China and Foreign Countries* (Hezuo jingji lilun yu shijian-zhongwai bijiao yanjiu), Beijing: China City Press, 1991, pp. 57-73.

42. Gu Shengzu, "Where Is Chinese Rural Surplus Labor Heading? (Zhongguo nongcun shengyu laodongli xiang hechu qu)," *Reform*, 1994, No. 4, pp. 79-87.

43. Small towns are the link between the city and the countryside, the "tail of the city, head of the countryside," with both features of the city and the countryside. They are the political, economic, and cultural centers of a certain area of the countryside, with relatively strong radiating capacities. In their extension, small towns have both a narrow and a broad sense. Small towns in the narrow sense usually refer to administrative towns (including towns in areas just outside city limits, according to the definition of random sample surveys by relevant departments and commissions of the State Council, such as the National Bureau of Statistics and the State Commission for Restructuring Economic Systems). Small towns in the broad sense refer to small market towns above a certain scale in addition to administrative towns; small market towns include the locations of township governments and the headquarters of more than two thousand state-owned farms as well as small market towns developed from administrative villages and the locations of clusters of TVEs. "Small towns" in this book refer to administrative towns.

CHAPTER FIVE

REFORM OF THE BANKING SYSTEM AND DEVELOPMENT OF THE SECURITIES MARKET

The financial system, which consists of various financial institutions (commercial banks, insurance companies, etc.) and financial markets (the money market, the bond market, the stock market, etc.), is one of the most important pillars of a modern economy. A key objective of the transition from a planned economy to a market economy is to reconstruct the financial system to adapt to a market economy.

5.1
The Concepts of "Money" and "Finance" in a Planned Economy

The certificates of credit in a certain form issued by central banks of various countries of planned economy (such as ruble in the Soviet Union or Renminbi (RMB) in China before the 1980s) are used only for measurement of the amount of labor provided by laborers and for the economic accounting of enterprises. According to Marxist political economy, such certificates are "no more 'money' than a ticket for the theater."[1] They are only tokens of the share of each member of the society in the total output and "do not circulate."[2]

1. Money is "passive" in that it is used only as a tool for pricing and accounting. Accordingly, measures like "cash administration" are used to restrict and control the use of cash in order to prevent the "spontaneity" of resource allocation. Only industrial and commercial enterprises are allowed to obtain credit from the state bank, while credit among different enterprises ("commercial credit") is strictly prohibited.

2. The bank is only considered as the cashier for the state fiscal system, and one institution played the roles of both the central bank and commercial banks, resulting in the so-called "mono-bank system."

3. The bank plays an insignificant role in inter-temporal allocation of financial resources. Its financing to enterprises is limited to only credit financing for "non-budgeted working capital" (i.e., the part of working capital that is not employed perennially).

4. Households and individuals are not allowed to participate in any financial activities other than opening deposit accounts in the bank.

On the eve of the founding of the People's Republic of China in 1949, CCCPC began to build its state bank on the basis of the preexisting banks in the Liberated Area of North China. From 1948 to 1978, the People's Bank of China (PBC) had been the only state bank in China, integrating the functions of the central bank such as financial supervision with those of policy banks and commercial banks such as savings and loans. In 1956, during the Socialist Transformation Campaign, all private financial institutions were merged into the PBC, and a centralized and unified financial system thus came into being. The PBC was not only the financial supervisor and money issuer but also the state bank dealing with banking activities. As the state bank, the PBC established an organizational structure characterized by vertical command chain across the nation, unified the issuance of the Chinese currency RMB, and exercised unified supervision of various kinds of financial institutions. Moreover, it was in charge of adjusting money demand and supply to foster the fast development of the state sector of the economy through money issuance and monetary policy.

5.2
The Changes in China's Financial System
in the 1980s

After the commencement of the reform and opening up in the late 1970s, people's communes were replaced by households as units of agricultural production, which greatly expanded the scope of monetary activities; non-state industrial and commercial enterprises, which operated independently and were somewhat market-oriented, began to emerge; and state-owned enterprises (SOEs) were given more decision-making power in financing. These factors enhanced the role of banks as financial intermediaries and called for restoring the various functions of the financial system. Beginning from the mid-1980s, China accelerated its financial reform. By the late 1980s, a rudimentary financial system came into being.

5.2.1 Changes in Enterprise Financing

After the commencement of the reform and opening up, things changed. First, the State Council stipulated in June 1983 that SOEs should gradually switch to bank loans to supplement their insufficient working capital. Second, in order to improve the supervision over investment in capital construction through "paid use," fiscal appropriations for investment in capital construction were replaced by bank loans in 1985 after years of trial. Those loans would be provided by the restored People's Construction Bank of China (the predecessor of the China Construction Bank) according to state planning of capital construction. The interest and principal of these loans were to be repaid as per contracted period and year respectively. As a result, fiscal appropriations as a source of financing were gradually replaced by bank loans. Before 1979, about two-thirds of the fixed asset investment of SOEs was financed by fiscal appropriations from the government. By the mid-1980s, however, the proportion had decreased to one-quarter.[3] In addition, some enterprises began to raise funds through the securities market.

Meanwhile, non-state sectors have been developing gradually since the early 1980s. Non-state enterprises had to support their operations through self-financing, as they could not get fiscal appropriations from the government.

5.2.2 The Introduction of New Financial Instruments and the Start of the Capital Market

Under the planned economic system, cash and bank deposits are the two major financial assets. After the commencement of the reform and opening up, the need for new financial instruments emerged with the increasing shares of household and corporate deposits in total national savings. The central bank took a series of actions to adapt to the changed situation. From 1980 to 1985, specialized banks began to discount commercial paper. In 1986, the PBC began to offer rediscount services to specialized banks and allowed commercial banks to trade financial assets. In 1981, the Ministry of Finance began to restore bond issues. In 1987 and 1988, the secondary markets of corporate bonds and treasury bonds were established respectively. In 1990 and 1991, the Shanghai Stock Exchange and the Shenzhen Stock Exchange were established successively for centralized trading of stocks. Moreover, investors began to trade treasury bond futures in these two exchanges in 1993 and 1994, respectively.

5.2.3 Changes in the Organizational Structure of Financial Institutions

The first step of the banking reform in China was to change the mono-bank system copied from the former Soviet Union. In 1979, the State Council decided that the Agricultural Bank of China (ABC) was to be restored to specialize in rural banking. The Bank of China (BOC) was split off from the PBC to specialize in foreign exchange business. The restored People's Construction Bank of China (PCBC) became the bank specializing in financing investment in fixed assets. In 1983, the State Council decided that the PBC was to focus on its function as the central bank and transfer all saving and loan businesses to the newly established Industrial and Commercial Bank of China (ICBC).

Besides these nationwide specialized banks, smaller banks and non-bank financial institutions were also established in China. In the late 1970s, credit cooperatives were restored across rural China. In 1980, the People's Insurance Company of China (PICC) restored its domestic insurance operations, which had been stopped for nearly twenty years, and later Shenzhen Ping An Insurance Company (the predecessor of

Ping An Insurance (Group) Company of China, Ltd.) was established in 1988. After 1984, many local banks and non-bank financial institutions such as trust and investment companies and financial leasing companies were established. In 1987, two nationwide joint-stock commercial banks, Bank of Communications headquartered in Shanghai and CITIC Industrial Bank affiliated with the China International Trust and Investment Corporation (CITIC), were established (see Figure 5.1).

Figure 5.1   **Financial Institutions in China in the Early 1990s**

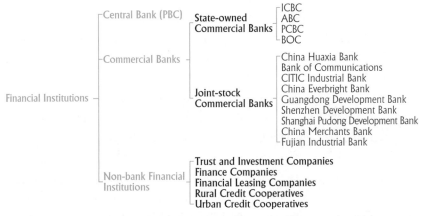

Source: The PBC, *China Financial Outlook*, 1994, Beijing: China Financial Publishing House, 1994.

5.2.4 Changes in the Central Bank's Approaches to Macroeconomic Control

As commercial financial institutions were gradually separated from the central bank, traditional approaches characterized by "unified control over deposits and loans" were discarded by the PBC. A new approach of "centralized planning, managing at different levels, linking deposits with loans, and controlling the balance" was adopted in 1979. In 1981, "controlling the balance" was replaced by "balance responsibility." In 1985, the approach was further changed to "centralized planning, partition of funds, actual loans linked to actual deposits, and mutual financing." Under this system, provincial branches of each specialized bank borrowed funds from provincial branches of the PBC according to predetermined credit quotas, and then allocated funds to its sub-branches at different levels. These sub-branches deposited the allocated funds in local branches of the PBC and withdrew the money when they needed it. Borrowing happened among different banks at the same level, among different levels within the same bank, and among commercial banks and the central bank.

China's financial system was always under strict administrative control by the central bank, with the typical characteristics of financial repression. The official interest rates were so set that the real interest rate at that time was often negative (see Table 5.1), and capital resources were not allocated efficiently by the market but rather allotted by administrative planning. The PBC was characterized by unclear functions, out-of-date means of adjustment, and an irrational organizational structure and financial system and therefore could not effectively perform its fundamental role in maintaining the stability of currency. Commercial businesses were not separated from policy-related businesses in specialized banks, which suffered from the combination of government administration and enterprise management. For businesses within the predetermined range, specialized banks had no independence as commercial banks due to strict control by the central bank. For businesses outside the predetermined range, specialized banks lacked effective constraints by the market mechanism. The rules for market entry were neither clearly defined nor strictly enforced. It was not rare for unqualified investors to get access to the market.

Table 5.1   **Real Interest Rate of Loans of State Banks (1985-1989)**

Year	Nominal Interest Rate [a]	Inflation Rate [b]	Real Interest Rate [c]
1985	4.68	11.0	-7.22
1986	4.68	7.0	-2.23
1987	6.69	8.8	2.11
1988	7.56	20.7	-13.14
1989	10.26	16.3	-6.04

a. Nominal interest rate = the (weighted average) annual interest rate based on which the PBC grants loans to financial institutions.

b. Inflation rate = retail price index (year on year).

c. Real interest rate = a - b.

Source: The Planning and Fund Department of the PBC, *Handbook of Current Interest Rates* (Lilyu shiyong shouce), Beijing: China Financial Publishing House, 1997.

5.3
The Banking Reform in the 1990s
and Future Perform

From 1993 to 1994, China experienced a round of hyperinflation that revealed the serious problems in its banking system and forced the government to deepen its reform of the banking system.

5.3.1 The Progress of the Banking Reform since 1994

According to the decision of the Third Plenary Session of the 14th CCCPC held in November 1993, the banking reform should be deepened with a market orientation from 1994, which mainly included the following aspects.

5.3.1.1 The Establishment of the Central Bank System

As afore mentioned, the primary task of the banking reform is to turn the PBC into a real central bank. To this end, the following measures have been taken.

First, switching the monetary policy from multi-level adjustment to single-level (central) adjustment. The end of 1998 witnessed the establishment of large branches of the PBC in nine major cities, replacing the original thirty-one provincial branches based on the administrative regions, to further eliminate interference of local governments in the central bank's monetary policy and financial supervision. In 1997, the Monetary Policy Committee was established as a consultative agency to improve monetary policy.

Second, making indirect adjustment the core of the macro adjustment system. According to the *Law of the People's Bank of China* adopted by the National People's Congress in 1995, the objective of the PBC was to maintain the stability of currency and thereby promote economic growth. The intermediate objective of the PBC changed from regulating credit quotas to regulating money supply. Starting in the third quarter of 1994, the PBC established a monitoring statistical index of money supply and published the data on a regular basis. Meanwhile, the reform of monetary policy tools was also in steady progress. The first was the launch of rediscount business in 1995. The second was the launch of open market operation on a trial basis in April 1996. The third was the reform of the credit control system. In 1998, credit quotas for state-owned commercial banks were replaced by indirect control based on asset-liability ratio management and risk management. The fourth was the improvement on the interest rate mechanism. A unified nationwide interbank lending market came into being in January 1996; limit on interest rate in the interbank market was removed on June 1; a new interest rate administration system on foreign currency was adopted in September 2000; and urban commercial banks and rural credit cooperatives began to enjoy an enlarged range of deposit and lending interest rates during 2001 and 2002.

5.3.1.2 The Reform of Commercial Banks and Other Financial Institutions

Commercial banks, the principal part of China's banking sector, were the focus of the banking reform. The major measures taken were as follows.

First, the four preexisting specialized state banks (the "Big Four") were transformed to wholly state-owned commercial banks. According to the *Commercial Bank Law of the People's Republic of China* of 1995, the "Big Four" should stop doing any non-bank business such as that of "trust and investment." These wholly state-owned commercial banks should adjust their disposition of branches and take back the power of their branches to grant loans without authorization from the headquarters.[4] All commercial banks should introduce modern management methods including asset-liability ratio management, internal risk control, conservative accounting, and loan classification.

Second, non-wholly state-owned joint-stock banks were established to foster competition within the banking sector. Besides those banks established before 1993, which are Bank of Communications, CITIC Industrial Bank, China Everbright Bank, Shenzhen Development Bank, Huaxia Bank, Pudong Development Bank, China Merchants Bank, Guangdong Development Bank, Fujian Industrial Bank, and China Investment Bank, two more joint-stock banks were established in 1995: China Minsheng Banking Corporation Limited and Hainan Development Bank, which targeted non-state sectors and the Hainan Special Economic Zone respectively. Meanwhile, Huaxia Bank, originally affiliated with Capital Steel Co., Ltd., and China Investment Bank were transformed into independent banking corporations while

China Everbright Bank became the first in China to introduce a foreign financial institution as a strategic investor. Urban credit cooperatives in cities also began to merge into urban commercial banks.

While reforming commercial banks, the PBC also reformed non-bank financial institutions. After consolidation, there were a total of 244 trust and investment companies by the end of 1997. The number of securities companies was 90 after their separation from the PBC. In 1998, the People's Insurance Company of China Group was split into three independent companies: the PICC Property, the Life Insurance Co. of China, and the China Reinsurance Co. In addition, there were eight branches of wholly foreign-owned insurance companies, one Sino-foreign joint venture insurance company and two insurance intermediaries in China.

5.3.1.3 The Reform of the Foreign Exchange Control System

Before the reform and opening up, China adopted a system under which all foreign exchanges from export were required to be surrendered at the official exchange rate and the use of foreign exchange was allocated according to a centralized plan. As a result, the exchange rate of RMB was extremely overvalued. After 1979, foreign exchange control was gradually loosened and the practice of unified control over revenues and expenditures in foreign exchange was broken up. A dual-track system of official exchange rate and market exchange rate was adopted. A certain proportion of foreign exchange retention was allowed to encourage exports.

In 1994, the Chinese government made great changes to its foreign exchange control system. After January 1, 1994, all foreign exchange revenue and expenditure under current account of domestic institutions was to be surrendered to and bought from banks, respectively. Domestic enterprises were to take back and sell their foreign exchange revenue under current account to banks at the market rate except the legal retained part. The government terminated the plan and the approval system for foreign exchange expenditure under current account. Instead, domestic enterprises could buy foreign exchanges from banks at the interbank market rate with valid commercial documents or an import license. The interbank foreign exchange market was established and the original dual exchange rates were merged into a single rate to allow for the managed floating exchange rate system. From the second half of 1996, foreign-invested enterprises were included in this foreign exchange surrendering and buying system, and the convertibility of RMB under current account was realized ahead of schedule. On December 1 of the same year, China formally accepted Article 8 of the *International Monetary Fund Agreement*, thereby undertaking obligations of IMF members such as avoiding restrictions on current account and avoiding discriminating monetary policy.

The reform of the foreign exchange control system played an important role in the fast development of China's foreign trade and economic relations and in the further improvement of balance of payments after 1994.

5.3.1.4 The Establishment and Improvement of the Financial Supervision System

The modern financial system is a complex system consisting of three sectors of banking, securities, and insurance, which have their respective features and should be supervised in different ways. Taking into consideration the development stage of the financial sectors, the ability of financial supervision, and the segregated operation of the three sectors, the Chinese government decided to adopt a segregated supervisory structure. In the first half of 1993, the China Securities Regulatory Commission (CSRC) was spun off from the PBC as a specialized agency in charge of supervision over the securities market. Similarly, the China Insurance Regulatory Commission (CIRC) was spun off from the PBC in November 1998 as a specialized agency in charge of supervision over insurance services, insurance companies, and the insurance market. In March 2003, the PBC transferred its role of supervision over commercial banks to the newly established China Banking Regulatory Commission (CBRC). Hence, a segregated supervisory structure for banking, securities, and insurance was formed.

5.3.2 New Challenges for the Banking Reform in the New Millennium

Although the last two decades of the twentieth century witnessed great achievements in China's banking reform, there are still many problems unsolved. Hence, the impact of China's accession to the WTO at the end of 2001 has been especially significant. How to reduce financial risks and enhance the competitive capacity of Chinese banks in both domestic and foreign markets is therefore a big challenge ahead.

5.3.2.1 Ensure the Stability of the Banking System

Research on financial crises in the twentieth century demonstrates that the scope and degree of financial crises largely depend on the degree of banking crises. After the East Asian financial crisis, the Chinese government took a series of measures to reduce the proportion of non-performing loans (NPLs) and increase the capital adequacy ratio of state-owned banks. China issued special treasury bonds of RMB 270 billion in 1998 to enhance the capital adequacy of state-owned banks. In 1999, four asset management corporations (AMCs), including Cinda, were established to take over NPLs of RMB 1,400 billion from the Big Four. By mid-2002, however, the NPLs of the Big Four rose to RMB 1,700 billion. Moreover, none of them except the Bank of China met the capital adequacy requirement of the *Basle Accord*.

It is therefore urgent for the Chinese government to reduce the NPLs ratio of state-owned banks and increase their capital adequacy to decrease financial risks. Possible measures are as follows: (1) the state makes additional capital investment; (2) the state disposes of the NPLs for a second time; (3) the banks solve the problem by themselves through improving management; (4) the state reduces business tax on these commercial banks to enhance their ability of reducing NPLs (the current tax rate is 8 percent; the central government has already removed its part of the tax of 3 percent and local governments should also remove the remaining 5 percent); (5) the banks establish a prudent financial system, implement the five-category loan classification system, and increase provisions for non-performing loans; and (6) the banks reduce their exposure of risks in the capital market.

5.3.2.2 Reform State-Owned Commercial Banks

The root cause of the Big Four's problems lies in their poorly defined relations of property rights and lack of proper governance structure. Although they are nominally state-owned banks, the owner is actually absent. As they have been regarded as administrative organs by the government for a long time, they not only lack a strict system of board of directors in a real sense but also have no normalized procedure for the appointment and dismissal of their presidents. As a result, without pressure from the government, no one really cares about the financial risk and economic efficiency of state-owned banks. Hence, the transformation of state-owned commercial banks into joint-stock banking corporations has become one of the most important reform tasks.

The reform of SOEs in the past twenty years was characterized by negligence of institutional transformation and overemphasis on IPO financing. In order to quicken the process of initial public offering (IPO), many enterprises "carve out" their core assets for IPO while leaving a large amount of non-core assets to the original enterprises as remaining enterprises (usually the so-called "authorized investment institutions"), and this practice hindered further reform. In view of this, institutional transformation should be given priority in the reform of state-owned commercial banks to change their ownership and governance structures in substance. Meanwhile, private enterprises, institutional investors and individuals both at home and abroad should be allowed to buy sufficient proportion of shares when establishing joint-stock limited banking corporations. Based on the shareholder diversification, healthy corporate governance of commercial banks should be established.

5.3.2.3 Develop Non-state Banks Aggressively

Whether the financial sectors should be opened to private participation has been a longtime controversy on which no agreement has been reached in the financial circles in China. However, this should no longer be a problem since China's accession to the WTO. China promises to give foreign banks the same treatment as Chinese banks within five years after the accession. *Opinions on Promoting and Guiding Domestic Private Investment* and *Opinions on Policies and Measures to Speed Up the Development of Service Industries during the Tenth Five-Year Plan Period* promulgated by the State Planning Commission on December 11 and December 3 of 2001 also provided respectively and specifically, "domestic private investment should be encouraged and permitted in all areas where foreign investment is encouraged and permitted;" in financial sectors that are heavily dominated by the state sector, restrictions on market entry of non-state sectors should also be loosened gradually to offer them the same treatment as the state sector, thereby enabling them to participate in the development of the financial sectors on a large scope.

The reform and opening up experience of more than twenty years demonstrates that to establish a micro foundation for a market economy, effort should be devoted to the reform of SOEs and even more effort should be devoted to the development of nonstate enterprises. Non-state enterprises not only develop faster than SOEs but also impose exterior competitive pressure. Similarly, it is necessary to open the financial sectors to non-state sectors and strongly encourage non-state financial institutions.

1. Continue the reform of joint-stock commercial banks and urban commercial banks. There have been eleven joint-stock commercial banks since the establishment of Bank of Communications, the first one of this kind, in 1987. More than one hundred urban commercial banks were established during the reform of urban credit cooperatives in the late 1990s. These joint-stock banks still possess the characteristics of the old system, as they were initially set up and controlled by government or SOEs. More private capital both at home and abroad should be allowed to be invested in these banks to facilitate their transformation and help them establish effective corporate governance and lawful operations on the basis of a diversified ownership structure.

2. Open the banking sector to non-state capital and allow citizens to establish non-state banks. In July 2003, Great Wall Financial Research Institute, a private institution of economists and financial professionals, put forward a plan for the trial operations of five non-state banks, which were ready to apply for establishment to the China Banking Regulatory Commission.

3. Reorganize rural credit cooperatives. Many credit cooperatives emerged in rural areas during the campaign of "cooperative transformation of agriculture." They were expected to perform better after the commencement of the reform and opening up. In fact, however, most credit cooperatives have suffered huge losses due to poor operation. Since 1999, local governments in some regions have consolidated original rural credit cooperatives into rural credit cooperative unions at the county level or above. However, such measures may be far from enough to solve the fundamental problems of credit cooperatives, poorly defined property rights and insider control, etc. As to existing rural credit cooperatives, the key is to adopt different forms of property rights to restructure and transform themselves into real financial enterprises. For those localities that really need rural credit cooperatives, it is imperative to clearly define their property rights and restore their nature of being cooperatives of their members.

4. Normalize and develop informal financing. In the context of financial repression, informal financing tends to flourish to meet the huge demand of enterprises for financing in localities where non-state sectors are developed. Possible forms of informal financing include loans among individuals, "underground banking houses," and "money-pooling organizations."[5] For most localities, the following actions are needed: (1) legalization; (2) normalization; and (3) establishment of the credit system.

5.3.2.4 Switch from Specialized Banking to Universal Banking

According to the current *Commercial Bank Law of the People's Republic of China*, the system of specialized banking should be adopted in the financial sectors and commercial banks are not allowed to be involved in insurance and investment banking businesses. However, the experience of developed countries shows that universal banking is a trend of development. Financial institutions with universal banking in disguised form, such as financial holding companies, are emerging in China.

Universal banking may lead to extremely high financial leverage ratios due to the repeated cross-investment among different financial businesses. Such situations are conducive to illegal financial activities such as insider trading and market manipulation and thus cause great financial risks. Consequently, an effective China Wall should be established among the subsidiaries of a financial holding company under universal banking in order to internalize the China Wall among different businesses under specialized banking. Moreover, to minimize financial risks, it is essential to combine internal control and external supervision, rather than solely rely on the latter.

5.4
The Development of China's Money Market

5.4.1 The Current Situation of China's Money Market and Its Problems

According to the *Interim Regulations of the PRC on the Administration of Banks* issued in January 1986 by the State Council, specialized banks can call money from each other at negotiated interest rates.

Since 1987, interbank lending, interbank repo, and commercial paper have come into being. By 1996, a unified national interbank lending market had emerged among the headquarters of sixteen commercial banks, with a total trading volume of RMB 587.2 billion in 1996. Starting in 2000, the same treatment was given to authorized branches of commercial banks, insurance companies, securities companies, securities investment funds, finance companies, and rural credit cooperative unions and the trading volume in 2000 reached RMB 672.8 billion. In 1997, the interbank repo market started to operate at the China Foreign Exchange Trading Center. By the end of 2000, the cumulative trading volume in the interbank repo market had reached RMB 1,600 billion with 650 trading members. The commercial paper market started much earlier. In 1982, commercial paper acceptance and discount business within the same city first appeared in Shanghai on a trial basis. In 1985, the PBC issued *Provisional Regulations on Acceptance and Discount of Commercial Paper* followed by *Trial Procedures of the PBC on Rediscount* in the next year, which gave permission for rediscount business. By the end of 2000, the cumulative trading volume of commercial papers had reached RMB 674 billion and that of discount had amounted to RMB 631 billion.[6] Today, the interbank lending market, the interbank repo market, and the commercial paper market form the major part of China's money market.

However, many problems still exist in the current Chinese money market:

1. Inadequate financial tools. The development of China's money market has been mainly in the interbank lending market and the interbank repo market while other markets are less developed. First, the treasury bond market, which should be the most important part of the money market, is not yet fully developed due to the lack of treasury bills with maturity less than one year. Second, transferable certificates of deposit, which were issued in large volume only in the late 1980s, have disappeared due to the stagnation of the market after 1990 caused by the low interest rate set by the PBC. Third, the commercial paper market is inactive despite the issuance every year.

2. Low liquidity and inactive trading. China's money market had long been dominated by commercial banks until 1998 when the PBC allowed foreign banks and insurance companies to enter the interbank bond market. In 1999, 283 rural credit cooperative unions, 20 investment funds, and 7 finance and securities companies

were also permitted to enter the interbank bond market. Since then the situation has improved. However, the commercial paper market is fragmented, and its trading is separated in thousands of dealers across the country, making commercial paper only a payment tool of enterprises or a substitute for loans. Not surprisingly, a large amount of commercial paper is actually sunk.

3. Fragmented market. China's money market has long been fragmented. Regional interbank lending markets based in large cities like Shanghai, Beijing, Wuhan, Shenyang, Chongqing, Xi'an, and Guangzhou are characterized by wide gaps in lending interest rates and different trading rules among them. As a result, the liquidity of the money market is rather low.

4. Imperfect market infrastructure. A sound market infrastructure, including a trading network, a unified quotation system, a unified bond depository and clearing system for settlement of cash and securities, has been absent in China's money market.

The money market price cannot accurately reflect money demand and supply due to the fragmented market, inadequate market tools, and low liquidity. As a result, it is impossible to form an accurate benchmark interest rate and to enable it to function as a transmission mechanism of monetary policy.

5.4.2 Further Development of China's Money Market

Generally speaking, the development of the money market is to achieve two objectives: to establish a market system with sufficient liquidity of monetary assets and to provide the central bank with an effective transmission mechanism of monetary policy. Since 2000, China's money market has been moving toward these objectives. For example, in 2000, the PBC permitted twelve securities companies to enter the interbank lending market and the Industrial and Commercial Bank of China was allowed to open a commercial paper department in Shanghai, the first of its kind in mainland China. Moreover, the PBC Shanghai selected seven prefecture-level (city-level) branches in Zhejiang and Fujian provinces for repurchase of commercial paper on a trial basis. Meanwhile, four PBC branches, located respectively in Hangzhou, Fuzhou, Ningbo, and Xiamen, were authorized to examine and approve rediscount and repurchase of commercial paper of more than RMB 5 million per deal. The conditions for starting the rediscount and repurchase of commercial paper were also loosened. Moreover, the PBC Shanghai planned to further promote commercial paper acceptance business in large cities and to encourage financial institutions in these cities to engage in discount and cross-sector rediscount business for qualified enterprises. Commercial banks under the jurisdiction of the PBC Shanghai were encouraged to open specialized windows for commercial paper business.

Interest rate liberalization has been a hot issue in China's financial reform. In 2000, officials of the PBC once asserted that China would make steady progress in the reform of liberalizing interest rates in the next three years. Steps of the interest rate reform were to take the following order: (1) foreign currencies before Renminbi (i.e., liberalizing the interest rates for deposits and loans in foreign currencies before those in Renminbi); (2) loans before deposits (i.e., liberalizing the interest rates of loans before those of deposits); (3) rural before urban (i.e., liberalizing the interest rates in rural areas before those in urban areas); and (4) large deposits before small deposits (i.e., liberalizing the interest rates of large deposits before those of small deposits). However, the liberalization of interest rates (i.e., the determination of equilibrium prices of funds by market) also needs some other conditions such as a sound and unified money market and independent commercial banks. Thus, the gradual liberalization of interest rates will still be one of the most important tasks in China's future financial reform.

5.5
The Development and Improvement
of the Securities Market

During the few decades before the reform, there was no securities market in China at all. Only after the launch of marketization reform at the end of the 1970s had the securities market in China begun to take shape and develop gradually.

5.5.1 The Development of China's Securities Market since the Reform and Opening Up

China's securities market started in 1980, when Fushun Office of Liaoning Branch of the PBC issued stocks for enterprises, and 1981, when the Ministry of Finance issued treasury notes. From 1991 to 2002, the accumulative total value of securities issued in China reached more than RMB 5 trillion and a securities market with a comparatively complete set of securities has taken shape.

China's stock market has developed very rapidly. By the end of 2002, there were 1,220 listed companies in the Shanghai Stock Exchange and the Shenzhen Stock Exchange, the total number of shares of which amounted to 587.462 billion. By the end of 2002, the total capitalization of floating shares had reached RMB 1.3 trillion and the total trading amount of the stocks amounted to RMB 3 trillion. Currently, there are 126 securities companies with more than 2,900 securities business units and more than 100,000 employees all over the nation. The number of stock accounts was once recorded at 68 million. The fast development of the stock market has significantly changed the financing structure of enterprises. During the first one-and-a-half decades of the reform, the financing of enterprises was dominated by long-term credit financing, a natural result of the policies of full loan financing for working capital adopted in 1983 and substituting fiscal appropriations with bank loans for fixed asset investments in 1985. Since 1992, other types of financing, especially equity financing, have become an important form of corporate financing. From 1987 to 2001, the total amount of equity financing by listed companies amounted to RMB 623.3 billion.

China's bond market has experienced three phases in its development. The first phase is characterized by the immature over-the-counter (OTC) bond market represented by counter trading of bearer certificates. The second phase is characterized by the exchange bond market, such as the Shanghai Stock Exchange. The third phase is characterized by the mature OTC bond market represented by the interbank bond market. Currently, China's bond market consists of the interbank bond market as the OTC market and the Shanghai Stock Exchange and the Shenzhen Stock Exchange as the exchange market. After 1997, China's bond market, especially the treasury bond market, experienced fast growth. By the end of 2002, the total balance of China's bond assets had reached RMB 3.4 trillion, among which negotiable bonds were worth RMB 2.8 trillion. The total annual bond trading reached RMB 13.4 trillion, implying average daily trading of more than RMB 50 billion. The bond market attracted all kinds of institutional investors and individual investors, and was obviously overrunning the stock market in terms of any indicator. However, China's bond market is still dominated by treasury bonds and financial bonds issued by policy banks, while the market for corporate bonds is underdeveloped. In 2002, the bond financing by the government and enterprises was RMB 592.9 billion and RMB 32 billion respectively. Hence, the major functions of China's bond market are to provide investment tools for institutional and individual investors, to raise funds to support government financing, and to help the central bank switch to indirect adjustment by monetary policy, rather than to help with the effective allocation of capital resources among enterprises.

Table 5.2 **The Financing Structure of Chinese Enterprises** (RMB billion, %)

Year	Total amount of financing	Loans in local and foreign currency[a]		Equity financing[b]		paper financing[a,c]		Bond financing[a]	
		Increase	%	Increase	%	Increase	%	Increase	%
1996	1,158.0	1,114.0	96.2	42.5	3.7	6.4	0.5	-4.9	-0.4
1997	1,258.3	1,140.0	90.6	128.5	10.2	-2.5	-0.2	7.7	-0.6
1998	1,281.4	1,152.0	89.9	84.0	6.5	29.4	2.3	16.0	1.3
1999	1,207.6	1,072.1	88.8	94.1	7.8	29.4	2.4	10.2	1,0
2000	1,587.2	1,288.7	81.2	210.4	13.3	79.8	5.0	8.3	0.5
2001	1,401.6	1,252.4	89.4	116.9	8.3	17.6	1.3	14.7	1.0

Note: Foreign currency is translated into local currency based on the current average exchange rate.
   a. Loans in local and foreign currency, commercial paper financing, and bond financing by financial institutions all refer to the increase in the current year.
   b. Equity financing in local and foreign currency includes rights offers and convertible bonds.
   c. Commercial paper financing = increase in ending balance of bank acceptance -increase in ending balance of bank discount, because the discounted part has been counted as indirect financing in loans of financial institutions.
   d. Bond financing in 2001 refers to bonds issued that year as the balance was not reported.
   Source: The PBC and the CSRC.

5.5.2 Problems in China's Securities Market and Proposed Solutions

China's current securities market suffers from many problems, i.e., the corporate bond market is underdeveloped and the stock market is hindered by inappropriate positioning, overspeculation, and poor regulation, etc., which have hindered the proper functioning of China's securities market.

5.5.2.1 Extremely Underdeveloped Corporate Bond Market

After 1992, equity financing began to grow, while bond financing remained an insignificant channel for enterprise financing. In 2002, loans of financial institutions increased by RMB 1,920 billion. The total amount of funds raised from the securities market reached RMB 1,060 billion, of which RMB 627.8 billion was treasury bonds, RMB 307.5 billion was financial bonds issued by policy banks, RMB 96.2 billion was stocks, and RMB 32.5 billion was corporate bonds.[7] Corporate bonds accounted for only 3 percent of the total financing of the securities market and was even more insignificant compared with bank loans.

Moreover, corporate bonds account for only a small share of China's bond market, demonstrating again the underdevelopment of China's corporate bond market. Government bonds are often preferred by financial institutions and other investors as a tool of liquidity management because of their safety in terms of credit risk. In comparison, corporate bonds are regarded as a typical tool of capital investment. In the global context, the percentage of corporate bonds in the bond market has been increasing recently while that of government bonds has been decreasing. Corporate bonds accounted for 23.8 percent of the American bond market in 1990 and the figure increased to 30.3 percent by the end of 2001. However, the major tools of China's bond market are treasury bonds and financial bonds issued by policy banks with the state-owned commercial banks as the key investors, showing a strong flavor of government credit. The development of corporate bonds will facilitate the establishment of private credit in the bond market and promote the transition of the bond market from a government-credit-dominated to a private-credit-dominated market.

The extremely underdeveloped corporate bond market in China can be attributed to many factors, the key ones among which are three.

First, the functional positioning of corporate bonds is not appropriate. Corporate bonds are often regarded by the government as a tool for raising funds for fixed asset investment and are always bundled with fiscal appropriations and bank loans when planning departments consider projects. To facilitate the healthy development of China's corporate bond market, the first task is to get rid of this improper mindset.

Second, there are few sophisticated institutional investors in the corporate bond market. In China, however, individual investors still account for the majority of corporate bondholders, which has resulted in two consequences. The first is that individual bondholders have little demand-side discipline over issuers. For such a complicated financial product with credit risk as corporate bonds, only institutional investors can exert effective demand-side discipline over issuers. It is often difficult for individual investors to accurately understand the credit risk and corresponding interest rate of corporate bonds because they lack the ability to conduct professional analysis. The second is that without institutional investors such as funds and insurance companies, it will be hard to expand the corporate bond market.

Third, the liquidity of bonds is low due to the absence of an OTC market. Currently, there are only a small number of corporate bonds with high credit rating listed and traded in the Shanghai Stock Exchange and the Shenzhen Stock Exchange with daily trading volumes less than RMB 50 million; most corporate bonds cannot meet the basic requirements to be listed in exchanges. As a result, the issuance cost of corporate bonds in the primary market is high due to the inactive secondary market, which hinders the further development of corporate bonds.

Measures that can be taken to solve these problems are as follows: (1) bring more institutional investors into the corporate bond market by launching corporate bond funds with corporate bonds as the key investment, allowing banks to invest in corporate bonds, and lifting the limitation on insurance companies to invest in corporate bonds; (2) replace the approval system for bond issuance by the verification system and remove the limitation on the interest rate of corporate bonds gradually to let the market set the price; (3) allow corporate bonds to be traded on the OTC bond market; and (4) set up China's own credit rating companies, and discipline them by new laws and regulations and institutional investors, allowing a virtuous cycle of the development of the credit rating system and the corporate bond market.

5.5.2.2 Inappropriate Positioning of the Stock Market and Problems Incurred

During a fairly long period after China's stock market was established, the administrative authorities believed that the basic function of the stock market was to raise capital for enterprises, especially for SOEs, and adopted the policy that "the stock market should serve SOEs." Accordingly, the administrative authorities in charge of securities took the following measures.

First, SOEs were given top priority in IPO approval to raise funds and get out of financial difficulty. In developed market economies, the setup and IPO of companies follow the registration system. China, however, adopted the administrative approval system, or the substantive examination system. Before 2000, a company planning to be listed in exchanges had to first get recommendation from the provincial government and then get approval from the CSRC. After that, there were still many procedures of administrative approval regarding the IPO price and size. SOEs obtained the most chances, while few chances were given to non-state enterprises. It was not until March 1998 that the first non-state listed company, Sichuan New Hope Agribusiness Co., Ltd. (code: 000876) in Sichuan Province, appeared with controlling interest by the non-state enterprise, New Hope Group. In addition, private capital acquired the controlling interests of several listed companies through back-door listing.

Second, stock prices were often manipulated to raise more funds for companies with listing qualifications. The administrative authorities helped listed companies to enjoy high premiums in IPO and rights issue by making encouraging speeches from time to time and "boosting the market with policies." Moreover, they also tried to boost stock prices by adjusting the supply and demand sides. Supply-side policies included (1) setting an IPO quota each year to limit the number of IPO; and (2) dividing stocks into "floating shares" and "non-floating shares" to allow only one-third of the shares to be traded on stock exchanges. Demand-side policy was to encourage various types of investors to buy stocks. As a result, the P/E ratio in the secondary market reached 40 to 60. Under such circumstances, even though listed companies issued stocks at the high P/E of around 20 set by the administrative authorities, the huge gap between IPO price and secondary market price still attracted numerous retail investors, who were not aware of the danger of bubbles in the stock market.

This practice of "the government boosting the market and SOEs grabbing the money" caused a series of disastrous effects. Some companies with very poor performance were able to issue stocks with high premiums only because they gained approval from the administrative authorities. These companies not only enjoyed risk-free high returns from the primary and secondary markets but also raised funds through rights offers with high premiums. As a result, the stock market was turned into a paradise for rent seeking. Most stocks were not worthy of investment because of their extremely high P/E and low growth rate. Therefore, investors could not count on long-term return; instead, they could only try to earn money through speculative buying and selling. As a result, a speculative atmosphere permeated the entire stock market, making it "a casino without rules."

The realities of China's securities market in recent years have demonstrated that it is impossible for SOEs to get out of financial difficulty only by "grabbing money" from the securities market. On the contrary, this will only lead to the ultimate collapse of China's securities market. As far as the primary market is concerned, quota allotment plus the approval system should be replaced by the registration system. The issue of "all floating" should be resolved in an appropriate way to realize the same benefits and rights for the same class of shares. Effective governance should be established in line with the *Company Law* in all listed companies, and internal monitoring by stockholders should be strengthened. Listed companies and the securities market should gradually upgrade themselves to international standards. As far as the secondary market is concerned, the government and supervisory institutions of securities exchanges should strengthen regulation over illegal activities, improve information disclosure, strictly implement trading rules of the stock market, and check and punish illegal activities.

5.5.2.3 Overspeculation and the Formation of Economic Bubbles

Because of the poor quality of listed companies and high stock prices in the secondary market resulting from the wrong positioning of the stock market, the P/E is too high. The average P/E of negotiable shares even reached a ridiculously high level of 100 to 200 in the early 1990s, making stocks not worthy of investment. Although the average P/E has been up and down several times since 1993, it remained at about 40 for a long time. Moreover, the cash dividends of listed companies account for only about one-tenth of their profits. It is impossible for investors to make profits from long-term investment. As a result, market participants can only try to profiteer from short buying and selling, which almost unavoidably leads to overspeculation.

In China, similar to what happened in the early stage of developed countries, over-speculation and economic bubbles also appeared in its infant securities market. With their privilege of conducting illegal activities without being punished, some individuals created speculation mania in the stock market, the futures market, and the real estate market, aggravating the problem of economic bubbles.

The fact that the government gave a boost to the stock market several times during its development, caused strong criticism and the "big debate on the stock market" in early 2001. However, the strong support from some leaders and the positive feedback effect of the "big bull market" drove the composite index of Shanghai Stock Exchange up to the historical high of 2,247.69 points on June 7, 2001. The inevitable plunge of stock prices afterwards trapped not only most retail investors but also the entire society.

Figure 5.2 **Monthly Chart of the Composite Index of Shanghai Stock Exchange* (from January 1999 to January 2003)**

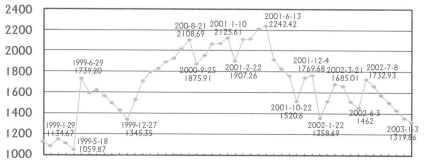

*The values demonstrated at each point are the closing index of the last trading day of each month, except for the specially marked points.

Source: Shanghai Stock Exchange.

The government can take the following possible measures to prevent overspeculation and economic bubbles: (1) abandon the wrong practice of "the government boosting the market and SOEs grabbing the money;" (2) speed up the reform of SOEs and improve the corporate governance of listed companies to lay a solid foundation for the development of the securities market; (3) adopt a prudent and stable monetary policy and other macroeconomic policies to maintain macroeconomic stability and to avoid violent fluctuation of the securities market; (4) come up with a solution acceptable to all relevant parties to the problem of non-floating shares to realize "all floating" as soon as possible; (5) speed up the legislation of securities trading, improve the regulation of various securities trading institutions and businesses, and strengthen the supervision of market to prevent new problems; and (6) remove limitation on the sphere of private investment to turn private capital into industrial investment and to turn bubble-generating "heat" into economy-driving "steam" for a new round of rapid economic growth.

Notes and References

1. This refers to the "certificate of labor" or "labor-money" put forward by Robert Owen (1771-1858), in whose communes a certain number of certificates of labor are granted to each member according to their work in exchange for their deserved consumer goods. According to Marx, "Owen presupposes directly associated labor, a form of production that is entirely inconsistent with the production of commodities. The certificate of labor is merely evidence of the part taken by the individual in the common labor, and of his right to a certain portion of the common produce destined for consumption." "Owen's 'labor-money,' for instance, is no more 'money' than a ticket for the theater." (See Karl Marx, *The Capital* (Ziben lun), Chinese edition, Vol. 1, Beijing: People's Publishing House, 1972, pp. 112-113.)

2. According to Marx, "In the case of socialized production, the money-capital is eliminated. Society distributes labor-power and means of production to the different branches of production. The producers may, for all it matters, receive paper vouchers entitling them to withdraw from the social supplies of consumer goods a quantity corresponding to their labor-time. These vouchers are not money. They do not circulate." (See Karl Marx, *The Capital* (Ziben lun), Chinese edition, Vol. 2, Beijing: People's Publishing House, 1972, p. 397.) Here Marx indicated that the voucher is different from currency because it does not circulate like currency, which "takes the form of a constant motion away from its starting-point" in the transaction and flows "from the hands of one commodity-owner into those of another." (See Karl Marx, *The Capital* (Ziben lun), Chinese edition, Vol. 1, Beijing: People's Publishing House, Chinese edition, 1972, p. 134.) Instead, it serves as a voucher to exchange for goods and returns to the state-owned bank where the voucher is issued after every deal settled.

3. *China Statistical Yearbook* (Zhongguo tongji nianjian), Beijing: China Statistics Press, various years.

4. Before this, branches of state-owned specialized banks were "legal persons" or "quasi-legal persons" and could provide credit services without authorization from the headquarters.

5. Lu Mai, *The Development of Non-state Sectors in West China* (Xibu diqu de minying bumen de fazhan), mimeograph, 2001.

6. Xie Ping, "Pension Insurance, Banking Sector and Money Market (Yanglao baoxian yu yinhangye ji huobi shichang) (2001)," Wei Jianing (ed.), *Pension Insurance and Financial Markets* (Yanglao baoxian yu jinrong shichang), Beijing: China Finance Press, 2002, p. 153.

7. Team of the Monetary Policy Analysis of the PBC, *Report on the Implementation of China's Monetary Policy in 2002* (2002 Zhong-guo huobi zhengce zhixing baogao), Beijing: China Finance Press, 2003.

Chapter Six

Reform of the Fiscal System

6.1
Government Finance in a Planned Economy

For most of the period from 1953 to 1979, the fiscal and taxation system in China displayed the following three basic characteristics:

6.1.1 Government Finance and Business Finance Were Integrated into a Unified National Financial System

Since a planned economy was a society-wide giant enterprise established on the basis of state ownership, the nature of its financial system was just as what was stated in a *Dictionary of Economics and Management* in the mid-1980s: "Since the financial system of a socialist country is built on the basis of public ownership of the means of production and the national economy is under the unified leadership of the State, government finance includes relations of distribution not only outside the realm of production, but also inside the realm of production. Hence, a socialist public financial system consists of state budget, bank credit, and business finance."

6.1.2 The Government Used Its Power to Raise the Budgetary Revenue, Which Mainly Came from State-owned Industry

Under a planned economy, the government was able to use its power of pricing to set very low prices for primary products, such as grain and other raw materials, to transfer the surplus generated by non-state sectors to state-owned industry and commerce and then to channel almost all the surplus of the national economy into the budget as profits and taxes of state-owned industry and commerce. Compared with other countries in the process of industrialization, the industrial sector in China had maintained very high profitability since the full establishment of the planned economic system in 1956. The situation gradually changed only after the commencement of the reform and opening up at the end of 1978. As such, from 1957 to 1980, profit remittance and tax payment from the industrial sector had always accounted for 50-66 percent of the government revenue.

6.1.3 There Were Huge Differences in Financial Burden Across Industries and Enterprises in Terms of Profit Remittance and Tax Payment

As the whole country was a giant enterprise, the economic unit called "enterprise" was just a workshop or a working team of the State Syndicate and all surpluses, be they taxes or profits, belonged to the state from the very beginning. The reason why some surpluses had to be turned in to the taxation department in the form of taxes was that in the economic accounting of enterprises under the planned economic system, taxes slimmed down profits, and profits in turn slimmed down costs. Hence, in designing tax rates, the principle of "reasonable profit" was usually adopted. By using tax rates as a lever, the government left SOEs with a planned profit rate equal to a certain rate of social average profit rate. Moreover, the government also made extensive use of the taxation policy to carry out its own agenda in industrial development by stipulating grossly different tax rates for different sectors and products. Therefore, under the planned economic system, the principle of equitable tax burden was not practiced; rather, a very complex tax rate structure with enormous difference was instituted. For instance, in 1980, the average rate of industrial and commercial tax was 18.9 percent for light industry (317 percent for the tobacco industry) but 4.6 percent for heavy industry. This resulted in the ratchet effect of "whipping the fast ox" and unfair competition among different industries and enterprises.

6.2
Fiscal Reform from 1980 to 1993

From 1979 to 1993, the Chinese government adopted measures of "power-delegating and profit-sharing" in the state sector and instituted material incentives to "bring into play" the enthusiasm of local governments and enterprises. By doing so, both the relations between the central and local governments and the relations between the government and state-owned enterprises had changed.

6.2.1 Changes in the Financial Relations between the Central Government and Local Governments

In 1979, there was a huge budget deficit and an enormous pressure on the central government finance. To bring into play the enthusiasm of local governments to increase revenue and reduce expenditure and to ensure the fiscal revenue of the central government, from 1980, the fiscal budgetary system of China was switched from the unitary system to the responsibility system, which not only offered incentives to local governments to increase revenue and reduce expenditure but also prevented the fiscal revenue of the central government from further declining.

6.2.1.1 The Revenue-Sharing System

In 1980, except in the three municipalities directly under the central government (namely, Beijing, Tianjin, and Shanghai) where "unified control over revenues and expenditures" was still practiced, a "revenue-sharing system" was introduced in all provinces and autonomous regions. Under this new fiscal administration system, revenue would be shared between the central and the local governments according to predefined formulae. In the twenty-six provinces and autonomous regions where the revenue-sharing system was practiced, four different formulae were adopted.

First, a formula of fixed-ratio fiscal responsibility was continually followed in Jiangsu Province. Jiangsu Province started with a fixed-ratio fiscal responsibility system in 1977. Under this system, the central government shared the revenue with the provincial government according to a ratio based on the historical ratios of provincial government fiscal expenditure to its revenue, and this ratio was supposed to be fixed for four years. In reality, this ratio was always adjusted each year through negotiations between the central and local governments. The ratio of revenue turned in to the central government to revenue retained by the provincial government was 58:42 in 1977, 57:43 from 1978 to 1980, and 61:39 in 1981.

Second, the system of "dividing revenue and expenditure, turning in a set quota or receiving a set subsidy," was implemented in Guangdong and Fujian provinces, which pioneered in the experiment of opening to the outside world. That was to set a fixed amount of turned-in or subsidy based on the final accounting of the revenue and expenditure of the two provinces in 1979, and once determined, this amount would remain fixed for five years. The fixed amount of turned-in for Guangdong Province was RMB 1 billion each year, while the fixed amount of subsidy for Fujian Province was RMB 1 billion. In the process of implementation, increased revenue and balance of expenditure were all retained for local use.

Third, in fifteen provinces including Sichuan, Shaanxi, Gansu, Henan, Hubei, Hunan, Anhui, Jiangxi, Shandong, Shanxi, Hebei, Liaoning, Heilongjiang, Jilin, and Zhejiang provinces, the system adopted was one of "dividing revenue and expenditure, taking different responsibilities according to different circumstances." The so-called "dividing revenue and expenditure" is to clearly divide the scope of revenue and expenditure between the central government and the local government according to administrative affiliation. The so-called "taking different responsibilities according to different circumstances" refers to the following: based on the predefined scope of revenue and expenditure and the budgeted revenue and expenditure of 1979, provinces with revenue exceeding expenditure would need to submit a fixed percentage of the surplus to the central government; provinces with revenue falling short of expenditure would receive a subsidy from the central government to be financed by a certain proportion of industrial and commercial tax; and provinces with revenue smaller than expenditure even though the central government gives up the entirety of industrial and commercial tax would receive additional central government subsidy in a fixed amount. During the five years of practicing the fiscal responsibility system, the local governments that had more revenue could spend more and vice versa, and the local governments should independently arrange their own budget and seek balance between revenue and expenditure.

Fourth, in the five autonomous regions, including Inner Mongolia, Xinjiang, Tibet, Ningxia, and Guangxi, and the three provinces with more minority nationalities, namely, Yunnan, Qinghai, and Guizhou, the fiscal system pertaining to national autonomous areas remained unchanged. The existing special treatment to national autonomous areas was still maintained, with improvement in two aspects: first, the concept of fiscal responsibility was to be adopted in these areas as well, with reference to the third system specified in defining the scope of revenue and expenditure and determining the amount of central government subsidy, which should remain unchanged for five years rather than one year; second, the portion of local revenue growth would all be retained by the local government and the amount of subsidy by the central government to national autonomous areas would be progressively increased by 10 percent every year.

In 1986, when contemplating coordinated reform in price, taxation, government finance, banking, and foreign trade systems, the State Council intended to replace the "revenue-sharing system" with the "tax-sharing system." However, with the miscarriage of coordinated reform, not only was the revenue-sharing system not abolished, but it was solidified into a formal system- the all-round fiscal responsibility system in 1988.

6.2.1.2 The All-Round Fiscal Responsibility System

The "all-round fiscal responsibility system" introduced in 1988 was the continuation and development of the revenue-sharing system of 1980. It included the country's thirty-seven provinces, municipalities, autonomous regions, as well as "cities specifically designated in the state plan" in six methods.

The first type was "responsibility for progressive increase in revenue". Specifically, the year-on-year increase of local revenue and the sharing ratio with the central government were determined on the basis of the actual revenue of 1987, the reasonable level of expenditure, and the growth rate in recent years. When the realized revenue falls with the range of the predetermined growth rate, it would be shared by the central government and the local government according to the predetermined sharing ratio. When the realized revenue exceeds the predetermined growth rate, the extra part of the revenue would be completely retained by the local government. When the realized revenue falls short of the predetermined growth rate, the local government would have to make up the gap with its own financial resources. This method was adopted by Beijing, Hebei, Liaoning, Zhejiang, Henan, and Chongqing.

The second type was "total sharing". Specifically, this involved a verification of base amounts of revenue and expenditure according to actual records of revenue and expenditure of the previous two years and determination of a sharing ratio based on the ratio of actual local government expenditure to its total revenue. This method was adopted by Shanxi, Anhui, and Tianjin.

The third type was "total sharing plus growth sharing," which was formulated by adding a component of growth sharing to the second type of contract. Specifically, the revenue of any given year would be split into two parts. The first was the base amount, which would be shared according to total sharing ratio; the second was the incremental portion, which would be shared according to another sharing ratio, namely, the "growth sharing ratio." This method was implemented in three regions, Dalian, Qingdao and Wuhan.

The fourth type was "responsibility for progressive increase in turned-in." Specifically, taking the turned-in revenue of 1987 to the central government as the base, a progressively increasing amount would be turned in according to a certain growth rate. This method was adopted by Guangdong and Hunan provinces.

The fifth type was "set quota for turned-in." This method was adopted by Shandong, Heilongjiang, and Shanghai. Specifically, based on the originally verified revenue and expenditure bases, a fixed amount for turning in would be collected from the difference between the base amounts of revenue and the expenditure. The amounts for turning in of the three regions were determined as follows: Shanghai RMB 10.5 billion; Shandong (excluding Qingdao City) RMB 289 million; and Heilongjiang (excluding Harbin City) RMB 299 million.

The sixth type was "set quota for subsidy." This method was practiced in Jilin, Jiangxi, Fujian, Shaanxi, Hainan, Inner Mongolia, Guangxi, Guizhou, Yunnan, Tibet, Qinghai, Ningxia, Xinjiang, Hubei and other provinces. Specifically, based on the originally verified revenue and expenditure bases, a fixed amount of subsidy would be granted to cover the difference between the expenditure base and the revenue base.

6.2.2 Changes in the Financial Relations between the Government and Enterprises

From 1979 to 1993, according to the requirements to "delegate power to and share profit with enterprises," the financial relations between the government and state-owned enterprises (SOEs) were adjusted, and the past practice of turning in all profits and taxes to the government finance and total fiscal allocation of all investments was replaced by the method of the "fiscal responsibility system" in various forms.

1. Since the end of 1978, the enterprise fund system, various forms of profit retention system, and system of responsibility for one's own profits and losses had subsequently been tried out in SOEs. With the exception of the three experimental units including the Capital Iron and Steel Corporation that had carried out the "system of responsibility for one's own profits and losses," the profit retention system was introduced in most of the other industrial and transportation SOEs, 6,600 of them by the early 1980s. Statistics showed that profits retained by industrial and transportation enterprises between 1978 and 1982 amounted to RMB 42 billion, certainly a considerable amount.

2. From 1984 to 1986, a reform of "substituting tax payment for profit delivery" ("tax for profit" in short) was carried out in all enterprises in two steps, wherein most profits of SOEs were turned in to the state finance in the form of enterprise income tax. In April 1983, the first step of "tax for profit" reform was implemented. The key measure introduced by the Method was to increase the proportion of enterprise income tax in the pretax profit of SOEs while reducing the proportion of profit turned-in so as to achieve a coexistence of tax payment and profit remittance. The large- and medium-sized SOEs would pay their income tax at a uniform rate of 55 percent and small SOEs at an eight-level progressive rate from 7 percent to 55 percent. In addition, due to considerable differences in the price environment of various enterprises, large- and medium-sized SOEs were also required to pay "regulation tax"- one rate for each enterprise according to their profits- to avoid unfair treatment in profit retention. Industrial and commercial income tax for collective and private enterprises was to apply an eight-level progressive rate from 10 percent to 55 percent. The statutory rate of income tax for foreign-invested enterprises was 33 percent; the rate was 15 percent for enterprises in special economic zones in addition to the privilege of "exemption from income tax in the first two years and reduction of income tax by half in the next three years." During the first step of the "tax for profit"

reform, a total of 107,145 industrial, transportation, and commercial enterprises were involved, of which 28,110 were industrial enterprises, 2,236 transportation enterprises, and 76,799 commercial enterprises.

On October 1, 1984, the second step of "tax for profit" reform was implemented. The key measures of the second step reform included a division of the income to be turned in to the state finance by SOEs into eleven tax categories and a gradual switch from the coexistence of tax payment and profit remittance to complete substitution of tax payment for profit delivery, with after-tax profits retained by enterprises. Specifically, the existing industrial and commercial tax was split into product tax, value-added tax, business tax, and salt tax; resource tax was imposed on certain mining enterprises; four categories of local taxes, namely real estate tax, land use tax, vehicle and vessel tax, and urban maintenance and construction tax, were restored or created; income tax was collected from profitable SOEs; and regulation tax was levied on large SOEs.

3. In 1987, the enterprise contracting system of "fixing the base quota, guaranteeing the remittance, retaining what exceeds the quota, and making up what falls short of the quota" was introduced into SOEs on a full scale. Although it was prohibited time and again by the central government by means of document dispatch, the common practice in various localities was that all taxes payable by the enterprise, including turnover tax and enterprise income tax, were all included in the fixed base quota; whenever the enterprise incurred a loss, government tax revenue would be affected. In this case, it was easy for enterprises to "retain what exceeds the quota" but difficult for them to "make up what falls short of the quota." Hence, "being responsible for profits but not losses" became a common practice. Statistics showed that during the period from 1987 to 1991, total unpaid taxes of contracted enterprises amounted to over RMB 5.1 billion, of which only 37 percent, or RMB 1.9 billion, was made up by enterprises themselves, while the remaining RMB 3.2 billion became the loss in government budget.

6.2.3 Institutional Defects of the Fiscal Responsibility System

Although there were differences between the "revenue-sharing system" and the "all-round fiscal responsibility system," they are nevertheless both variants of the fiscal responsibility system. It was originally intended that implementation of the "revenue-sharing system" and the "all-round fiscal responsibility system" was to define the rights and responsibilities of the various levels of fiscal units and to give play to the "two enthusiasms" of the central and local governments while ensuring stability of the budgetary revenue of the central government. However, the implementation of this system had displayed several serious drawbacks.

6.2.3.1 Unstable Fiscal Revenue Base Made State Financial Resources Insufficient for the Government to Fulfill Its Social Duties

As mentioned, the main feature of the traditional fiscal and taxation system was that the state achieved its fiscal revenue in the form of taxes and profits turned in by state-owned industrial and commercial enterprises by taking advantage of the central government's pricing power and the monopolistic position of SOEs. After over a decade of reform, dramatic changes had taken place in China's economic structure. Many non-state enterprises joined the competition, which drove down the profitability of SOEs. At the same time, the reform of power delegating and profit sharing enabled local governments and enterprises to try all means to turn in less tax and keep more revenue. What is worse, the management of tax collection was ineffective and local governments often reduced taxes on their enterprises or exempted their enterprises from paying taxes beyond their authority. Consequently, the share of fiscal revenue in the national economy was decreasing every year (see Table 6.1), while it still had to fund most of the existing activities. The resulting deficit increased so dramatically that the government could not even sustain its basic social services.

Table 6.1 **Fiscal Revenue, Expenditure and Deficit as Percentages of GDP (%)**

Year	Fiscal Revenue	Fiscal Expenditure	Fiscal Deficit
1978	34.8	34.5	-0.3
1981	27.3	29.4	2.1
1986	25.2	27.4	2.2
1991	18.4	21.8	3.3
1992	14.2	17.7	3.4

Source: Christopher J. Heady, Wing Thye Woo, and Christine P. Wong, *Fiscal Management and Economic Reform in the People's Republic of China*, Hong Kong: Oxford University Press, 1995. See Chinese edition, Beijing: China Financial and Economic Publishing House, 1993, p.12.

6.2.3.2 Rapid Decrease of the Budgetary Revenue of the Central Government

The fiscal responsibility system expanded the power of local governments to control their fiscal revenue without corresponding constraint mechanism, encouraging local fiscal institutions to act in local interests. At the same time, the budgetary revenue of the central government had only seen a short period of stability after the implementation of the revenue-sharing system in 1980, and began to decrease in 1986 (see Table 6.2). In the early 1990s, approximately half of the expenditure of the central government had to be financed by borrowing from banks.

Table 6.2 **Central Fiscal Revenue as Percentages of Total Fiscal Revenue and GDP (%)**

Year	As Percentage of Total Fiscal Revenue	As Percentage of GDP
1978	15.52	4.85
1979	20.18	5.73
1980	24.52	6.30
1981	26.46	6.40
1982	28.61	6.55
1983	35.85	8.26
1984	40.51	9.28
1985	38.39	8.59
1986	36.68	7.63
1987	33.48	6.15
1988	32.87	5.19
1989	30.86	4.86
1990	33.79	5.35
1991	29.79	4.34
1992	28.12	3.68

Source: The National Bureau of Statistics, *China Statistical Yearbook* (Zhongguo tongji nianjian), Beijing: China Statistics Press, various years.

6.2.3.3 Slackening Fiscal Discipline and Throwing Fiscal System into Chaos

The government shifted the burden of some expenditure items, including part of the expenses of administrative organs and the costs of primary education that should have been covered by the government finance, to the units concerned, forcing them to fund themselves by "raising funds" and "creating extra income." As a result, the scale of "extra-budgetary" revenue and expenditure continually expanded and "private coffers" proliferated through imposition of various kinds of charges and quotas in a multitude of names, which encouraged the unhealthy tendency to "marketize" public welfare undertakings, such as arbitrary charges in disguised forms for compulsory education, public health service, and other public services. Together with rampant corruptive practices like rent-setting and rent-seeking by government departments and making deals between power and money, all these aroused discontent of the society.

In spite of the impact to the fiscal revenue and expenditure, the fiscal responsibility system has negative effects on effective resource allocation and market system establishment.

For one thing, it resulted in "unfair treatment" and "whipping the fast ox" among various regions. Under the fiscal responsibility system, the key parameters were the sharing ratios of various regions, which were determined through one-to-one bargaining between the central government and the local government in question on the basis of historical data. Because of this, all kinds of unfair circumstances would inevitably occur and the system encourages people to seek benefits not from reform of government public service, but from making use of the public authorities to engage in "rent seeking."

Secondly, it intensified the drive to market segregation and hindered formation of a unified market. Based on administrative affiliation, the "revenue-sharing system" and the "all-round fiscal responsibility system" designated the profits and enterprise income tax of an SOE as fixed revenue of the government to which the enterprise was affiliated. To increase revenue, local governments at all levels employed all available means to expand the scale of capital construction and set up local SOEs by government investment on the one hand; while on the other, they widely exploited such measures as regional trade barriers, discrimination in taxes and fees, subsidy in disguised form so as to protect their "own" enterprises from external competition, resulting in widespread "vassal economy" of local protectionism, market segregation and tendencies of the market "dicing, stripping, slivering and mincing" across the country. Meanwhile, on this basis, pressure groups backed by vested interests emerged, thereby obstructing advance of market-oriented reform such as the tax-sharing system.

All-Round Reform of the Fiscal System in 1994

In response to the shortcomings of fiscal responsibility system, *the Decision on Issues Regarding the Establishment of a Socialist Market Economic System* was made by the Third Plenary Session of the 14th CCCPC to start an all-round reform of the fiscal system. Compared with all the previous reforms, the reform design was committed to the adjustment of the structure of intergovernmental fiscal distribution and stressed on normalized, scientific, and impartial relations of intergovernmental fiscal distribution. The fundamental framework of a fiscal and taxation system compatible with a market economy was established, because the reform proceeded fairly successfully.

6.3.1 Main Requirements of the Third Plenary Session of the 14th CCCPC for Fiscal and Taxation System Reform

Two key measures of the fiscal system reform in the near future defined by the Third Plenary Session of the 14th CCCPC are as follows:

The first measure was to replace the fiscal responsibility system with a tax-sharing system based on a reasonable division of authority between the central and local governments and establish mutually independent tax collection systems for the central and local governments. Taxes necessary for safeguarding the national rights and interests and implementing macro-control were categorized as central taxes while those directly related to economic development were shared between the central and local governments. Categories of local taxes were augmented to increase local tax revenue. The proportion of fiscal revenue in GNP would be raised gradually through developing the economy, improving efficiency, and tapping new sources of revenue and the ratio of central fiscal revenue to local fiscal revenue would be set at a more reasonable level. The system of revenue return and transfer payment from the central to the local would be established to adjust income distribution across regions and, particularly, to aid the development of underdeveloped regions and the rejuvenation of old industrial bases.

The second measure was to reform and improve the taxation system according to the principle of unified tax law, equitable tax burden, simplified tax structure, and fair division of power. A system of turnover tax would be instituted with value-added tax (VAT) being the principal part. Consumption tax would be levied on a few commodities, and business tax would continue to be levied on most non-commodity operations. Income tax rate for SOEs would be lowered and state key energy and transportation projects fund and state budget regulation fund would be eliminated. Enterprises would pay taxes as required by law and the profit distribution between the state and SOEs would be straightened out. At the same time, enterprise income tax and personal income tax would be unified, the tax rates would be normalized and the tax base would be broadened. Some new taxes would be imposed, some old ones would be adjusted, cases of tax reduction and exemption would be reviewed, and tax collection management would be tightened up to close tax loopholes. The multiple budget system would be improved and normalized, and the government public budget and the state assets operation budget would be established. If necessary, social security budget and other budgets would be created. Fiscal deficit would be under strict control. The fiscal deficit of the central government would be solved through issuance of long-term and short-term government bonds instead of overdrawing at banks.

6.3.2 The Tax-Sharing System for Fiscal Budget

Tax-sharing system is a budget system commonly adopted by the market economy countries implementing fiscal federalism. The features of the fiscal system are to plot out expenditure range according to the budget duties and responsibilities made by different levels of government, to classify sources of income among budgets of all levels according to the characters of different taxes and to balance the public service level among different regions through the transfer payment given by the central government to the local governments. In the mid-1980s, the Chinese government once considered replacing the "fiscal responsibility system" with a "tax-sharing system" during the period of the Seventh Five-Year Plan (1986-1990), but the idea was aborted later on. In 1992, the experiment with the tax-sharing system reform was restored. According to the *Decision on Issues Regarding the Establishment of a Socialist Market Economic System* adopted at the Third Plenary Session of the 14th CCCPC, starting on January 1, 1994, the tax-sharing system would be implemented nationwide. The following are the four main contents of the system.

1. On the basis of separating the functions of the government from those of the enterprise, define functions of governments at provincial, county (county-level city), and township (town) levels and divide authority among governments at different levels according to their functions.

2. According to the principle of matching authority with financial power, define the scopes of expenditure of governments at different levels according to their authority. The central government finance would mainly assume outlays necessary for state security, foreign affairs and operation of the central government organs and expenditure necessary for adjusting the structure of the national economy, coordinating regional development and implementing macro-control as well as expenditure for the development of undertakings under direct control of the central government. The rest would be in the scope of local government expenditure.

3. According to the nature of benefits and the principle of effective collection and management, divide tax revenue according to different tax categories. Taxespertaining to safeguarding the national rights and interests and implementing macro-control would be categorized as central taxes; taxes linked closely to local economic and social development, scattered in sources, and suitable for local collection and management would be categorized as local taxes; principal taxes with stable revenue and large amount would be categorized as central-local shared taxes. The proportion of central fiscal revenue should be increased to about 60 percent in total fiscal revenue, while the proportion of central fiscal expenditure would be kept at about 40 percent in total fiscal expenditure.

4. Establish a system of formula-based transfers step by step and transfer part of central fiscal resources, which equals to about 20 percent of total fiscal revenue, to local governments with lower levels of revenue so as to gradually reduce the difference in the level of government services across regions.

Fixed revenue of the central budget includes: customs duties, consumption tax and VAT per the customs, consumption tax, income tax of enterprises under the central government, income tax of local banks, foreign-invested banks and non-bank financial institutions, revenue collectively turned in by the railway department, headquarters of various banks and head offices of various insurance companies (including business tax, income tax, profits, and urban maintenance and construction tax), as well as profits turned in by enterprises under the central government. With regard to export tax rebates for foreign-trade enterprises, except the 20 percent assumed by local governments in 1993 that was listed in the base to be turned in by local governments to the central government, all subsequent export tax rebates would all be assumed by the central finance.

Fixed revenue for local government budget includes: business tax (excluding business tax collectively turned in by the railway department, headquarters of various banks, and head offices of various insurance companies), income tax of local enterprises (excluding income tax of the aforementioned local banks, foreign-invested banks, and non-bank financial institutions), profits turned in by local enterprises, urban land use tax, personal income tax, fixed asset investment regulation tax, urban maintenance and construction tax (excluding the portion collectively paid by the railway department, headquarters of various banks, and head offices of various insurance companies), real estate tax, vehicle and vessel tax, stamp tax, slaughter tax, agricultural/animal husbandry tax, agricultural specialties tax, farmland use tax, deed tax, estate and gift tax, land appreciation tax, as well as revenue of paid state land leasing.

Central-local shared revenues are VAT and resource tax. For VAT, the central government would share 75 percent while local governments would take the remaining 25 percent. Resource tax would be classified according to different resource varieties: land resource tax would go to local government revenue while offshore petroleum resource tax would go to central government revenue. Securities exchange stamp tax would be shared equally between the central government and the local governments.[1]

6.3.3 Basic Requirements of the Taxation System Reform

Basic requirements of the taxation system reform were: normalizing the taxation system according to the principle of unified tax law, equitable tax burden, simplified tax structure and fair division of power; establishing a taxation system compatible with a market economy; straightening out distribution and promoting fair competition. The main points are as follows.

1. Implement a new system of turnover tax (indirect tax) with VAT being the principal part. Turnover tax after the reform consists of VAT, consumption tax, and business tax, uniformly applicable to domestic-invested and foreign-invested enterprises. After calculation, according to the principle of "neither too much nor too less," the normal VAT rate is set at 17 percent of the added value, with a preferential rate at 14 percent.

2. Unify income tax for domestic-invested enterprises. Simplify and unify the income tax rate for enterprises of different ownership. A unified enterprise income tax would apply to all Chinese enterprises, including SOEs, collective enterprises, private enterprises, as well as corporations and other forms of joint ownership enterprises.

3. Unify personal income tax. The focus of the 1994 reform was to consolidate the existing personal income tax, personal income regulation tax, as well as income tax of urban and rural individual business owners to establish a unified personal income tax. A progressive rate would be adopted for personal come tax.

4. Tighten up tax collection and management. Establish two tax collection systems, namely the State Administration of Taxation and local taxation bureaus. Central taxes and central-local shared taxes would be collected by the State Administration of Taxation, while the local taxes would be collected by the local taxation bureaus. Along with the work to tighten up tax collection and management, arbitrary imposition of charges and quotas and "extra-budgetary revenue" of governments at all levels would be straightened out and the retained items would be managed within the legal framework of budget revenue.

6.3.4 The Impact on Finance Made by the Reform of Tax-sharing System

The fiscal operation after the reform proved that it was a successful one with very positive effects. First, the tax-sharing system changed the structure of the original fiscal responsibility system where multiple systems coexisted. It normalized the intergovernmental fiscal distribution relations and established a restraint mechanism wherein governments at all levels performed their own functions, carried out their own duties, and gained their own benefits as well as an attachment mechanism wherein benefits and expenses were shared between upper-level and lower-level governments. In addition, it rationalized the relations of authorities and responsibilities among governments at all levels. Second, fiscal transfer payment by the central government was strengthened considerably and formed a reasonable vertical distribution mechanism of financial resource. The promulgation of the *Method for Fiscal Transfer Payment during the Transition Period* initially established a normalized horizontal equalization mechanism of financial resource, which was favorable to the gradual narrowing of the gap in the level of government services across regions. Third, the tax-sharing fiscal system effectively facilitated the adjustment of industrial structure and the optimization of resource allocation, strengthened budget constraint to local government finance, and promoted reasonable economic behaviors of local governments. By earmarking for the central government, most of VAT from industrial products and all consumption tax, the tax-sharing system, to a great extent, limited local protectionism and market fragmentation; whereas, by earmarking for the local government tax categories from the tertiary industry and agriculture-related tax categories, the tax-sharing system stimulated enthusiasm of the local government to develop the tertiary industry as well as farming, forestry, animal husbandry, and fishery. After the downward coasting in 1995, the proportion of fiscal revenue in GDP began to climb up in 1996, rising year after year, while the proportion of fiscal deficit in GDP began to decline in 1996.

Table 6.3 **Fiscal Revenue and Deficit as Percentages of GDP**

Year	Fiscal Revenue (RMB Billion)	Fiscal Expenditure (RMB Billion)	Balance of Revenue and Expenditure (RMB Billion)	GDP (RMB Billion)	Fiscal as Percentage of GDP (%)	Balance of Revenue and Expenditure as Percentage of GDP (%)
1995	624.220	682.372	58.152	5,847.81	10.7	0.99
1996	740.799	793.755	-52.956	6,788.46	10.9	0.78
1997	865.114	923.356	-58.242	7,446.26	11.6	0.78
1998	987.595	1,079.818	-92.223	7,834.52	12.6	1.18
1999	1,144.408	1,318.767	-174.359	8,206.75	13.9	2.12
2000	1,339.523	1,588.650	-249.127	8,940.36	15.0	2.79
2001	1,638.604	1,890.258	-251.654	9,593.33	17.1	2.62

Note: Starting in 2000, fiscal expenditure includes domestic and overseas debt payment of interest expense.

Source: The National Bureau of Statistics, *China Statistical Yearbook* (Zhongguo tongji nianjian) 2002, Beijing: China Statistics Press, 2002.

After the East Asian financial crisis in 1998, China implemented a proactive fiscal policy dominated by bonds issuance to finance increased expenditure. Therefore, starting in 1998, deficit and the proportion of deficit in GDP increased rapidly.

6.4
Reform of the Fiscal and Taxation System after 1994

Even though the fiscal and taxation system in China switched to a new track in 1994, it nevertheless had a number of serious drawbacks mainly in the following aspects: (1) straightening out and normalizing the "extra-budgetary revenue," (2) further improving the tax-sharing system, and (3) establishing the framework of public finance.

6.4.1 Straightening Out "Extra-Budgetary Revenue"

Governments at all levels in China had the so-called "extra-budgetary revenue." During the early period after the founding of the PRC when a highly centralized system of unified control over revenues and expenditures was implemented, extra-budgetary revenue was limited only to agricultural surtax and production revenue of institutional units. In 1957, extra-budgetary revenue was equivalent to 8.5 percent of budgetary revenue. During the Great Leap Forward, the scope of extra-budgetary funds began to expand as a result of the economic system reform and transfer of fiscal authority to lower levels. After the commencement of the reform and opening up, budgetary revenue was declining, but extra-budgetary revenue of governments at all levels saw a big increase each year for the following three reasons.

1. In the process of the reform, fiscal revenue was decreasing while government functions remained more or less the same and government institutions and staff were even expanding. To support government administration, new sources of revenue were created outside of the budget-collecting charges to make up insufficient tax revenue. For instance, the central government began to collect fees for "state key energy and transportation projects fund" in 1980; in 1989, fees were also collected

for "state budget regulation fund." There were more cases of local governments obtaining extra-budgetary revenues to finance expenditures.

2. After the implementation of the "revenue-sharing system" and transfer of fiscal authority to lower levels, local governments at all levels began to enjoy more and more power to control the local economy. Consequently, some administrative organs began to concoct various pretexts to extort excessive fees.

3. In the marketization process, for quasi-public goods where service cost and beneficiaries could easily be identified, such as highway facilities, the method of paid supply should be adopted as much as possible in the first place; and yet, with the unsound rule of law and the integration of government administration with enterprise management, this kind of charges were subject to neither market constraint nor administrative regulation. This provided administrative organs or quasi-administrative organs with a motive to expand their own revenue to concoct various pretexts for high charges.

As of the early 1990s, creating extra-budgetary revenue had become a common phenomenon from the central government to local governments. By the end of 1996, there were more than 130 items of charges expressively stipulated by the central government and 46 items of construction fees, surcharges, and funds approved by the central government; after aggravating at every lower level of local governments and competent departments, according to incomplete county and county-level city statistics, there were over 1,000 various items of charges and over 420 various kinds of funds. An investigation by the Office on Alleviation of Enterprise Burden of the State Council in 1997 revealed that all sorts of unreasonable burdens on industrial SOEs amounted to RMB 50-60 billion or so, accounting for 20 percent of their achieved profits and taxes and exceeding the total of their achieved profits of the same year.[2] According to the result of a straightening-out registration and level-upon-level tabulation by competent departments of various kinds of funds nationwide, the national total of fund revenues in 1995 amounted to RMB 203.4 billion, equivalent to 32.6 percent of the fiscal revenue of the same year. An investigation on extra-budgetary funds by the Ministry of Finance in 1996 showed that at the end of 1995, the national total of extra-budgetary funds collected with approval from governments at the provincial level and above was RMB 384.3 billion, equivalent to 61.6 percent of the fiscal revenue of the same year. Even after several rounds of clean-up by competent state departments, there were still 344 items of departmental charges/administrative and institutional charges and 421 departmental funds in 1997 at the central level.[3] Items of charges at the provincial level and below were even more numerous. For instance, in a county-level city in Zhejiang Province, there were over 1,000 items of charges in 1995. A prefecture-level city had approximately 4,000 items of charges.[4] According to estimates by some financial experts, in 1997, the national total of extra-budgetary charges by governments at all levels was RMB 750-1,200 billion, equivalent to 1-1.5 times of the fiscal revenue of the same year.[5]

The expansion of extra-budgetary revenue of the government resulted in a series of evil consequences such as widespread corruption and waste by government institutions and officials, unbearable heavy burdens on enterprises and residents, which aroused strong public discontent. In 1998, Zhu Rongji, then the new premier, declared to implement the "transformation of administrative fees into taxes," in an attempt to straighten out and reorganize items of extra-budgetary revenue. The straightening-out and reorganizing scheme included five items. First, to conduct a thorough clean up of all types of existing charges and to resolutely abolish obviously unreasonable items of charges with unfavorable public reactions. According to an analysis, items of charges already abolished or about to be abolished could well exceed a quater of the items of charges at that time. Second, to conduct the "transformation of administrative fees into taxes" for most items of charges that were necessary to be retained. On the whole, the scope of transformation into taxes included items that payers could not directly benefit from as well as items of construction charges. Third, to distinguish charges for public welfare from administrative and institutional charges. Charges by public welfare undertakings such as schools and hospitals should be strictly straightened out and distinguished; abolishment must be carried out if necessary; items necessary for retention should be disconnected from administrative organs; responsibilities should be clarified among the government, public welfare units and the public; items of charge should be strictly defined. Moreover, market mechanism could be introduced into these public welfare units to enhance their quality of service through competition. Fourth, to strictly normalize charges by intermediaries such as auditing, accounting, appraisal, and law firms. In the past, these intermediaries used to be affiliated with administrative organs, though their business was mainly enterprise behavior. Owing to their special relations with the government, there were often many practices of unreasonable charges. These intermediaries must be pushed onto the market and separated from government operations completely. Fifth, to retain a few items of charges. Items of charges that could neither be abolished nor transformed should be maintained as government-stipulated fees. These items to be maintained mainly include four categories: (1) charges on certificates and licenses for registration according to law; (2) charges by law courts on lawsuits; (3) franchised operation charges, such as taxi license plates; and (4) environmental protection fees, which mainly targeted polluting enterprises.[6]

One important aspect in straightening out and normalizing extra-budgetary revenue was rural tax and fee reform, which has been adequately discussed in Chapter 4.

By the turn of the century, efforts in straightening out and normalizing extra-budgetary revenue had paid off. According to the report by the Ministry of Finance, the record-high ratio of extra-budgetary revenue to budgetary revenue of the Chinese government was 1:1; but by 2000, the ratio had dropped to 0.28:1. In 2001, the Ministry of Finance carried out a reform in all budgetary units to separate revenue from expenditure. The focus of the reform was to disengage revenue from expenditure, separate collection from payment, and abolish extra-budgetary funds step by step by bringing them under budget control. In 2002, the Ministry of Finance stipulated that all departmental extra-budgetary revenue should be brought under budget control or special fiscal account control,[7] and thirty-four central government departments achieved this goal. Starting in 2003, all administrative and institutional charges and revenues from fines and confiscations should be turned in to the special fiscal account,[8] which signified the end of extra-budgetary revenue.

6.4.2 Further Improving the Tax-Sharing System

According to theories of intergovernmental fiscal relations and overseas experiences in the implementation of the tax-sharing system, a complete tax-sharing fiscal system should include the following aspects: (1) there should be a clear-cut and reasonable division of authority among governments at all levels, (2) government at all levels should have a set of normalized and stable revenue systems, and (3) a sound transfer payment system should be set up with public service equalization as the basic objective. In the last aspect, the tax-sharing system set up in 1994 had its obvious drawbacks.

First, when the "new taxation system" was implemented in 1994, the central government adopted the buffer measure of guaranteeing the "1993 base number" to protect the original interests of wealthier regions. According to the new system, the incremental central revenue from consumption tax (central tax) and VAT (central-local shared tax, with a central share of 75 percent) in excess of the central revenue from tax receipts in 1993 would be returned to the local government as compensation to guarantee that its revenue after implementing the new system would not be less than its actual revenue in 1993 (the 1993 base number). The portion left after compensation for the 1993 base number would be shared between the central and local government budgets by the ratio of 7:3. The reform met with little resistance as local governments were happy with the idea to set up the 1993 base number. However, due to the unscrupulous exaggeration of the base number in the last quarter of 1993 by some local governments, most of the incremental revenue from the two taxes was returned to local government budgets such that the central government budget was left with an insufficient amount for transfer payment to less-developed provinces and autonomous regions, thereby aggravating the imbalance of fiscal resources across regions.[9]

Second, according to the basic principles of public finance, the respective responsibilities of the central and local government finance should be divided in line with the range of benefits brought by the public goods: the central government should be responsible for providing nationwide public goods, such as income redistribution and macro-control, whereas the local governments should be responsible for providing regional public goods with limited range of beneficiaries, such as local administrative services and public security. Division of authority among governments at different levels by the current fiscal and taxation system was also unreasonable. Governments at the county and township levels were assuming many duties of nationwide public services, including popularizing the nine-year compulsory education and public medical service, taking on heavy duties of expenditure and yet without corresponding sources of revenue. The combination of heavy duties and inadequate transfer payments resulted in enormous differences in the level of public services. Across provincial-level units, the ratio of highest and lowest budget expenditure per capita rose from 6.1 in 1990 to 19.1 in 1999.[10]

Third, the 1994 reform of the tax-sharing system failed to address the issue of the unequal distribution of fiscal resources across regions by transfer payment. The reform didn't give local governments adequate right of taxation to obtain additional revenue nor the right to raise public construction funds through borrowing.

Since 1995, the central government had taken out a certain amount of funds from its own incremental revenue for transfer payment. However, the fiscal resources of the central government available for transfer payment were limited and therefore it was very difficult to adjust the vested local interests. There were also technical problems such as incomplete statistical data and imperfect measurement method in the design of a transfer payment system. Because of this, the Ministry of Finance decided to temporarily implement a method for fiscal transfer payment during the transition period and promulgated the *Method for Fiscal Transfer Payment during the Transition Period*. It selected some objective and policy factors and adopted a relatively standard method to make limited transfer payment. The basic principles followed by the fiscal transfer payment during the transition period were: (1) not to adjust the vested local interests, (2) to be fair and just, and (3) to set priority and give special care to minority regions.

Specifically, the fiscal transfer payment amount during the transition period was composed of objective-factor transfer payment amount and policy-factor transfer payment amount. Objective-factor transfer payment amount was calculated and determined mainly by taking reference to the balance between the standard fiscal revenue and the standard fiscal expenditure of various regions as well as the objective-factor transfer payment coefficient. The standard fiscal revenue was calculated and determined by adopting the methods such as "standard tax base ∗ standard tax rate" and "revenue base ∗ (1 + relevant factor growth rate)," respectively, according to different tax categories; while the standard fiscal expenditure was calculated and determined by adopting different methods mainly according to classifications of staff outlay (excluding the health care and urban construction systems), public outlay (excluding the health care and urban construction systems), health care undertakings expenses, urban maintenance and construction expenses, social security expenses, pension for the disabled and families of the deceased and social relief expenses, expenditure for supporting agricultural production, and expenditure for comprehensive development of agriculture. Policy-factor transfer payment was calculated and determined mainly based on the difference between the standard fiscal revenue and expenditure and policy-factor transfer payment coefficient of the minority regions. The formula for calculation of the fiscal transfer payment amount of various regions was as follows: fiscal transfer payment amount of certain region = objective-factor transfer payment amount of the region + policy-factor transfer payment amount of the region.[11]

In implementation, this transfer payment system displayed considerable randomness, which not only affected further deepening of the reform of the tax-sharing fiscal system, but also encouraged the phenomenon of visiting officials of central departments for money (paobuqianjin). A normalized fiscal transfer payment system was yet to be established and improved in the future reform.

6.4.3 Realizing the Transition toward Public Finance System

After over two decades of reform, the fiscal system continually invested a great deal of financial resources in SOEs in competitive fields. However, in competitive sectors, SOEs are less market-oriented and competitive than non-state enterprises. Correspondingly, the government lacks adequate resources to support public services in the fields of public security, compulsory education, and public health care.

In response to this situation, in 2000, the Chinese government proposed the goal of "establishing a framework of public finance compatible with the requirements of a socialist market economy." The primary task of establishing a preliminary framework of public finance was to "further adjust and optimize the structure of fiscal revenue and expenditure, gradually reduce investment in profitable and business fields, rigorously cut down administrative and institutional expenses, push business institutions onto the market and use the financial resources mainly for meeting the common needs of the society and for social security."[12] To this end, the state finance should adapt to the needs of transforming government functions, further adjust and optimize the structure of expenditure, and gradually normalize the scope of public finance expenditure. In the meanwhile, it should also gradually withdraw from ordinary competitive fields, reduce its financial aid to business development projects and applied research projects in enterprises, and increase its input in education, science and technology, health care, public security, social security, and infrastructure construction.[13]

In line with this effort, reform was also carried out in the following aspects of the budget system.

6.4.3.1 Deepen the Departmental Budget Reform

A reform of the departmental budget system was kicked off in the second half of 1999 to reflect both extra-budgetary and budgetary funds in departmental budgets according to a unified standard and to make the budgeting process more serious, scientific, and normalized. In 2000, budgets of four departments, namely the Ministry of Education, the Ministry of Agriculture, the Ministry of Science and Technology, as well as the Ministry of Labor and Social Security, were submitted to the National People's Congress for examination and approval. In 2001, the number was increased to twenty-six departments, with their budgets more specific in contents and more standardized in format. In 2002, all budgeting units of the central government prepared their budgets according to the unified standard and a new classification of government revenues and expenditures. By having unified control over budgetary and extra-budgetary funds, all departments increased the transparency of their revenues and expenditures. Meanwhile, the departmental budget reform of local governments also sped up toward unification and standardization. Departments at the provincial and prefecture/city levels in public security, law court, industrial and commercial administration, environmental protection, and family planning were all required to implement departmental budgets. Government finance at the provincial level should expand the scope of departmental budgets as much as possible, while government finance at the prefecture/city level should make preparations for the departmental budget reform.

6.4.3.2 Advance the Reform of the Fiscal and Treasury Administration System

To implement the reform of a centralized treasury receipt and payment system is to transform the decentralized budget receipt and payment system, which was established during the reform of administrative decentralization and featured by multiple accounts, to a modern treasury management system with a unitary treasury account wherein all deliveries and appropriations are to be received and paid by the treasury. Implementation of this reform is of great significance to ensure safe and effective operation of government funds, enhance the efficiency of government funds, and prevent corruption at the very source. In 2001, the State Council approved the Reform Program of the Fiscal and Treasury Administration System jointly proposed by the Ministry of Finance and the People's Bank of China. At the same time, an experiment was also conducted at the six central government departments including the Ministry of Water Resources, the Ministry of Science and Technology, the Office of Legislative Affairs, the Ministry of Finance, the Chinese Academy of Sciences, and the National Natural Science Foundation of China. In 2002, experiments in reform were further extended to twenty-three central government departments, and carried out in Anhui, Sichuan, Fujian, Chongqing, Liaoning, Heilongjiang, Jiangsu, and Shandong. In addition, direct fiscal appropriations were also tried out for special funds for the central government to subsidize local governments.

6.4.3.3 Implement the Government Procurement System

According to the new requirement to prepare departmental budgets, government procurement budgets should be prepared, a centralized procurement catalogue should be compiled, and centralized government procurement should be implemented. Relevant methods for implementation should be worked out to institutionalize the government procurement under the rule of law. At the same time, the scope of direct appropriation should be extended, and a public bidding system should be introduced for government procurement to ensure the separation between administration and execution of government procurement. The auditing of government procurement should also be tightened up. In 2001, the government procurement amounted to RMB 65.3 billion nationwide, and in 2002, the figure reached RMB 100 billion, which is still expanding today. It should be pointed out that the departmental budget reform and supporting reforms of the centralized treasury receipt and payment system and the government procurement system were only part of the effort to establish a framework of public finance. These measures centered on solving the problem of the supervision in the process of supplying public goods. To ensure the efficient supply of public goods, it is also necessary to solve the problem of revealing preference of the public for public goods. Hence, the fundamental measure to advance the budget system reform, establish a public finance system, and improve the efficiency of public goods supply is to reform and improve the system of the National People's Congress, strengthen its power in the preparation and execution of government budget as the legislative body, and institutionalize the government budget system under the rule of law.

6.4.4 Proposals for New Reform Measures

With the elapse of the five-year transition period after the accession to the World Trade Organization (WTO), it is necessary for China to accelerate its taxation system reform in line with the fundamental principles of the WTO and the international practice. In 2000, a research group on the topic of "Further Fiscal and Taxation System Reform in China," composed of both Chinese and foreign economists, proposed suggestions focusing on the following items.

6.4.4.1 Improve Value-Added Tax

Improving value-added tax (VAT) mainly includes two aspects: first, to convert production VAT to consumption VAT; second, to extend VAT coverage.

The current production VAT system allows the enterprise to deduct the input tax included in purchased raw materials, not the input tax included in fixed asset. Therefore, there is the problem of double taxation on capital goods, which can be avoided when production VAT is converted to consumption VAT.

After the VAT conversion, some existing preferential tax policies need corresponding adjustments: (1) switch from the current policy of import-stage VAT exemption for foreign-invested and domestic-invested projects on imported equipment to a policy of "collection first and deduction later" in principle, (2) abolish the current VAT rebate for foreign-invested enterprises on homemade equipment, and (3) abolish the current income tax deduction for technological upgrading on homemade equipment.

Moreover, the VAT coverage should be expanded according to the principle of multistage collection. As a first step, industries closely related to economic development, such as construction and installation, transportation, warehousing and leasing, and post and communications, should be included into the VAT coverage. When conditions are ready, the VAT coverage can further expand to real estate, some services, and the entertainment industry, leaving the banking and insurance industry and some other services to business tax. By expanding the coverage, the VAT chain is well connected and its neutrality and deduction functions can be brought into full play.

6.4.4.2 Normalize Taxation on Imports and Exports

Limited by the present fiscal and administrative capacities of China, the export tax rebate system in China has been changed many times since the taxation system reform but is still imperfect and incomplete, which distorts the VAT mechanism and lowers the competitiveness of Chinese products in the international market. Therefore, China should make active use of the export tax rebate mechanism permitted by the WTO, and further deepen the reform of taxation on imports and exports. Specific measures include the following.

1. Unify and normalize preferential taxation policies for imports, and establish an open, impartial, transparent, and effective system of tax collection and management for imports, which is supportive to the collection and management of import duty and domestic turnover tax and in line with the international practice.

Adjust import taxation policies, restore taxation on imported fixed assets (including real estate) for production and operation use, and allow deduction in the subsequent stages.

2. Adapt to the new environment after the WTO accession, further improve the export tax rebate system, properly adjust export tax rebate policies, and gradually realize the objective of zero tax rate for exports. In line with the international practice, further expand export tax rebate coverage and include service trade and travel shopping export into export tax rebate coverage. Adopt effective preferential taxation measures to encourage imports and exports of high-tech products.

6.4.4.3 Adjust Consumption Tax and Business Tax Policies

In terms of consumption tax adjustment, aside from the realized adjustment of consumption tax rates for tobacco and liquor products and standardization of their tax base, consideration should be given to increasing the consumption tax rates on cars with large displacement engines and properly adjusting the tax rates

文化中國

and brackets of vehicles and motorcycles. In addition, some of the luxury goods and products closely related to environmental protection may also be brought into the coverage of consumption tax.

With regard to business tax adjustment, aside from the tax rate increase for the entertainment industry, the preferential policies to foreign-invested enterprises should be adjusted. The business tax exemption for intra-zone business receipts of foreign-invested financial institutions established in the special economic zones (SEZs) in the first five years should be abolished to ensure equitable tax burden on domestic-invested and foreign-invested enterprises.

6.4.4.4 Reform the Enterprise Income Tax System

The main problems with the existing enterprise income tax system include: separate income tax laws and regulations for domestic-invested and foreign-invested enterprises, inequitable tax burden across regions, unreasonable division of tax revenue between the central and local governments according to administrative affiliation, and irregular tax base. To solve all these problems, the enterprise income tax system reform needs to be carried out in the following lines.

Unify the enterprise income tax systems for domestic-invested and foreign-invested enterprises and consolidate the two laws, namely, the *Interim Regulations of Enterprise Income Tax of the People's Republic of China* and the *Enterprise Income Tax Law of Foreign-Invested Enterprises and Foreign Enterprises of the People's Republic of China*; normalize the tax base, define the scope and standard of pretax deduction in reference to the international practice, and unify the depreciation levels of domestic-invested and foreign-invested enterprises; straighten out and normalize the current preferential policies according to the principle of unified tax law, equitable tax burden, maintaining industry-specific preferential treatment, and phasing out region-specific preferential treatment; transform the existing practice of tax collection according to administrative affiliation; and reform the means of enterprise income tax collection.

The Ministry of Finance has pledged to gradually unify the enterprise income tax on domestic-invested and foreign-invested enterprises according to the principle of national treatment, and to create a more equitable tax environment for competition among all kinds of enterprises.

6.4.4.5 Reform the Personal Income Tax System

Main contents of the personal income tax reform include: (1) transforming the pure schedular tax system into a mixed tax system combining comprehensive tax and schedu-lar tax-including regular income such as wages and salaries, remuneration for personal services, and business income into the comprehensive tax category while retaining the schedular tax collection for other sources of income and (2) strengthening the tax collection method combining withholding at sources and filing tax returns by individuals, establishing an information processing system for individual earnings and large payments, and setting up an interdepartmental information exchange system and a third-party information reporting system of personal income to ensure effective collection.

Given the fact that interest income tax belongs to the central government, sharing personal income tax revenue between the central and local governments should be further clarified. The main consideration is that, as an important tax category with an income redistribution function, personal income tax is generally taken as a shared tax according to taxation theories and the international practice; moreover, after implementing the mixed tax system of comprehensive tax and schedular tax, the collection and refund of comprehensive income tax as well as information gathering also need cross-regional coordination and processing. As to the method of sharing, the preliminary view is that for the time being, it is proper that the central government exclusively enjoys taxes on investment income, including interest, dividends, and bonuses, while taxes on other income items are enjoyed by the local government.

Adjustment of the personal income tax rate is also under discussion. The purpose to implement the progressive tax on income is to redistribute income and narrow the gap between the rich and the poor. However, the American experience tells a different story. Extremely complicated and highly costly and distortionary, the American system of progressive income tax has created a situation where the ordinary citizens have a heavy burden while the rich always have ways to evade. Consequently, the progressive tax has in fact degenerated into a regressive tax.[14] Therefore, there are experts, both home and abroad, who advocate a uniform rate for personal income tax and at the same time, there are other scholars who favor a progressive tax rate.[15]

6.4.4.6 Reform and Improve Local Taxation System

As the economic situation changes, problems in the current local taxation system, such as two tax systems for the same tax object, excessively limited tax coverage, and unreasonable tax categories, have become more and more prominent. Accordingly, there is a need to speed up the reform and improvement of the local tax categories and establish local taxes with property tax and act tax as the mainstay. Detailed contents include: to consolidate the two different tax systems so that the tax burden will be the same for Chinese and foreign enterprises and citizens; abolish the outdated tax categories such as banquet tax; and impose new tax categories such as estate tax and securities transaction tax.

6.4.4.7 Speed Up the Transformation of Administrative Fees into Taxes

Discussions of the academic community and policy circles have focused on the following issues.

1. Rural taxation system reform. The on-going rural tax and fee reform is only the interim goal of the rural taxation system reform, and the final goal should be the gradual abolition of the existing agricultural tax and the establishment of a rural income tax system.

2. Social security financing. How to finance the public expenditure of social security, especially the implicit debts for repayment of pension funds of older employees of SOEs, has long been an issue of heated debates over the recent years. As to whether to transform social security contribution into social security tax or not, there has never been a consensus among different government institutions and the academic community. In this regard, there will be further discussions in Chapter 8 of this book.

3. Feasibility of transforming administrative fees into taxes in the aspects of urban maintenance and construction and resource protection. A suggestion is to transform administrative fees into taxes and to abolish all irregular charges.

4. Feasibility of replacing educational surcharge with tax.

5. Feasibility of transforming pollution fees into environmental protection taxes.

6.4.4.8 Adjust Taxation Rights

Based on the principle established in the *Law on Legislation of the People's*

Republic of China and the overall arrangement of transforming administrative fees into taxes, the next important issue is to transfer the taxation rights to lower levels.

Among the eight aforementioned items of the fiscal and taxation reform, some items have been approved by the Third Plenary Session of the 16th CCCPC in October 2003 and are expected to be implemented in the subsequent years.[16]

Notes and References

1. Since 2002, the ratio for sharing securities exchange stamp tax between the central and local governments has been changed to 97:3.

2. Yang Zhigang, "Fund Analysis of the Chinese Government (Zhongguo zhengfu zijin fenxi)," *Comparison of Economic and Social Systems* (Jingji shehui tizhi bijiao), 1998, No. 5.

3. *China Financial and Economic News* (Zhongguo caijing bao), April 29, 1998.

4. Jia Kang, "Basic Thinking on Tax and Fee Reform: Separation and Consolidation (Shuifei gaige de jiben silu: fenliu guiwei)," *Reform* (Gaige), 1998, No. 4.

5. According to the estimate by Jia Kang and Zhao Quanhou, fiscal revenue (total budgetary revenue) in 1996 was RMB 740.499 billion; after deducting extra-budgetary funds of the "state-owned enterprise and competent departments," government budgetary charges were RMB 83.587 billion; government extra-budgetary charges amounted to RMB 389.377 billion, estimated outside-system charges RMB 597.971 billion, government extra-budgetary charges plus estimated outside-system charges totaled up to RMB 987.305 billion, equivalent to 1.33 times of the total fiscal budgetary revenue. See Jia Kang and Zhao Quanhou, "Theoretical Analysis Framework and International Comparative Studies of the Tax and Fee System and Exploratory Discussion on Tax and Fee Reform in China (Shuifei tizhi de lilun fenxi kuangjia, guoji bijiao yanjiu yu Zhongguo de shuifei gaige tantao)," Liu Rongcang and Zhao Zhiyun (eds.), *Front Line of China's Financial Theories* (Zhongguo caizheng lilun qianyan), Vol. 2, Beijing: Social Science Literature Publishing House, 2001, p. 449.
6. *China Economic Times* (Zhongguo jingji shibao), November 2, 1998.
7. Xiang Huaicheng, "Report by Minister of Finance Xiang Huaicheng at the Fifth Session of the Ninth National People's Congress on Central and Local Government Budget Performance in 2001 and Budget Draft in 2002 (Caizhengbu BuzhangXiang Huaicheng zai Di Jiu Jie Quanguo Renmin Daibiao Dahui Di Wu Ci Huiyi shang guanyu 2001 nian zhongyang he difang yusuan zhixing qingkuang ji 2002 nian zhongyang he difang yusuan caoan de baogao) (March 6, 2002)," *China Business Post* (Caijing shibao), March 7, 2002.
8. "All Charges and Fines Go to the Treasury from This Year: The Termination of 'Extra-Budgetary Revenue' " (Shoufei fakuan jinnian qi tongjiao guoku, 'yusuan wai shouru' zhongjie)," *China Business Post* (Caijing shibao), January 3, 2003.
9. In 1997, the average financial resources per capita for population supported by the local finance nationwide was RMB 16,314; Shanghai, with RMB 53,566, being the highest, equivalent to 328 percent of the national average, Jiangxi Province, with RMB 10,850, being the lowest, or just about 66 percent of the national average, the absolute difference between the highest and the lowest was RMB 42,761, with relative difference of 3.96 times.
10. Huang Peihua, Deepak Bhattasali et al., China: *National Development and Local Finance* (Zhongguo: guojia fazhan yu difang caizheng), Beijing: CITIC Publishing House, 2003, p. 4.
11. Objective-factor transfer payment of a region = (standard fiscal expenditure of the region - standard fiscal revenue of the region) * objective-factor transfer payment coefficient; objective-factor transfer payment coefficient = (sum total of central government transition budget - sum total of policy-factor transition)/sum of balance of standard revenues and expenditures of the regions where standard fiscal expenditure exceeds standard fiscal revenue; standard fiscal revenue of a region = local standard fiscal revenue at the same level of the region + central government revesubsidy to the region + rated original system subsidy to the region - original system quota of turned-in revenue of the region + settlement subsidy to the region + other subsidies to the region; standard fiscal expenditure of a region = standard staff outlay of the region + standard public outlay of the region + standard health care undertakings expenses of the region + standard

urban maintenance and construction expenses of the region + standard social security expenses of the region + standard expenses of pension for the disabled and families of the deceased and social relief of the region + standard agricultural production support expenditure of the region + standard agricultural comprehensive development expenditure of the region; policy-factor transfer payment of a region = (standard fiscal expenditure of the region - standard fiscal revenue of the region) $*$ policy-factor transfer payment coefficient.

12. Li Lanqing, "Speech by Vice Premier Li Lanqing at the Opening Ceremony of the Seminar on Government Finance for Pro-vincial/Ministerial-Level Officials (Li Lanqing Fuzongli zai Shengbuji Ganbu Caizheng Zhuanti Yanjiuban Kaibanshi shang de jianghua)," *Xinhua News* (Xinhuashe Beijing dian), November 20, 2000. 24

13. Lou Jiwei, "Fiscal Reform and Development in China after Accession to WTO (Jiaru WTO hou de Zhongguo caizheng gaigeyu fazhan) (2002)," Wang Mengkui (ed.), *China after Accession to WTO* (Jiaru Shimaozuzhi hou de Zhongguo), Beijing: People's Publishing House, 2003, pp. 27-31.

14. Robert Hall and Alvin Rabushka, "Chapter 4: The Flat Tax and the Economy," *The Flat Tax*, 2nd edition, California: Hoover Institution Press, 1995. See also Wang Zeke, "Heavy Cost of the Federal Individual Income Tax of the USA (Meiguo Lian-bang geren suodeshui de chenzhong daijia)," *Comparative Studies* (Bijiao), Vol. 3, Beijing: CITIC Publishing House, 2002, pp. 163-170.

15. Lawrence J. Lau, "Some Thoughts on a Comprehensive Individual Income Tax for China (Youguan Zhongguo shixing zonghe geren suodeshui de yixie sikao)," *Comparative Studies* (Bijiao), Vol. 2, Beijing: CITIC Publishing House, 2002, pp. 129-141.

16. *Decisions of the CCCPC on Issues Regarding the Improvement of the Socialist Market Economy System* approved by the Third Plenary Session of the 16th CCCPC proposed the reform of the taxation system. It includes reforming export tax rebate system, unifying enterprise tax system, converting production VAT to consumption VAT, improving consumption tax, appropriately expanding tax base, revising personal income tax, implementing an integrated income tax system of consolidated and classified taxes, granting local government proper tax administration authority under the premise of unified tax administration, creating conditions for unifying urban and rural taxation system, etc.

CHAPTER SEVEN

OPENING TO THE OUTSIDE WORLD

In the late 1970s, the Chinese government started to experiment with a new policy of opening up (kaifang), or opening to the outside world (duiwai kaifang). After more than two decades, the opening to the outside world of China has improved a lot. Particularly, with China's accession to the World Trade Organization (WTO) in November 2001, China is entering a new state of all-round opening up.

7.1
The Evolution of China's Foreign Economic Relations and Development Strategy

Since 1949, China's foreign economic and trade relations have undergone four stages of different strategies.

7.1.1 Self-Seclusion (1949-1971)

Neither before nor after the founding of the People's Republic of China (PRC) did the Chinese leadership consider establishing an entirely closed economy. However, the out-break of the Korean War in 1950 and the subsequent blockade of China by the United States and its allies forced China to cut itself off from the West. After 1956, in order to adapt to the centrally planned economic system, the Chinese government established a foreign trade system characterized by state monopoly. All the import and export businesses of an industry were monopolized by a state-run national import and export corporation[1] established by the industry. Import and export were carried out according to the mandatory plan assigned by the State Planning Commission: exports were purchased according to the state plan while imports were transferred and distributed according to the state plan, with the state finance system responsible for all profits and losses. Under this system, the function of import and export trade was defined as "supplying what each other needs," and it played only the role of "regulating supply and demand" with foreign countries.

After the Great Leap Forward was launched in 1958, and especially after the political and economic relations with the USSR ruptured in the early 1960s, the Chinese leadership emphasized self-reliance, encouraged every region to have "independent economic setup," and adopted the self-seclusion policy in foreign economic relations. From then until the 1970s, foreign trade in China was basically stagnant (see Table 7.1).

Table 7.1 **China's Share in World Trade**

Year	World Trade Volume (US$ billion)	China's Share in World Trade (%)
1953	2.37	1.5
1957	3.11	1.4
1959	4.38	1.9
1962	2.66	0.9
1970	4.59	0.7
1975	14.75	0.8
1977	14.80	0.6

Source: General Agreement on Tariffs and Trade (GATT), *International Trade*, from N. Lardy, *China in the World Economy*, Washington, D.C: Institute of International Economics, 1994, P.2

7.1.2 Import Substitution (1972-1978)

During the later half of the Great Cultural Revolution, the gaps in industry, technology, and management between China and industrialized countries grew even more apparent. Mao Zedong sensed the danger of a long period of self-seclusion: it would be impossible to achieve industrialization, let alone the ideal of "surpassing Britain and catching up with the United States," a goal set in earlier years. As a result, China improved its relations with the United States and normalized diplomatic relations with Japan in 1972, and adopted a policy of developing trade relations with Western countries. Especially during 1977-1978, China imported many sets of large-scale manufacturing and mining equipment. In 1978 alone, China signed contracts totaling US$7.8 billion for equipment related to chemical fertilizers and metallurgy, among other industries, which were for twenty-two large-scale projects. Import and export trade rapidly grew, with the total import and export volume 39 percent higher in 1978 than it was in 1977. However, at this time, China's purpose for developing foreign trade was not to build an open economy, but rather, to establish an economic system of independence and self-reliance by import substitution.

7.1.3 Combination of Export Orientation and Import Substitution (1978-2001)

Deng Xiaoping pointed out, "The present world is open. One important reason for China's backwardness after the industrial revolution in Western countries was its closed-door policy... The experience of the past thirty or so years has demonstrated that a closed-door policy would hinder construction and inhibit development."[2] "The lessons of the past tell us that if we don't open to the outside, we can't make much headway... If we isolate ourselves and close our doors again, it will be absolutely impossible for us to approach the level of the developed countries in 50 years."[3] Hence, he demanded that "actively developing relations, including economic and cultural exchanges, with other countries on the basis of the Five Principles of Peaceful Coexistence" would "enable us to make use of capital from foreign countries and of their advanced technology and experience in business management."[4]

Opening to the outside world under the leadership of Deng Xiaoping included the adoption of an export-orientation strategy, which was mainly to fully exploit China's comparative advantages in labor-intensive industries and to earn foreign exchange through "three supplied and one compensation (sanlaiyibu)," namely, processing supplied materials, processing according to supplied samples, assembling supplied parts, and compensation trade.

It has to be pointed out that although the authorities had decided on the foreign trade policy of export orientation, because of their lack of clear understanding of the differences between import substitution and export orientation, government officials in practice continued to execute the policy of import substitution. The export orientation strategy was not implemented immediately. For instance, from 1985 to 1992, China maintained an average statutory tariff rate above 43 percent. Until 1993, China still maintained a dual exchange rate system, and the official exchange rate of RMB was significantly overvalued.[5] Under such conditions, many processing enterprises actually served the domestic market.

7.1.4 An Open Economy (after 2002)

China is a contracting state of the General Agreement on Tariffs and Trade (GATT), the predecessor of the World Trade Organization (WTO). In 1986, China applied to restore its status as a contracting state of the GATT. This very act signified China's determination to further open itself to the outside world and to integrate itself into the world economic system. Subsequently, the Chinese government instituted reform measures in many areas related to trade. For example, tariff barriers were significantly lowered, most import quotas were abolished, and the laws and the law enforcement system were improved, which push forward the opening up of Chinese economy. In November 2001, China acceded to the WTO officially. China accepted the rules of globalization comprehensively and the Chinese economy is being transformed into a open one day by day.

7.2
The Spatial Evolution of Opening to the Outside World

China's opening to the outside world has been advancing step by step in several stages and at several levels, with coastal regions as the strategic focus.

In the early 1980s, China began to establish bases for opening to the outside world in a few coastal cities. The reason for this decision was that, with a vast territory and many years of planned economic system it would be impossible to quickly establish the domestic market and to fully implement the policy of opening to the outside world to integrate with the international market. Therefore, with experience learned from other countries in establishing special economic zones (SEZs), the Chinese leadership exploited the advantages of some coastal cities such as Shenzhen of being close to Hong Kong, Macao, and Taiwan and being the hometown of a large number of overseas Chinese in order to create a "micro climate" for a market economy, to attract foreign capital, technology, and management, and to develop export-oriented industries. Specific steps taken included:

1. In May 1980, it was decided to implement special economic policies and flexible measures of opening to the outside world in both Guangdong and Fujian provinces.

2. In August 1980, SEZs were set up in Shenzhen, Zhuhai, Shantou, and Xiamen as experiments. SEZs are "regional export-oriented economies regulated mainly by market forces." Imported goods for self-use by enterprises in SEZs were exempted from tariffs and consolidated industrial and commercial tax. Tariffs and consolidated industrial and commercial tax on imported goods for sale were reduced by half; for the sale of self-produced goods within SEZs, consolidated industrial and commercial tax was also reduced by half.

3. In May 1984, it was decided to further open fourteen coastal port cities, namely, Dalian, Qinhuangdao, Tianjin, Yantai, Qingdao, Lianyungang, Nantong, Shanghai, Ningbo, Wenzhou, Fuzhou, Guangzhou, Zhanjiang, and Beihai (including Fangchenggang), and to offer foreign-invested enterprises there preferential treatment similar to that provided SEZs.

4. In February 1985, it was further determined to designate the Yangtze River Delta, the Pearl River Delta, the Xiamen-Zhangzhou-Quanzhou Triangle in South Fujian, the Jiaodong Peninsula, and the Liaodong Peninsula as open economic regions.

5. In April 1988, it was decided to establish the Hainan Special Economic Zone.

By then, the overall pattern of all-round opening to the outside world in coastal regions was basically set up. Opening up in coastal regions greatly promoted the regional economic development as well as the reform and opening up and the economic development of the whole nation.

First, these open regions made effective use of international resources, actively participated in international competition, and became pioneers of opening to the outside world in China. According to statistics, by the end of 1990, the accumulated investment in capital construction over the prior decade completed by the first four SEZs in Shenzhen, Zhuhai, Shantou, and Xiamen exceeded RMB 30 billion; a number of large-scale infrastructure and industrial projects had been completed. Foreign direct investment (FDI) in the fourteen coastal open cities during the Seventh Five-Year Plan (1986 - 1990) exceeded US$10 billion; more than two thousand of the "three categories of foreign-invested enterprises" (i.e., Sino-foreign equity joint ventures, Sino-foreign contractual joint ventures, and wholly foreign-owned enterprises) were put into operation. Opening to the outside world promoted the development of export-oriented sectors. The total export volume of the twelve coastal provinces, autonomous region, and municipalities in 1990 was approximately US$40 billion, accounting for about two-thirds of the total national export volume.

Second, opening to the outside world in these regions promoted rapid economic growth, making them the most vigorous regions. All-round opening up attracted a great deal of foreign investment and generated a great deal of foreign trade, which in turn led to rapid development. Gross value of industrial output in the first four SEZs jumped from only RMB 5.5 billion in 1985 to RMB 49.5 billion in 1990, an increase by eight times in only five years, with an average annual growth of 50 percent.

Third, these regions played a key role in connecting inland China with the international market. Enjoying their unique position as gateways to the outside world, these coastal open regions could fully play the role of connecting the inside of China to the outside world, and vice versa. By absorbing foreign capital, technology, and management, and developing export trade, these regions could gradually develop and strengthen themselves; then, they could gradually transfer foreign capital, technology, and management skills to inland regions so as to promote development there, as well. In addition, these SEZs and coastal open regions also daringly explored new economic systems and operating mechanisms, thus accumulating experience, setting up models, and providing references for economic system reform in the whole nation; they became the testing ground for reform. Opening to the outside world in the 1980s prepared China and provided experience for further opening to the outside world in the 1990s.

7.2.2 Expanding the Regions Open to the Outside World in the 1990s

In the 1990s, the Chinese government proposed the "four-along strategy" to further open China to the outside world.

1. "Along the coast" referred to development focused on coastal China from the Bohai Sea to the Beibu Gulf (Gulf of Tonkin).

2. "Along the border" referred to development focused on the border regions of Xinjiang, Inner Mongolia, and Heilongjiang to strengthen economic and trade exchange with countries of the Commonwealth of the Independent States (CIS) and development focused on the border regions of Yunnan and Guangxi to open trade routes to South Asia and Southeast Asia.

3. "Along the river" referred to the overall development and opening up of the Yangtze River Valley downstream from Chongqing, with the development of Pudong in Shanghai as the flagship; from there, the goal was to link the east and the west and to generate influence to the south and the north.

4. "Along the railway" referred to the regions along the railroad from ports in East China to the Altai Mountains in Xinjiang Autonomous Region, as part of the Eurasian "continental bridge" within Chinese territory.

Opening to the outside world in various regions across China in the 1990s was carried out in two directions. First, the territory along the banks of the Yangtze River was to be gradually built into another vast open belt after coastal regions of China, with the development and opening up of Pudong in Shanghai as the "head of the dragon." This plan had the greatest strategic significance in expanding open regions in the 1990s. In April 1990, the Chinese government made a strategic decision to develop and open Pudong New Area in Shanghai. Deng Xiaoping, in his South China tour in 1992, made an important speech, pointing out that Shanghai had significant advantages in terms of human resources, technology, and management. Besides,

當代中國經濟改革

Shanghai could generate influence in the Yangtze River Valley, which was the largest highly industrialized region in China. On both sides of the Yangtze River were comprehensive industrial bases with a high degree of specialization in Shanghai, Nanjing, Wuhan, and Chongqing, among others. As the Yangtze River economic belt possessed technological strength and covered a vast inland area, it could open itself to the outside world to a wider extent and at a higher level than other regions. No other region could substitute for the Yangtze River Valley because of its existing industrialization. Moreover, the Yangtze River economic belt boasted convenient transportation and a mature cultural environment. It could fully tap international resources by expanding its opening up process and attracting investment to stimulate the growth of local and inland economies. Therefore, in 1993, after implementing the development of Pudong in Shanghai, the Central Committee of the Communist Party of China (CCCPC) and the State Council decided to apply the opening-up policy to the five cities of Wuhu, Jiujiang, Wuhan, Yueyang, and Chongqing. As a result, Pudong in Shanghai, as the flagship in the development and opening up, would further strengthen its influence and leading role, and, at the same time, the largest highly industrialized belt in the Yangtze River Valley would be realized following the lead of the Pudong area.

Second, the process of opening up in inland provinces and autonomous regions was accelerated. Inland cites along the border were further opened up, to push the economic development of inland provinces and autonomous regions forward. The inland provinces and autonomous regions of China have vast territories and abundant natural resources, and opening these areas to the outside world would facilitate the exploitation of these advantages. In 1993, the CCCPC and the State Council decided to open eleven provincial capital cities- Hefei, Nanchang, Changsha, Chengdu, Zhengzhou, Taiyuan, Xi'an, Lanzhou, Xining, Guiyang, and Yinchuan. In addition, the provincial capital cities of the four coastal and border provinces and autonomous regions of Harbin, Changchun, Hohhot, and Shijiazhuang were made open cities. They were allowed to enjoy the same preferential policies as those of coastal open cities, which infused vitality into the development of these provinces. Thus, by the mid-1990s, a new pattern of all-round, multi-level, wide-scope opening to the outside world was well underway.

文化中國

7.2.3 Development Prospects of Special Economic Zones

The strategy of gradual opening to the outside world by starting with SEZs was developed to cater to the requirements of government management capacity and the system reform during the transition from a closed economy to an open economy. In the process of the reform and opening up, SEZs had been the showcase and testing ground, and had become the bases to utilize foreign investment, increase exports, and set up modern industries, especially modern manufacturing.

With the basic framework of a market economy in place and the accession to the WTO, the continuation of preferential treatment to enterprises in SEZs, such as reduced or exempted taxes, became nonconducive to the establishment of a large unified domestic market of fair competition, or to the reduction of disparity between coastal and inland regions. The Chinese government promised that after the accession, policies not in conformity with the WTO principles, such as national treatment and most-favored-nation (MFN) treatment, would no longer be adopted in SEZs. This meant that the policies extended exclusively to SEZs must be adjusted, and their primary functions must be changed, allowing them to win new competitive advantages through institutional innovations rather than through preferential policies such as tax incentives.

A new trend at the turn of the century was that many foreign enterprises shifted orders from their factories in other regions to those in China, or set up new plants in China to produce products for the international market. A consequent topic is whether China will become a world-class manufacturing base, or a "world factory." Perhaps the real problem lies in how much benefit it can bring to indigenous enterprises and people in China.

7.3
Foreign Direct Investment

Since the inception of reform and opening up in the late 1970s, the Chinese government has adopted a series of preferential policies to attract foreign investment, the achievement of which has drawn worldwide attention.

7.3.1 Growth and Characteristics of Foreign Direct Investment in China

Foreign direct investment attracted by China has been growing year by year. Since 1993, China has been the largest recipient of FDI among developing countries. By the end of 2002, the total number of foreign-invested enterprises approved nationwide was 424,196; the total contract value of FDI reached US$828 billion; and the total utilized value of FDI stood at US$448 billion. For the first time, China surpassed the United States to become the country using the largest amount of FDI in the world.

Figure 7.1 **Foreign Direct Investment in China** (US$ billion)

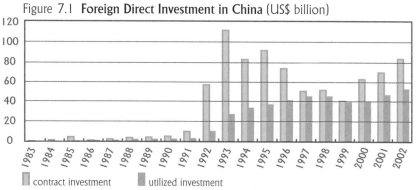

■ contract investment　　■ utilized investment

Source: The National Bureau of Statistics, *China Statistical Yearbook* (Zhongguo tongji nianjian), Beijing: China Statistics Press, various years.

In terms of the sources of investment, East Asia has been most important for China, and among them, the Hong Kong Special Administrative Region has been the largest supplier of FDI in the form of individual as well as enterprise investment. Investment from other parts of the region also takes Hong Kong as its springboard. As of 2002, accumulated utilized investment from Hong Kong had reached US$204.9 billion. Taiwan is another important source of investment. Although statistics showed that accumulated utilized investment from Taiwan was only US$33.1 billion, fourth place among investment sources, the true amount is much higher, given the fact that many Taiwanese invest through a third place or party to avoid restrictions imposed by the Taiwan authorities on investing in mainland China. This accounts for why Hong Kong, the Virgin Islands, and the Cayman Islands are important gateways for outside investment. According to estimates, the actual investment from Taiwan was about two to three times more than the official statistics showed. Thus, Taiwan is in fact the second largest source of FDI in mainland China. In addition, developed countries such as the United States, Japan, and European countries are also important sources of investment (see Table 7.2).

Table 7.2 **China's FDI by Origin** (US$ billion)

Country (Territory)	Utilized Investment in 2002	Accumulated Utilized Investment
Hong Kong (China)	17.861	204.875
Virgin Islands	6.117	24.388
U.S.A	5.424	39.889
Japan	4.190	36.340
Taiwan (China)	3.971	33.110
South Korea	2.721	15.199
Singapore	2.337	21.473
Cayman Islands	1.180	3.803
Germany	0.923	7.994
U.K.	0.896	10.696

Note: Accumulated utilized investment was accumulated from 1978.
Source: Ministry of Commerce, PRC.

Most FDI from the East Asian region comes to China to take advantage of the low cost of production factors such as labor, and is mainly engaged in labor-intensive production, with products primarily exported to their traditional markets. As a result, an interesting "triangular trade" phenomenon has formed. Large quantities of inputs are imported by mainland China from South Korea, Japan, and Taiwan (China), which are assembled or processed in China and then exported to developed markets, such as the United States and Europe. As a result, the original trade surplus of these East Asian economies with the United States has now become the large trade surplus of China with the United States. In 2001, China replaced Japan as the number one source of trade deficits with the United States. At the same time, these East Asian economies generated a great trade surplus with China.

In terms of the sector distribution of FDI in China, it is mainly found in manufacturing. By the end of 2001, manufacturing accounted for 70 percent of the total number of foreign-invested enterprises, 56 percent of total investment, and 60 percent of registered capital. FDI in the service industry was mainly concentrated in real estate. Shares of the primary industry in total investment and registered capital of foreign-invested enterprises were quite low, less than 2 percent (see Table 7.3). This is partly because China has comparative advantages in manufacturing, i.e., low costs of production and strong supporting capacity of domestic industries, and partly because China has long imposed rigorous restrictions on foreign investment in service industries.

Table 7.3 **Sector Distribution of Foreign-Invested Enterprises at the End of 2001**

Sector	Number of Enterprises		Total Investment		Registered Capital		Foreign Registered Capital	
	Number	%	US$ million	%	US$ million	%	US$ million	%
Total	202,306	100.00	875,011	100.00	505,795	100.00	359,683	100.00
Farming, Forestry, Animal Husbandry, and Fishery	4,752	2.35	9,135	1.04	6,180	1.22	4,763	1.32
Mining and Quarrying	1,047	0.52	3,282	0.38	2,317	0.46	1,462	0.41
Manufacturing	141,668	70.03	491,322	56.15	305,250	60.35	214,931	59.76
Production and Supply of Electricity, Gas, and Water	1,268	0.63	49,505	5.66	20,039	3.96	11,606	3.23
Construction	5,139	2.54	21,547	2.46	11,862	2.35	7,743	2.15
Geological Prospecting and Water Conservancy	128	0.06	4,237	0.48	1,545	0.31	1,412	0.39
Transport, Storage, Post, and Telecommunications	3,499	1.73	41,442	1.734	20,432	4.04	15,163	4.22
Wholesale and Retail Trade and Catering Services	12,249	6.05	24,592	2.81	15,585	3.08	11,311	3.14
Banking and Insurance	74	0.04	2,089	0.24	1,965	0.39	1,415	0.39
Real Estate Management	11,925	5.89	149,094	17.04	72,244	14.28	55,536	15.44
Social Services	16,169	7.99	56,274	6.43	34,020	6.73	23,188	6.45
Health Care, Sports, and Social Welfare	469	0.23	2,774	0.32	1,543	0.31	1,128	0.31
Education, Culture and Arts, Radio, Film, and Television	530	0.26	1,390	0.16	982	0.19	675	0.19
Scientific Research and Polytechnic Services	1,851	0.92	4,334	0.49	2,752	0.54	2,171	0.60
Others	1,538	0.76	13,994	1.80	9,079	1.80	7,179	2.00

Source: The National Bureau of Statistics, *China Statistical Yearbook* (Zhongguo tongji nianjian), Beijing: China Statistics Press, 2003. Percentages are calculated by the author.

In terms of the regional distribution of FDI in China, investment is mainly concentrated in coastal regions. In 2002, FDI in twelve coastal provinces, autonomous region, and municipalities accounted for 87.43 percent of the national total. The main reasons were that these areas were the first to be opened to the outside world and had a better investment environment, higher level of economic development, and a better industrial base. It should be noted that the disparity in investment environment between coastal and inland regions has become increasingly large as a result of the first mover advantage. Inland regions have lagged far behind in many aspects, such as infrastructure, institutional environment, cadres' mindset, and supporting capacities of local industries. Obviously, the concentration of FDI in coastal regions is not conducive to reducing the gap in regional development.

Foreign investment in the early years was mainly in the form of Sino-foreign equity joint ventures and Sino-foreign contractual joint ventures (i.e., Sino-foreign cooperative enterprises). Wholly foreign-owned enterprises gained popularity in subsequent years, and today, they have become the primary form of foreign investment in China. In 2002, they accounted for 65 percent of the total number of FDI projects, 69 percent of contract investment, and 60 percent of used investment. In addition, other forms of investment, such as BOT financing and securities financing have also been introduced into China. Generally speaking, foreign investment may take the form of sole investment or joint venture according to the investors' free will. The *Catalogue for the Guidance of Foreign Investment Industries* formulated by the government only imposes restrictions on the share of foreign investment in certain service sectors and particular manufacturing industries as allowed by China's WTO accession protocol.

A new form of FDI is to participate in the reform of China's state-owned enterprises (SOEs).The first important measure in the reform of SOEs is to define property rights. The reform can either be "restructuring on the spot"- defining property rights, dividing shares, and establishing a corporation system while maintaining the existing ownership structure- or "restructuring with outside investment"-transforming SOEs into mixed-ownership companies or companies controlled or wholly owned by new investors by introducing new domestic and foreign capital. "Restructuring with outside investment" is of particular significance, as it can help China's SOEs overcome the difficulties in breaking down the old institutional framework and the inadequacy of self-owned capital, thus accelerating the process of corporatization.[6]

7.3.2 Promoting the Growth of Local Enterprises

In the early stage of the reform and opening up, China's policy toward foreign capital was centered on preferential treatment because foreign investors then were unfamiliar with the investment environment in China and were still doubtful about the opening-up policy. Furthermore, China's infrastructure and other conditions were also backward, and there were many restrictions on and discrimination in charges against foreign-invested enterprises. With great changes in China's economic environment, the focus is being shifted from "preferential treatment" to "impartiality" in attracting foreign investment.

Since 1995, China has adjusted its policy on charges and taxes on foreign capital by, for instance, repealing consolidated industrial and commercial tax, imposing value-added tax (VAT), consumption tax, and business tax, abolishing the tax exemption for foreign-invested companies on imported cars, and merging the two exchange rates. Most foreign investors believe that a fair taxation environment for all enterprises is instrumental in attracting more foreign investment. At the same time, this policy adjustment can curb fake foreign investment and optimize the FDI structure.

Creating a sound competitive environment does not mean the immediate removal of all restrictions on investments by foreign citizens or of all protections for domestic infant industries. In recent years, the Chinese government has formulated a series of policies in accordance with the international practice to increase the attractiveness of China's industry to foreign capital, to regulate the behavior of various parties, and to encourage the entry of foreign investors and guide them into the normal track.

In 1995, the State Planning Commission, the State Economic and Trade Commission, and the Ministry of Foreign Trade and Economic Cooperation jointly issued the *Interim Regulations on the Guidance of Foreign Investment Directions* and the *Catalogue for the Guidance of Foreign Investment Industries*. The *Regulations* and the *Catalogue*, to be adjusted according to changes in circumstances, divided foreign investment projects into four categories: "encouraged," "restricted," "prohibited," and "permitted." Foreign investment projects of the "encouraged" and "permitted" categories enjoy preferential treatment according to laws and regulations. Foreign investment projects of the "restricted" category require approval by the ministries and commissions of the State Council or governments of provinces, autonomous regions, or municipalities directly under the central government, and cities specially designated in the state plan.

The new edition of the *Catalogue for the Guidance of Foreign Investment Industries* issued on March 31, 2002 listed three categories of industries: "encouraged," "prohibited," and "restricted." In the meantime, it further expanded the industries open to foreign investment.

Since 2001, in accordance with commitments made during negotiations for the accession to the WTO, China has successively amended the *Law of PRC on Wholly Foreign-Owned Enterprises*, the *Law of PPC on Chinese-Foreign Equity Joint Ventures*, and the *Law of PRC on Chinese-Foreign Contractual Joint Ventures* and abolished performance requirements for foreign-invested enterprises in export, local content, balance of foreign exchange, transfer of technology, and establishment of R&D units, thereby providing a legal guarantee to grant national treatment to foreign-invested enterprises in the aforementioned aspects.

In a word, the Chinese government adopted effective measures to improve the soft environment for foreign investment in the following aspects.

1. Improve the policy and legal environment for foreign investment; promote administration according to law; maintain stability, continuity, predictability, and operability of policies and laws regarding foreign investment; and create a unified, stable, transparent, and predictable legal and policy environment.

2. Maintain and improve a fair and open market environment; resolutely suppress arbitrary inspections and imposition of charges, quotas, and fines on foreign-invested enterprises; break local protection and trade monopolies; protect intellectual property rights and crack down on infringement and piracy; improve the complaint system for foreign-invested enterprises.

3. Further open trade in services.

4. Encourage foreign investors to invest in high-tech industries, basic industries, and supporting industries.

5. Take active measures to attract more multinationals to invest in China.

6. Encourage foreign investment in the central and western regions of China.

7.4
The Development of Import and Export Trade

The basic content of China's strategy of opening up was the development of foreign trade, which benefited not only from the reform of the foreign trade system but also from the enormous inflow of FDI. As a logical outcome of the spatial evolution of opening to the outside world, coastal regions in China were the main bases both for foreign capital utilization and foreign trade development.

7.4.1 The Process of the Reform of the Foreign Trade System

Since 1979, China has conducted a series of reforms in its foreign trade system and gone through a transition from a plan-oriented foreign trade system to a market-oriented foreign trade system.

7.4.1.1 Reform of Trading Rights

The government implemented several measures in reforming trading rights. These are as follows.

1. Transferred part of the trading rights to lower levels. Under the planned economic system, foreign trade was monopolized by twelve national import and export corporations. The monopoly in foreign trade hindered the realization of export potential. To encourage the initiatives of local governments and industrial departments, the central government gradually expanded their power to grant trading rights to foreign trade enterprises and export-oriented production enterprises; to approve the establishment of foreign-invested enterprises; and to approve "processing supplied

materials, processing according to supplied samples, assembling supplied parts, and compensation trade." At the same time, the government also expanded the trading rights of enterprises. Only exports that were huge in volume, significant to the national economy and the people's livelihood, particularly hot on the international market, or with special requirements were managed by specialized national import and export corporations affiliated to the Ministry of Foreign Trade and Economic Cooperation. The trading rights in all other merchandise were granted to local branches of national import and export corporations and foreign trade companies of industrial departments. All provinces, municipalities, autonomous regions, and cities specially designated in the state plan opened ports with direct trading rights to engage in foreign trade within an approved scope. Furthermore, the central government also approved the establishment of a new batch of specialized national import and export corporations affiliated to various ministries of industry and granted trading rights in products and supplies to a number of qualified large- and medium-sized enterprises. Except for a few categories of merchandise to be monopolized by national import and export corporations and another small portion subject to quota or license control, most merchandise can be freely exported and imported by enterprises with trading rights.

2. Granted production enterprises with trading rights in their own products and supplies and explored approaches to the integration of industry and trade, of technology and trade, and of production and marketing. In view of the long-existing problems in quality, variety, and packaging as a result of the separation between industry and trade and between production and marketing, the central government approved some large-sized key industrial enterprises and enterprise groups to directly engage in foreign trade. It also helped to set up joint-ownership enterprises to integrate trade, industry, agriculture, and technology, and began to experiment with various forms to integrate industry and trade as well as production and marketing.

3. Granted foreign-invested enterprises with trading rights in their own products and supplies; that is, foreign-invested enterprises were entitled to manage the import of raw materials, parts, and components for self-use and the export of their own products.

4. Implemented policies conducive to the development of processing trade. China introduced bonded supervision over imports necessary for processing activities.

At the same time, it abolished non-tariff barriers, such as licenses and quotas for processing import, except for some sensitive merchandise. These policies helped to avoid distortion caused by high tariffs and non-tariff barriers to trade, and effectively promoted the development of processing trade.

Table 7.4   **Reduction in the Average Statutory Tariff Rate in China**

Year	Average Tariff Rate (%)
1992	43.2
1993	39.9
1994	35.9
1996	23.0
1997	17.0
2000	16.4
2001	15.3
2002	12
2003	11

Note: Tariff rates in the table are calculated without weighting.

Source: Yin Xiangshuo, *The Process and Achievements of China's Foreign Trade System Reform* (Zhongguo duiwai maoyi gaige de jinchenghe xiaoguo), Taiyuan: Shanxi Economy Press, 1998, pp. 94-95; and other materials.

5. Granted private production enterprises with trading rights in their own products and supplies. In September 1998, the State Council approved the reform that granted private production enterprises and scientific research institutions with trading rights in their own products and supplies from 1999. Since then, the share of non-state enterprises in total national import and export volume experienced a substantial increase.

7.4.1.2 Reduce Tariff Protection

In 1982, the average statutory tariff rate was 56 percent in China. In 1992, the figure was cut to 43.2 percent. The process of reducing tariff rates was accelerated in recent years. In 2003, the average tariff rate dropped to 11 percent (see Table 7.4). By the end of the post-WTO transitional period, the average tariff level in China will reach a level equivalent to that of other developing members of the WTO.

7.4.1.3 Gradually Abolish Non-tariff Barriers

Non-tariff barriers in China include trading rights restrictions, import quotas, import licenses, list of import substitutes, import invitation-for-bids (IFB) requirements on specific merchandise, as well as quality and safety standards. Quotas and licenses introduced in the early 1980s were the most important non-tariff barriers. By the end of the 1980s, licensed merchandise had reached fifty-three categories, accounting for as much as 46 percent of all imported goods. In the 1990s, China gradually reduced the categories of licensed merchandise. By the end of the 1990s, less than 4 percent of taxable import merchandise was subject to the restriction of import license. In negotiations for the accession to the WTO, the Chinese government committed to remove all import quotas and licenses and to gradually abolish, within two to four years after the accession, the compulsory IFB requirement on the import of four major categories of goods, specifically, scientific apparatus, building equipment, agricultural equipment, and medical equipment.

7.4.1.4 Formulate and Establish Systems and Policies to Encourage Exports

These policies include export incentive funds to reward foreign trade enterprises and export production enterprises, several adjustments in foreign exchange rate based on the development of foreign trade and price variation of domestic merchandise, product tax/value-added tax rebates for export merchandise, preferential export credit for foreign trade enterprises and export production enterprises, and a system of foreign exchange retention from export proceeds.

1. Reform of the foreign exchange control system. Under the traditional domestic-oriented planned economy, foreign-related economic activities including import and export were regulated by the plan; foreign exchange was allocated by the government; and the role of exchange rate was insignificant. With the development of foreign economic relations, the impact of exchange rate on foreign-related economic activities became much more prominent. From 1981 to 1993, the government adjusted the official exchange rate many times. In 1994, the official exchange rate of RMB was merged with the market rate under a managed floating exchange rate system, and the convertibility of the Chinese currency (RMB) under the current account was achieved within three years. However, after the East Asian financial crisis of 1997, to relieve pressure on neighboring countries and to stabilize the overall situation of the world economy, China adopted the measure of intervention by the central bank to stabilize

the exchange rate of the Chinese currency, which restricted considerably its floating band. At present, we need to restore the floating nature of the exchange rate of the Chinese currency when the right opportunity comes along.

2. Tax rebates for exports. It is a common international practice that exported products are not subject to domestic turnover tax, such as product tax and value-added tax (VAT). After the taxation system reform of 1994, China stepped up its effort to promote exports by tax rebates and began to offer VAT rebates on exports.

Nevertheless, as export tax rebates were huge in amount, lengthy in process, and complex in formality, the slow implementation of export tax rebates affected export growth as an important policy factor.

7.4.2 The Development of Foreign Trade

7.4.2.1 The Gross of Trade Increases Rapidly and China is already a Trade Giant in the World

During the twenty-three years from 1978 to 2001, the volume of China's foreign trade increased by twenty-five times (see Figure 7.2). Correspondingly, China's rank in world trade jumped from No. 32 in the early stage of the opening up to No. 6. Import and export of some key categories of merchandise occupied important positions in the international market, making China an important player in the world trade system.

Figure 7.2 **Growth of China's Foreign Trade (1978-2001)**

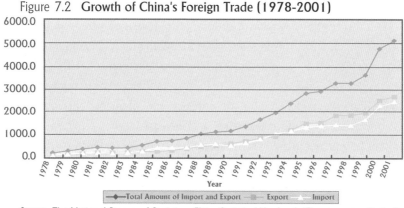

Source: The National Bureau of Statistics, *China Statistical Yearbook*, (Zhongguo tongji nianjian), Beijing: China Statiistics Press, various years.

Processing trade was the key driver of trade expansion in China. In these twenty-three years, the average growth rate of foreign trade in China was far higher than the average growth rate of world trade. The expansion of China's economy and the resulting improvement of its international competitiveness were two basic reasons for the high growth of foreign trade in China, but the most important reason was the rapid development of processing trade. Starting in the late 1970s, China adopted a policy of developing businesses of "processing supplied materials, processing according to supplied samples, assembling supplied parts, and compensation trade." In the mid and late 1980s, China implemented the opening-up strategy of large-scale import and export. As this strategy was geared to the international trend of industrial relocation and exploited China's comparative advantages in the low costs of factors such as labor and land in the international division of labor, enormous success was achieved. From 1980 to 2001, the average annual growth rate of processing export reached 29.4 percent while the average annual growth rate of processing import reached 24.1 percent; the average annual growth rates of processing export and import were 19.8 percentage points and 13.8 percentage points higher than other forms of export and import respectively. The shares of processing export and import in total export and total import were 59.2 percent and 41.5 percent respectively.

With the continuous growth of foreign trade, China's trade dependence ratio also increased correspondingly.[6] In 2002, the trade dependence ratio of China reached 49.6 percent, and export dependence ratio 26.0 percent (see Table 7.5). Compared with the international standard, (1) the increase of the Chinese trade dependence ratio conformed to the international trend because the world average export dependence ratio increased from 14 percent in 1970 to about 25 percent in 1997; (2) the current trade dependence ratio of China is still below the world average; (3) if the difference in GDP structure of various countries is taken into consideration, the trade dependence ratio of manufacturing in China is lower than that of developed countries such as the United States and Germany, and far below the level of the so-called "small open economies;" (4) a high proportion of processing trade leads to exaggeration of the degree of depen dence of China's economy on the international market when measured by the trade dependence ratio; and (5) if the influence of exchange rates is eliminated, according to the trade dependence ratio calculated by PPP (purchasing power parity), China's degree of openness (8.5 percent) is equivalent only to the average level of low-income countries (8.4 percent), and far below the average levels of middle-income countries (16.7 percent) and high-income countries (38.7 percent).[7]

Table 7.5 **Trade Dependence Ratio of the Chinese Economy** (% of GDP)

Year	1978	1980	1985	1990	1995	1997	2002
Total Imports and Exports	9.8	12.6	23.0	30.0	40.3	36.1	49.6
Total Exports	4.6	6.0	9.0	16.1	21.3	20.3	26.0
Total Imports	5.2	6.6	14.0	13.9	19.0	15.8	23.6

Source: The National Bureau of Statistics, *China Statistical Yearbook* (Zhongguo tongji nianjian), Beijing: China Statistics Press, various years.

7.4.3 Problems Demanding Immediate Solutions

China is already a trade giant in the world. Yet the following problems demand immediate solutions if China wants to become a trade power.

First, export suffers from poor merchandise mix and low grade. Over the past twenty years, the export mix of China's foreign trade has quickly been transformed from primary-product dominance in the early stage of the opening up to finished-product dominance (see Table 7.6). However, the process and production activities that China engages in are still concentrated on the labor-intensive, low-value-added part of production. Few of the exported products contain technology with Chinese intellectual property rights. Moreover, most Chinese exports are sold at low prices as a result of the lack of their own marketing network.

233

Table 7.6 **China's Export Merchandise Mix** (Total National Exports = 100)

Year	1980	1985	1990	1995	2000	2002
Primary Products	50.2	50.6	25.5	14.4	10.2	8.8
Foodstuffs	16.5	13.9	10.6	6.7	4.9	4.5
Other Agricultural Products	9.5	9.7	5.7	2.9	2.1	1.7
Fossil Fuel	23.5	26.1	8.4	3.4	3.2	2.6
Others	0.8	0.9	0.8	1.4	0.05	0.03
Finished Products of Processing Industry	49.8	49.4	74.5	85.6	89.8	91.2
Chemical Products	6.2	5.0	6.0	6.1	4.6	4.7
Textiles and Other Light Industrial Products	22.1	16.4	20.3	21.1	17.1	16.3
Electromechanical Products	4.7	2.8	9.0	21.1	33.1	39.0
Miscellaneous (including Ready-Made Clothes)	15.7	12.7	20.4	36.7	34.6	31.1
Others Non-Classified	1.2	12.5	18.7	-	0.09	0.02

Source: The National Bureau of Statistics, *China Statistical Yearbook* (Zhongguo tongji nianjian), Beijing: China Statistics Press, various years.

Given the global glut of production capacities, labor-intensive products are now experiencing cutthroat competition in the international market. Therefore, although China's export volume has grown rapidly, its trade terms[8] are deteriorating. What is worse, due to the low grade of export merchandise, China's export can adopt only the strategy of "winning by sheer numbers." With protectionism in international trade on the rise, this strategy is likely to meet with unfair treatment. At present, China is facing more antidumping investigations than any other country in the world. Because of the so-called "non-market economy provisions"[9] of fifteen years in China's WTO accession protocol, Chinese enterprises are at a disadvantage in responding to antidumping investigations. Moreover, China's export products are also faced with the risk that importing countries may quote special safeguard provisions against them. Faced with the proliferation of international technical and "green" trade barriers, Chinese export merchandise is in an unfavorable position in international competition as a result of its low grade. With the advent of the twenty-first century, the international economic circles began to spread a new "China threat theory", adding new uncertainties to the external environment of China's exports.

Second, China's export market is over-concentrated in a few countries. In terms of market structure, China's exports are concentrated in the three big markets of the United States, Japan, and Europe. China, in particular, is highly dependent on the U.S. market, with 40 percent of China's exports of final products going there. An important reason for this is that a number of neighboring economies have relocated to China their production activities of final products that are intended to be exported to the United States, forming a unique "triangular trade" phenomenon. In this case, China imports large quantities of intermediate goods from Japan, South Korea, and Taiwan, and then exports them to the U.S. market after assembling and processing.

To address the over-concentration problem in the short run, China must accelerate the implementation of a market diversification strategy. It needs to further develop traditional markets such as the United States, Japan, Europe, and ASEAN for new export growth; to vigorously exploit the Russian market, regulate Sino-Russian trade order, and expand Sino-Russian bilateral trade; to promote the export of products to India by focusing on engineering projects and overseas processing and assembling; and to develop markets in the Commonwealth of the Independent States (CIS), Middle East, Latin America, Africa, and South Asia.

Third, the development of service exports is lagging behind. In recent years, the proportion of service exports in total exports of the various trade powers in the world continuously increased. In 1999, service exports of these countries equaled 24 percent of their merchandise exports. In contrast, the development of service exports in China was slow: its ratio to merchandise exports was 15 percent lower.

7.5
Prospect of China's Opening to the Outside World

Chinese government took opening policy firmly, and after fifteen years of tough negotiations, China finally entered the WTO. China's accession to the WTO has further shown to the domestic and international communities that to establish an open market economic system is the committed policy of the Chinese government.

7.5.1 China Will Enter a New Era of All-Round Opening to the Outside World

China's commitments upon the accession are mainly in two areas: one is to open markets, including merchandise markets and service markets; the other is to accept the WTO rules and to revise relevant Chinese laws and regulations according to these rules.

Fulfillment of the commitments upon the accession will trigger extensive and profound changes in social and economic life in China. In terms of opening markets, over the past more than twenty years, under unilateral and bilateral frameworks, the degree of market opening increased significantly . But, as a whole, the absolute level of market protection was still high-higher than developed economies and developing economies as well.

After the accession, China's overall degree of market opening is parallel to the level of developing members, and in some sectors, it goes beyond the average level of developing members. Therefore, from a relatively closed economy to a relatively open economy, China will experience significant increase in the degree of market opening. In terms of revising laws and regulations, China has just set up a general framework of a market economy, and some reforms of critical importance to the market economic system, such as the establishment of a unified domestic market, SOE reform, and reform of the investment and financing system, have not yet achieved breakthroughs. The WTO rules are the basic requirements for an open market economic system. To deepen the economic system reform in line with the WTO rules is fundamentally consistent with the reform objective of establishing a socialist market economic system in China.

To fulfill the commitments to open the domestic market and to revise laws and regulations means less discretion and flexibility in the future to control the opening pace. It is certainly an unprecedented task to realize such extensive market opening and system adjustment in such a short period.

During the first year after the accession, the Chinese government earnestly fulfilled its commitments, actively responded to challenges by accelerating reform, and regarded challenges as opportunities for reform and development. First, China revised its laws and regulations and issued a number of judicial interpretations according to its commitments and the WTO rules while abolishing a number of judicial interpretations not in conformity with the WTO rules. Thirty ministries and commissions under the State Council reviewed 2,300 department regulations regarding merchandise trade, service trade, intellectual property rights, and investment, of which 830 were abolished and 325 were revised. Local governments reviewed more than 190,000 local laws and regulations. Second, administrative organs at various levels reviewed all their items of administrative approval; departments of the central government alone had more than 3,600 items reviewed, nearly half of which were abolished by May 2004. Third, China reduced its trade protection level. According to China's WTO accession protocol, after January 1, 2002, China reduced import tariff on merchandise of over 5,300 tariff codes, with the average statutory tariff rate down from 15.3 to 12 percent: the average tariff on agricultural products was reduced from 18 to 15.8 percent, and the average tariff on industrial products was reduced from 14.7 to 11.3 percent. Finally, China loosened its restrictions on market access for foreign investment in the service sector. In the retail sector, in 2002, China approved the establishment of eight joint ventures, which would open twenty-eight stores. In the banking sector, on November 7, 2002, the United Overseas Bank of Singapore officially opened its first branch in China. The Bank of East Asia, Credit Lyonnais, ABN AMRO Bank, and Deutsche Bank AG were either waiting for approval from the People's Bank of China or busy preparing for branch establishment. When China officially entered the WTO on December 11, 2001, it had already removed client restrictions against foreign banks on handling foreign exchange business and allowed these banks to operate RMB business in Shanghai, Shenzhen, Tianjin, and Dalian. Starting on December 1, 2002, the People's Bank of China further opened RMB business to foreign-invested financial institutions in Guangzhou, Zhuhai, Qingdao, Nanjing, and Wuhan. In the insurance sector, seven foreign-invested corporations have obtained their business licenses.

Earnest fulfillment of its commitments won high praise for China from the international community. The WTO carried out seventeen reviews of China's trade policies for the transition period. Results of the reviews indicated that China's fulfillment of its commitments upon the accession to the WTO was generally good. The American Chamber of Commerce made a general evaluation of the first nine months after the accession, with the result being "generally not bad."

The anticipated serious consequences did not occur in the first year after the accession, thanks to the active response of the government and enterprises. The expectation of adverse impact generated great momentum for further economic reform, adjustment of industry structure, and development of imports and exports. Sectors such as banking and automobile production that were once expected to meet major challenges have accelerated their reform and restructuring and achieved unprecedented development. Taking advantage of the global output reduction in bulk agricultural products resulting from natural calamities, agriculture has avoided adverse impact of import surge; at the same time, the product mix of agriculture has been adjusted, and international market expansion has been strengthened. Meanwhile, foreign economic and trade relations have been exceptionally active. While the growth of global trade was only 1 percent, export growth in China reached 20 percent in 2002, making it the sixth largest trade power in the world. Moreover, in utilization of foreign capital, China surpassed the United States for the first time, becoming the largest recipient of FDI in the world.

One important lesson from the first year after the accession is that opportunities always exist along with challenges. The key to success is to turn the table by a proactive attitude and a correct strategy. If handled properly, pressure can be turned into motivation, challenges into opportunities, and disadvantages into advantages.

7.5.2 Active Participation in Regional Economic Cooperation

Since the 1990s, regional economic integration has experienced rapid progress, becoming a prominent trend parallel with economic globalization. China has several alternative schemes: "10 + 1 (ASEAN + China)," "10 + 3 (ASEAN + China, Japan, and South Korea)," "China, Japan, and South Korea," and the Shanghai Cooperation Organization, among others. In 2002, China reached a framework agreement with ASEAN concerning the establishment of a free-trade area before 2010. At the same time, China is also cooperating with policy research units in Japan and South Korea to study the issue of Northeast Asia regional cooperation. With the process of regional cooperation, such as the "10 + 1" and "China, Japan, and South Korea," regional cooperation organizations in East Asia comparable to the European Union and the North American Free Trade Agreement may eventually emerge.

In the globalization of the world market, a system of orderly competition needs to be established to protect the equal rights of people of all countries. In the past two decades, developing countries have been advocating such a new order by consultation on an equal footing among all countries. However, over a considerably long period of time, developed countries reacted indifferently to this proposal. It was not until the end of 1997 when the financial crisis in East Asia dealt a serious blow to the economy of South Korea, which was newly accepted as a member of the so-called "rich countries' club," the Organization for Economic Cooperation and Development (OECD), that statesmen from developed countries began to realize that economies of all countries in the world are intimately related to each other and bound by a common cause. Since then, developed countries have adopted a more active attitude in salvaging countries ravaged by crisis and in preventing its spread. The financial crisis in countries like Russia and Brazil in 1998 further proved the necessity for international cooperation and the establishment of a healthy international economic system by joint efforts.

From October 3 to 5, 1998, the "Group of Seven" (G7)-the United States, Japan, Germany, France, the United Kingdom, Canada, and Italy-convened in Washington, D.C., where it discussed world economic issues of common concern (the G7 Economic Summit). At the same time, finance ministers from twenty-two countries attending the annual meetings of the International Monetary Fund (IMF) and the World Bank also discussed the issue of the world financial order. Participants also put forward many suggestions and declarations. It is a positive sign. It indicated that more and more people realized the necessity of establishing a sound international economic order by consultation on an equal footing among all countries. China, as an influential developing country, should actively participate in the establishment of a new international economic order to seek steady development of the world economy.

文化中國

Notes and References

1. National corporations under direct administration of the foreign trade department of the central government included China National Cereals, Oils and Foodstuffs Import and Export Corporation, China National Native Produce and Animal By-Products Import and Export Corporation, China National Textiles Import and Export Corporation, China National Silk Import and Export Corporation, China National Light Industrial Products Import and Export Corporation, China National Arts and Crafts Import and Export Corporation, China National Chemicals Import and Export Corporation, China National Machinery Import and Export Corporation, and China National Metals and Minerals Import and Export Corporation, among others.

2. Deng Xiaoping, "Building a Socialism with a Specifically Chinese Character (Jianshe you Zhongguo tese de shehuizhuyi) (June 1984)," *Selected Works of Deng Xiaoping* (Deng Xiaoping wenxuan), Vol. 3, Beijing: People's Publishing House, 1993, p. 64.

3. Deng Xiaoping, "Speech at the Third Plenary Session of the Central Advisory Commission of the Communist Party of China (Zai Zhongyang Guwen Weiyuanhui Di San Ci Quanti Huiyi shang de jianghua)" (October 1984), ibid, p. 90.

4. Deng Xiaoping, "Hold High the Banner of Mao Zedong Thought and Adhere to the Principle of Seeking Truth from Facts (Gaoju Mao Zedong sixiang qizhi, jianchi shishiqiushi de yuanze) (September 1978)," *Selected Works of Deng Xiaoping* (Deng Xiaoping wenxuan), Vol. 2, Beijing: People's Publishing House, 1994, p.122.

5. In 1993, the official exchange rate of RMB against the U.S. dollar was about 5.8, whereas the market exchange rate was between 11 and 12.

6. The trade dependence ratio is the index used to measure the degree of opening up and dependence of an economy on the in ternational commodity market, usually indicated by the ratio of total volume of imports and exports to GDP. Because imports and exports of most countries are balanced m the long term, some economists also use the export dependence ratio (ratio of exports to GDP) or import dependence ratio (ratio of imports to GDP) to indicate the degree of dependence on trade.

7. Long Guoqiang, "How to Look upon China's Trade Dependence Ratio (Ruhe kandai wo guo de waimao yicundu)," Development Research Center of the State Council of PRC, *Research Paper*, No. 2000-066, http://www.drc.gov.cn/e/index.htm; *China Economic Times* (Zhongguo jingji shibao), August 10, 2000.

8. Terms of trade refers to the ratio of average price of exported goods to that of imported goods. A decrease in this ratio means that the country must export more goods to exchange for the same amount of imported goods, indicating deteriorating terms of trade.

9. Within fifteen years after its accession to the WTO, China will still be considered a country with a nonmarket economy; this is one of the most important concessions made by China in its negotiations for accession to the WTO. This clause enables foreign enterprises to easily win antidumping lawsuits as long as it can be proven that the selling price of Chinese products is lower than the cost of the products in market economies.

CHAPTER EIGHT

SOCIAL SECURITY SYSTEM REFORM

After the founding of the People's Republic of China, a labor security system centered on urban state-owned work units was established. Workers covered by this security system received medical, pension, and other benefits from the state according to the stipulated benefit standards, protecting them against potential risks in life such as old age, illness, and death. Such protection was considered a fundamental right of workers. However, this kind of social security system was not only limited in coverage but also non-sustainable even within its limited coverage, as was evident after several decades of implementation. Meanwhile, the advance of economic reform, especially enterprise reform, posed an urgent need for the establishment of a social security system to cover the whole society as soon as possible to provide a social safety net and ensure stability amidst the great social transformation and economic restructuring.

8.1
The Social Security System and Problems before Reform

After the founding of the People's Republic of China, the Chinese government established a defined-benefit, pay-as-you-go social security system modeled on the precedents of the USSR and other socialist countries.

In February 1951, the central government issued the *Ordinance of the People's Republic of China on Labor Insurance*, stipulating that full-scale labor insurance to state employees and their dependents, such as old age insurance, medical insurance, and occupational injury insurance, be entirely planned by the state and implemented by enterprises. This *Ordinance* laid the foundation of social security for employees of state-owned work units. According to this *Ordinance*, the labor insurance system was first established in large industrial SOEs and was then gradually expanded to other industries such as state-owned commerce and trade. In rural areas, the practice of the traditional Chinese society was adopted with household provision as the major form of security.

Aside from the general feature of a pay-as-you-go system, the Chinese social security system was unique in that "work units" (factories, organs, and public institutions) were responsible for its implementation. Prior to the Great Cultural Revolution, the specific method for work units to implement social security was to deduct from income a fringe benefit fund in the amount of a fixed proportion of the payroll to cover the various items of labor insurance expenses. After the Great Cultural Revolution started, the fringe benefit fund was no longer enough to pay the social security expenses because of the increasing number of retired workers and the insufficient financial resources of enterprises amidst social turmoil. Since 1969, therefore, enterprises switched from deducting the labor insurance fund in the amount of a fixed proportion of the payroll to having pension, public medical service, and other labor insurance benefits listed under non-business expenditures. As a result, social security completely evolved into enterprise security.

In 1986, the State Council stipulated in the *Interim Regulations for the Implementation of the Labor Contract System in State-Owned Enterprises* that the pensions of new employees recruited under the labor contract system should be financed by pooling funds. While this somewhat changed the enterprise provision system of the Great Cultural Revolution era, the pension pooling remained small in scale and local in scope, and more importantly, the means of financing and management did not undergo corresponding adjustment to adapt to the economic reform. This situation continued until the early 1990s.

During the era of the planned economy, the social security system where "the state takes care of everything" was established and recognized as one of the major advantages of the socialist system. As work units were established as the grassroots organizations of the society under the planned economy, in which normal flow of labor force was no longer necessary, and workers and even their descendants could fully depend upon and adhere to their work units all their lives, the social security functions were quickly transmuted to "work-unit security." The contracting system reform of state-owned enterprises (SOEs) in the 1980s did not touch the labor and personnel system of enterprises, let alone lead to the emergence of the labor market or the market-oriented allocation of labor resources. Therefore, the issue of how to establish a social security system independent of the enterprise system was not raised. Though to a very limited extent, the labor contract system, introduced in 1986 for some new employees of SOEs, created an independent relationship between workers and enterprises and raised the issue of independent social security functions. This change, however, did not touch the fundamental issues of social security system reform, as "social pooling" was retained for pensions for workers under the labor contract system, which in fact was still a pay-as-you-go system administered entirely by the government.

8.1.2 Drawbacks of the Traditional Social Security System

The traditional social security system established during the era of the planned economy has its basic drawbacks in two fundamental aspects of efficiency and fairness.

8.1.2.1 Loss in Efficiency

First, it elicited the enthusiasm of the contributor. The defined-benefit, pay-as-you-go system is, in essence, an intergenerational transfer from the current generation of workers to the previous generation of workers, which dampens the working enthusiasm of the former. Especially when the aging of a society has reached a relatively high level, the working generation may have to support too many aged people, and the contradictions will become more prominent. Due to the Chinese

Social Security System Reform

policy of opposing birth control in the mid-1950s and the 1960s, China's population explosion caused serious social problems. In the early 1970s, the Chinese government was forced to switch to a policy of strict birth control and the birth rate dropped sharply. In the mid-1980s, the phenomenon of an aging population began to appear in China and was further aggravated in the 1990s. In some old SOEs, the ratio of the number of retirees receiving pension to the number of active employees had generally become very high (ranging from 1:3 to 1:1). With time, the enterprises' burden of pension and medical expenses increased, seriously affecting incentives for the current working generation.

Second, its operation cost was very high. As enterprise finance and government finance were integrated under the planned economy, social security funds always came from government finance, directly or indirectly, whereas employees themselves did not make any contribution. There was no connection at all between the payment of the social security benefits and the contribution of the beneficiary. Under such a financing structure, the beneficiary was tempted to seek high benefits, with work units vying with each other to raise payment standards. No one was motivated to supervise the revenue and expenditure of the social security fund. In the meantime, this style of management was also very likely to breed bureaucracy and to increase operation cost.

Third, it caused unfair competition among enterprises and obstructed the flow of workers among enterprises. With the aging of the population, the burden on enterprises was increasingly heavy. This was especially the case for old enterprises with numerous retired employees. Their cost for pension and medical care was abnormally high, and some of them were even running into great financial difficulties. In contrast, some new enterprises had a relatively light burden as the average age of their employees was low and consequently fewer funds were needed to support the aged, sick, and retired, which put the old enterprises at a disadvantage in competition. Meanwhile, different standards of social security in different enterprises also obstructed the free flow of employees.

Finally, the old system could not adapt to the needs of reform. During the reform, economic structure underwent great changes and enterprise restructuring was frequent. If the social security system fails to perform its security functions and to build a social safety net, resistance to reform will increase, or even social unrest will occur. Hence, the old social security system is particularly unfavorable to enterprise reform.

8.1.2.2 Deviation from Fairness

Under the old social security system, deviation from fairness did not lie primarily in the imparity between different cohorts or different generations of beneficiaries, but rather in the unbalanced relationship between the state and the individual as well as among different social groups. As the state monopolized all social security resources and bore all social security obligations to the individual simultaneously, the tight constraint on resources reduced the individual's disposable income to a minimum level and limited the consumer's right of free choice to a minimum scope.

It follows that the practice of the state- as the only producer and provider of consumer goods- to provide consumers with social welfare in kind can result in at least two direct consequences. One consequence is that the individual consumers are deprived of their right of free choice, and are fully subject to the decisions of the state as the producer, let alone the forming of social preferences regarding social security consumption through a public choice mechanism. Another consequence is that the state can carry out rationing in kind for different social groups at extremely low initial cost, resulting in hidden social inequality among different social groups.

First, under an urban-rural dual social structure, the state distributes most of the social security resources to urban residents. In China, the old social security system covered only some of urban residents (i.e., employees of SOEs and urban "big collectives"[1] as well as personnel of state organs), excluding unemployed urban residents and the vast number of rural residents. This constitutes a great unfairness to the latter.

Second, when social security resources were allocated in kind through work units, the level of benefits for each individual was dependent upon the availability of resources as well as the ability of work units to obtain resources under the planned allocation system. Because of this, there were great differences among different work units in terms of the welfare portfolio and levels of expenditure, resulting in a wide disparity in social security.

These aforementioned conflicts became more prominent after the inception of the reform and opening up. First, with the disintegration of the people's commune system, the simple and crude rural social security system, such as rural cooperative medical service, had nothing left and hundreds of millions of rural households were left without even minimal social security protection. Second, in urban areas, non-state sectors of the economy, including individual businesses, private enterprises, and Sino-foreign joint ventures experienced rapid development, yet their employees were not covered at all by social security services. Third, the traditional model of in-kind allocation of social welfare became increasingly incompatible with enhancing enterprise independence, expanding market exchange relations, and increasing consumer choices. With the weakening of the planned allocation of in-kind social welfare, social security was more and more dependent on enterprise finance. Therefore, inequality caused by enterprise security was almost inevitable when different enterprises had different market performance and different financial positions. In the event that an enterprise could no longer bear the burden of increasing demand for social security payment, employee pension and medical expenses were hardly guaranteed. If an enterprise went bankrupt in the process of enterprise reform, which is normal under a market economy, there would be no guaranteed resources to nourish the living and bury the dead. This posed a great threat to social stability.

8.2
Targets Established for Social Security System Reform

With the inherent defects of the old social security system increasingly prominent, its reform became more necessary than ever before. In November 1993, the *Decision of CCCPC on Issues Regarding the Establishment of a Socialist Market Economic System* was adopted at the Third Plenary Session of the 14th CCCPC, which established the targets for social security system reform.

8.2.1 Agreement Achieved on the Targets for Reform
Some economists in China began to explore in the early 1990s how to reform

the traditional social security system. After concluding the experience of social security of our country and the change process of social security system of other countries after World War II, they reached consensus on the goals for China's social security system reform.

They argued that the new system should be independent of the enterprise system to meet the needs of establishing and developing a market economy; it should not only embody social justice but also provide incentives for hard work and high savings to promote long-term economic development.[2]

First, the selection of a social security system should start from China's realities. China has a very low GDP per capita, and its primary goal is to realize rapid and sustainable growth after the economic take-off. As far as distribution is concerned, it needs to observe the principle of "giving priority to efficiency with due consideration to fairness." Starting from this fundamental principle, China should try to maintain the effectiveness of incentive mechanism in the selection of a social security system. While ensuring the basic social security, the new system should reinforce the incentive mechanism of "more pay for more work" and avoid the drawbacks of "big-pot meal" (i.e., indiscriminate egalitarianism).

Second, China should draw on the experiences of social security reforms in countries like Singapore and replace the pay-as-you-go system on benefit basis with a funding system (i.e., individual account system) on contribution basis. This is because the pay-as-you-go system is characterized by intergenerational transfer that breaks the connection between welfare benefits and insurance premium payments, which weakens the motive for contribution. It provides no incentive for pubic savings and is likely to create burdens on government finance.

Third, China should learn from the experience of countries like Chile and allow the beneficiary to entrust the administration and operation of the social security system to independent agencies, because direct administration by the government institutions is likely to create problems of low efficiency and corruption.

Last, attention should be given to its coordination with other social and economic reforms, particularly to its active role in promoting SOE reform and the formation of the capital market.

8.2.2 Targets for Social Security System Reform Established by the Third Plenary Session of the 14th CCCPC

In November 1993, the 14th CCCPC convened its Third Plenary Session and adopted the *Decision of CCCPC on Issues Regarding the Establishment of a Socialist Market Economic System*. One of the key elements of the *Decision* was to establish a new social security system in China, which decided that the individual account system should be introduced into the basic pension insurance and basic medical insurance, and that the administration of social security and the operation of social security funds should be separated. The basic requirements were as follows.

1. Establish a multi-layer social security system. Social security policies should be uniformed, and management should be legalized. The level of social security should be compatible with the level of social development and the bearing capacities of all parties. Social security schemes for urban and rural residents should be different. Social mutual assistance should be encouraged, and commercial insurance should be developed as a supplement to social insurance.

2. Determine the source of funds and means of security according to different types of social security. Emphasis should be given to the improvement of enterprise pension and unemployment insurance systems, the strengthening of social service functions to alleviate burdens on enterprises, the promotion of the adjustment of their organizational structures, and the enhancement of their economic benefits and competitiveness. The pension and medical insurance funds of urban employees should be jointly contributed by the work unit and the individual through a combination of social pooling and individual account. The unemployment insurance system should be further improved, with insurance premiums contributed by the enterprise in the amount of a certain proportion of its payroll. The industrial injury insurance system should be universally established. Old-age provision for farmers should be mainly household provision supplemented by community support.

3. The administration of social security should be separated from the operation of social security funds. The social security administration agencies exist mainly to exercise administrative functions. Supervisory organs of social security funds should be established with the participation of representatives from government departments

concerned and the public to supervise the receipts and expenses as well as the management of social insurance funds. While ensuring normal payment, safety, and liquidity of the funds, institutions in charge of social security funds may use social insurance funds mainly to purchase treasury bonds according to law to preserve and increase the value of social insurance funds.

If these rules can be implement seriously, we will get a multi-aspects social security system, and attract social power to shoulder the responsibilities with government. However, the concept for the government to monopolize all resources, rights, and responsibilities was so appealing that some institutions always doubted or even opposed the positive role played by non-government forces in the establishment of the social security system. By keeping away the non-government forces in the process, the reform deviated from the objectives established by the Third Plenary Session of the 14th CCCPC.

8.3
The Implementation of the Reform and Its Problems

According to the deployment of the Third Plenary Session of the 14th CCCPC, the establishment of the new social security system started in 1995, with a focus on the reform of the basic pension insurance system and basic medical insurance system for urban employees. While recognizing the impressive progress in the past decade in pension insurance, medical insurance, unemployment insurance, and occupational injury insurance, we are facing a number of pressing problems that demand immediate solution.

8.3.1 Pension Insurance Reform

Of the various items of the social security system, the pension system witnessed the fastest development. In terms of the number, the urban basic pension insurance had already covered 111 million employees, which including 36 million retirees[3].

The biggest difficulty in implementing the new pension insurance system with individual account is to provide pension funds for the retired and would-be retired employees (also called the "old ones" and the "middle ones," respectively). Under the old pay-as-you-go system, no individual account was opened, nor was any pension fund accumulated for the older employees. Thus, individual accounts opened for these older employees after pension insurance reform were basically empty. The balance of pension deposits in the hands of the government amounted to only a scanty RMB 30 billion, with a very unbalanced structure. In some old industrial bases where the proportion of older employees was relatively high, the pension system could no longer balance its revenue and expenditure. Under such conditions, the solution was for the state to repay the implicit debt by contributing to the pension fund that should have been accumulated for older employees (including both the "old ones" and the "middle ones"). During the long discussion of the social security system reform from 1993 to 1995, some economists and business leaders proposed two compensation schemes: (1) "cutting a chunk"[4] out of the existing state assets and (2) issuing "recognition bonds" by the Ministry of Finance.[5] However, because of the opposition from some government functional departments, neither compensation scheme was adopted. Therefore, the only option was to borrow from the "young ones" to support the "old ones" by using a social pooling fund collected from enterprises.

It was against this background that, at the national conference on planning the reform of the pension insurance system in March 1995, the State Council proposed two schemes to be adopted by each locality according to their local realities. As one of those two schemes was not very feasible because it did not provide a solution to the problem of how to source pension funds for older employees, a majority of local authorities opted for the alternative, which was called "big social pooling, small individual account."

According to this scheme, individual contributions made by an employee go to the individual account, and enterprise contributions go to the social pooling fund. At the retirement of an employee, if the deposits in his or her individual account are sufficient to pay the pension, then the payment is made in the same way as in Scheme I. If the deposits in the individual account are insufficient or the individual account is an "empty account", then the difference should be made up from the social pooling fund. Although this scheme alters the "fully funded" individual account to a "partially funded" one and, to a greater extent, its "social pooling fund" has the feature of a pay-as-you-go system, it provides a relatively practical method to settle the issue of the source of pension funds for the "old ones" and the "middle ones" by social pooling.

However, in fact, this scheme adopted the pay-as-you-go system and the individual account system for the "old ones" and the "young ones," respectively. In some old industrial cities where the proportion of the supported population was very high, the burden on enterprises to contribute to the social pooling fund was very heavy. According to a report by the United Nations Development Program (UNDP), the pension insurance premium rate in China on average was above 20 percent of the salary; when other insurance premiums were included, the gross rate of social security premiums was as high as 35 to 45 percent of the salary. In some old industrial cities like Shanghai, the pension insurance premium alone reached 28.5 percent of the salary of employees (of which 25.5 percent was collected from enterprises and 3 percent from individual employees[6]), whereas in some emerging cities, the premium rate of the social pooling fund was very low, putting the former in a disadvantageous position in competition. From a long-term point of view, this kind of practice was also susceptible to the danger of returning the pension system to the pay-as-you-go system on benefit basis.

These defects in the pension insurance system had the following negative consequences. First, enterprises participating in the pension insurance tended to delay or evade contribution. The collection rate of pension insurance fund contribution dropped year by year: from 95.7 percent in 1992 to 92.4 percent in 1993; 90.5 percent in 1994; 90 percent in 1995; and further down to 87 percent in 1996[7]. Second, 11 industries with young employees and good economic conditions established their own pension insurance system in order to evade large contributions, which caused more financial difficulty for the public pension insurance system. Third, non-state enterprises, especially foreign-invested enterprises, believed that it was unfair for them to contribute to the social pooling fund to compensate older employees of SOEs and therefore were not willing to participate. Fourth, when there were fund shortages, there was no choice but to divert the funds in the individual accounts of existing employees so that theirs became "empty accounts" as well.

To overcome these problems, the State Commission for Restructuring Economic Systems and the Ministry of Labor proposed an improvement scheme in June 1996, which came into effect in August 1997.[8] The core of this scheme was to unify the different schemes of various localities to establish the following framework: to set up individual accounts for employees at 11 percent of their salary, of which the individual would contribute 8 percent and the enterprise would contribute 3 percent; for the social pooling fund, the rate of enterprise contribution would be determined by the local government of the pooling area. Pension benefit payment would consist of two parts. The first part was the basic pension benefit, divided into several brackets according to the number of years of contribution, with payment in general not exceeding 25 percent of local average salary. The second part was the individual account pension benefit with monthly payment equal to the cumulative total of the individual account divided by 120. After the death of the employee or retiree, the individual account would not be inherited, but be used to comfort and compensate the bereaved family. Surrounding the framework, the reform scheme also proposed some other measures: to gradually increase the individual contribution rate, to gradually adjust the provision standard of basic insurance, and to improve fund operation, supervision, and management. In addition, the State Council also decided to hand over all the social pooling fund of pension insurance by industry to the local (provincial-level) insurance institutions for unified management.

The implementation of the unified system certainly played a role in improving pension financing and payment. It failed, however, in the transition from the old system to the new system to solve the most critical problem-the source of pension funds for the older employees whose payment still had to rely on social pooling and funds from the individual accounts of the existing employees.

Given the inherent defect, the basic pension insurance system began to fall into a payment dilemma in 1998: the current revenue was only RMB 145.9 billion while the expenditure amounted to RMB 151.16 billion. In 1999, twenty-five provinces / autonomous regions/municipalities across the country had deficits and funds diverted from individual accounts that exceeded RMB 100 billion. Under such conditions, the central government had to use tens of billions in its budget to fill the gap between revenue and expenditure of the basic pension insurance every year.

Amidst the mounting financial pressure of the basic pension insurance, two opposing policy propositions emerged. The first proposition advocated "substitution of contributions with taxes" for social security by imposing social security tax. This viewpoint maintained that basic pension insurance premiums, basic medical insurance premiums, and unemployment insurance premiums could be consolidated into a unified social security tax on the basis of various schemes of the social security system reform already launched by the state. In practice, collection of social security contributions was quite difficult. In many localities, therefore, these contributions were already collected by the tax authorities on a commission basis. If a social security tax was imposed, the collection of social security tax could be guaranteed with the aid of the *Law on the Administration of Tax Collection* and the tax authorities. However, this proposition was vehemently opposed because it was equivalent to deviating from the direction of reform stipulated by the Third Plenary Session of the 14th CCCPC and returning to a pay-as-you-go system. Under such strong opposition, the suggestion of switching to social security tax was not responded to by the government.

In early 2000, some collective protests and group incidents broke out in some localities, participated in by employees of SOEs who disliked the low compensation for "buying out employment guarantee." This state of affairs made the leadership of the Chinese government realize that to carry out SOE restructuring was particularly dangerous when there was no social safety net. Hence, the Chinese government invited some economists to offer suggestions on how to set up a new social security system, the most representative of which was the reform scheme of an old-age social security system proposed by Professor Lawrence J. Lau of Stanford University. According to his suggestion, the government should set up an old-age social security system composed of two parts: the "public basic pension" funded by the general tax revenue of the central government, and the "individual account in a central provident fund" funded by the contributions of employees and employers. The individual account in a central provident fund would be under the unified management of the "Administration Board of the Central Provident Fund" under the "Trust Council for the Central Provident Fund" of the central government. Domestic or foreign fund managers, banks, or other financial institutions would be selected and entrusted with operation and management[9]. Professor Lau also suggested that the state use the existing state assets to repay the implicit debt that the government owed to the social security fund for retired, active, and laid-off employees of state-owned work units. The idea behind this scheme gained applause from many economists and recognition from the government leadership. At the same time, a number of research institutions began to estimate the implicit debt of the government to the older employees of state-owned work units. According to estimates by the World Bank, this figure accounted for 46 to 69 percent of China's GDP in 1997; according to some economists, the figure varied from 71 to 94 percent of GDP that year; estimates by a research group of SCORES were as high as 145 percent. Even if we assume that the implicit debt accounted for only 30 percent of China's GDP in 1997, the total amount could still have exceeded RMB 2 trillion.[10] Therefore, in late 2000, the State Council made a resolution to set up the Council for National Social Security Fund.

As to how to replenish the individual accounts of the basic pension insurance, aside from the so-called "full replenishing" scheme of repaying all the implicit debt of the government to the older employees as mentioned earlier, there was also the so-called "partial replenishing" scheme proposed by the Ministry of Labor and Social Security. Partial replenishing referred to the scheme whereby only the individual contribution of the employee (5 percent of the salary at that time) was reckoned into the individual account, while the enterprise contribution (the average rate of contribution at that time was 20 percent) was used as the social pooling fund to make up the deficiency in the pension fund for the older employees. This scheme was similar to the scheme of 1995, namely "big social pooling, small individual account". Under this scheme, the role played by the individual account became insignificant, and there was no way to fully satisfy the pension requirement of the employee after retirement. Hence, it was certain that in the future the employee would still need another extensive plan of the pay-as-you-go system to make up for the deficiency in the pension fund. This idea, which was basically equivalent to the pay-as-you-go system and still had to rely on the government for financing, received wide criticism.

American economist Martin S. Feldstein believes that since the current real marginal product of capital in China is greater than the growth rate of aggregate wages, converting the social pooling portion under the pay-as-you-go system to a funded system will considerably reduce the government's financial burdens.[11] Economist Guo Shuqing is also a leading exponent advocating a fully funded system. He advocates that (1) a full individual account system can wholly link the benefits of pension insurance with its contributions and completely obliterate the "welfare big-pot meal;" (2) a full individual account system will dismiss any illusions of the people, and therefore is conducive to the smooth collection of contributions; (3) the government can hardly misappropriate; (4) the system is highly transparent with low management cost; (5) it can obtain the optimal effects of accumulation and appreciation; (6) due to the accelerating process of urbanization, without individual accounts, government pension insurance liabilities will be increasingly heavy as time goes by.[12] Hence, from the long-term point of view, a fully funded system can better give consideration to both fairness and efficiency.

In July 2001, the State Council decided to carry out experiments in Liaoning Province on the improvement of the urban social security system according to the instruction of the Ministry of Labor and Social Security. The main contents are as follows: Managing the individual account and the social pooling fund separately, with the individual account operated as a funded account; adjusting and improving the methods of pension calculation and payment; encouraging enterprises to set up enterprise annuities, and further stipulating that the total enterprise contribution within 4 percent of the total wage bill may be listed as cost expenditure.

Although adoption of the aforementioned method has somewhat improved the financial conditions of the pension insurance system of Liaoning Province, this kind of improvement was achieved only with special transfer payments from the central government. To support the experiments in Liaoning Province, the central government specially provided several billion RMB in financial support over the past few years to make up the deficit in the province's basic pension insurance. Furthermore, even if the central government finance could afford the necessary expenses, what would be set up when the Liaoning model is promoted nationwide would still be a pension insurance system dominated by the pay-as-you-go system, which could hardly be maintained in the long run. Out of this consideration, quite a few economists advocated returning to the basic thoughts on pension insurance of the Third Plenary Session of the 14th CCCPC as well as the compensation method drawn up in 2000.

Another layer of the urban pension insurance system in China is the annuities set up for employees by enterprises. This was called the "enterprise supplementary pension insurance system" before 2000 and was renamed "enterprise annuity" in 2000, with the intention to standardize the development of the enterprise supplementary pension insurance system based on established international practice. According to relevant regulations by the State Council, the enterprise may freely decide to set up a supplementary pension insurance plan for its employees according to its own financial position, with the funds extracted from the enterprise's self-owned fund for employee bonus and welfare and put into the employees' individual accounts. The enterprise may also freely choose the plan administrator.

However, the enterprise annuity plan has been developing very slowly. At the end of 2001, the number of employees participating in enterprise annuity plans nationwide was only 1.93 million, and the accumulated surplus amounted to RMB 4.9 billion.[13] There were three reasons for the relatively slow development. First, the burden of the contribution to the social pooling fund of the statutory compulsory social security plan was already quite heavy for many enterprises, so only a few enterprises with abundant financial resources were in a position to set up annuity plans. Second, there were no adequate incentives; for instance, it was still not clear whether preferential taxation policies should be provided for annuity contribution of enterprises. Third, there were some restrictions; for instance, it was stipulated by relevant departments that enterprises not participating in the basic pension insurance would not be eligible to set up enterprise annuity plans. And finally, the management and operation mechanism was not well established. In the most recent two years, financial institutions such as insurance companies have displayed rather high enthusiasm for the development of enterprise annuity plans. Participation of financial institutions will be instrumental to the development of enterprise annuity plans. Furthermore, one current viewpoint of the academic circles is to consolidate the individual accounts of the enterprise annuity and the basic pension insurance after its "replenishment," to enlarge the portion of Pillar II.

In 1990s, stock market of many countries broke out, so the cumulate individual account got suspicion. In western countries, notional defined-contribution schemes born. Some foreign economists, such as Peter Diamond in MIT, suggested China to choose this method.

Although voluntary individual savings pension insurance has long been deemed as the third layer of the pension insurance system, a clearly established institutional framework and development plan have not yet been in place. The source of financing for this layer can only be the transfer of residents' bank savings. However, to make it a pension plan capable of providing for old age and distinct from the ordinary savings, it is still necessary for financial institutions to develop it as a new type of financial product adapted to provide for old age and then launch it in the market. Marketing this type of financial product needs special promotion, such as exemption or deferment of interest income tax.

Aside from enterprise employees, there is yet another important group of pension beneficiaries- employees working in such public institutions as government offices. For the pension insurance of this group, the funded system with contributions has never been implemented; rather, the traditional pay-as-you-go system has been used for financing. However, with the establishment of the civil service system and advance of the reform of the personnel management system, the tradition of lifetime employment will soon be obsolete, considerably raising the urgency to reform the pension insurance system of public institutions. The new system should adapt to the requirement of the personnel management system reform, and, likewise, should establish individual pension insurance accounts for employees of public institutions and set up specific fund plans with joint contributions of individuals and public institutions as employers to achieve the integration with enterprise pension insurance plans in both institutional arrangement and operation mechanism.

8.3.2 Medical Insurance System Reform

The reform of the medical insurance system for employees in China started in the late 1980s. With the advance of economic system reform, both the government and enterprises became more aware of the incompatibility of the traditional public health service system and the new economic system. The government and enterprises bore all expenses, offering no incentive for patients to reduce medical expenses, resulting in a rapid increase in medical expenses. At the same time, medical institutions took this opportunity to increase service costs, blindly importing medical equipment that caused inefficient resource allocation. Pressured by the rapid increase in medical costs, financing for medical expenses became all the more difficult. In view of these problems, in March 1989, the State Council transmitted with endorsement the "Main Points of the 1989 Economic System Reform" of SCORES, and decided to carry out reform experiments on the medical insurance system in four cities: Dandong, Siping, Huangshi, and Zhuzhou. Meanwhile, some other localities carried out experiments on their own initiative. This type of reform attempt lasted until 1993. The main objectives of the reform included shifting part of the medical expenses to individual employees, decentralizing the authority for management of medical outlays, and implementing social pooling for medical expenses for retirees as well as for employees with major diseases. However, these reform measures did not succeed in stopping the rapid increase in medical expenses, and thus it became increasingly difficult for low- and medium-income classes to access medical care.

In 1993, the Central Government began to experiment with a reform in Zhenjiang of Jiangsu Province and Jiujiang of Jiangxi Province, with a combination of social pooling and individual account as its core content. In April 1996, based on the experience in these two cities, the State Council approved *Opinions on the Expansion of Experiments on the Reform of the Medical Security System* jointly issued by four ministries and commissions including SCORES, and expanded the experiments to over fifty cities across the country. The key points of this scheme are as follows.

1. To establish a medical security system including four layers: (i) the basic medical insurance system as social behavior; (ii) the supplementary medical insurance system as enterprise behavior; (iii) the commercial medical insurance system as individual behavior; and (iv) public medical assistance.

2. To feature the basic medical insurance system as "low standard, wide coverage." A low standard carries two meanings: (i) to moderately lower the standard of contribution of employing units and (ii) to guarantee only the basic medical

care. Wide coverage also contains two meanings: (i) to widen the scope of medical insurance beneficiaries and (ii) to extend the service of medical insurance to include medical care, drugs, and services.

3. On the basis of basic medical insurance, to put into play the complementary roles of supplementary medical insurance and commercial medical insurance, and to finally have public medical assistance cover all that is left.

4. To implement unified management of basic medical insurance by the labor and social security department of the government.

Cities participating in these experiments studied possibilities based on the aforementioned *Opinions* and created many forms of the combination of social pooling and individual account, such as social pooling for major illnesses.[14]

Based on the expanded experiments, the State Council issued in 1998 the *Decision on the Establishment of the Basic Medical Insurance System for Urban Employees*, and decided to establish the system by the end of 1999.The *Decision* adheres to the principle of "low standard, wide coverage" and the combination of social pooling and individual account, mandating that all urban employers participate in a basic medical insurance system administered on a local basis. The contributions of the employer and the individual were 6 percent and 2 percent, respectively, of the payroll, among which 30 percent of the employer contribution was put into the individual account.

Up to December 2002, a total of ninety-four million people nationwide participated in the basic medical insurance system; the balance of the basic medical insurance fund nationwide amounted to RMB 45 billion.[15] However, such chronic problems as high medical outlays, scarce medical resources, and their grossly imbalanced allocation still persist.

As the medical insurance reform involves the reform of financing and payment mechanisms on the demand side of the health care market, it must coordinate with the system reform on the supply side of the health care market and improve the information asymmetry between the consumer and the supplier in the medical service market so that correct market prices can be set to optimize the allocation of medical service resources. However, the slow progress in the reform of the medical service management system makes it difficult for the medical insurance reform as the demand side to achieve its anticipated results alone.

The most visible sign of the mismatch between the two reforms is that over the past years, the practice of allocating medical service resources by the administrative control system as was under the planned economic system has never changed; resources have been highly concentrated in big cities in the form of state-owned hospitals while small and medium cities and vast rural areas have been in severe shortage of resources. At the same time, the entry of domestic private capital and foreign capital has been stringently restricted. The government operates ordinary medical institutions (i.e., nonpublic medical facilities) that are supposed to be business operations, resulting in a great amount of public resources thrown into them without fully meeting their needs. Yet private capital is forbidden to enter the medical service market. Such institutional distortion and restriction on market entry result in a persistent shortage of medical service and therefore increases the cost considerably. In view of such a medical service system, the existing medical insurance plan can only be a high-cost plan with low accessibility for the low-income cohort. Taking the opportunity of medical insurance reform, some regions have attempted to separate the management of medical services and drug sales and to reduce medical expenses by changing the situation of subsidizing medical services by drug sales; however, the results are not very obvious. Reform of the medical service management system will involve many other aspects. For example, medical professionals may have a personnel management system independent of hospitals, and they may be granted qualification for practicing medicine independently, enabling them to provide service on a contract basis independent of hospitals. This will not only increase the income of medical professionals but also improve the unbalanced distribution of medical service resources among different regions. Additionally, this will promote competition among hospitals.

As the financing, payment, and management mechanisms for the demand side of the health care market, the medical insurance plan cannot ignore the underlying features of the health care market as an imperfect market. An effective medical insurance plan should look after any possibility of market failure in the health care market. According to the analysis of Kornai and Eggleston,[16] a co-payment mechanism that requires patients to bear part of the expenses will be instrumental in limiting the budget constraint on demand. A medical insurance plan that requires individuals to bear a portion of their medical expenses will help to control the inordinate growth of medical expenses. However, given the fact that the health care market is plagued by information asymmetry, the pressure from medical service suppliers for increasing costs can only be resisted by strengthening the extent of organization of the medical insurance plans. As the extent of organization increases, the ability of patient organizations to access information and to bargain over prices with medical institutions will also improve. Hence, the reform of the medical insurance system in China is not simply a problem of financing and management, but of strengthening the ability of policyholders as consumers to influence the market prices by enhancing their extent of organization.

8.3.3. Unemployment Insurance

In 1986, China introduced the *Enterprise Bankruptcy Law* and the labor contract system in SOEs. To conform to the requirements of the SOE reform, the State Council issued the *Interim Regulations on Unemployment Insurance of State-Owned Enterprises*, thereby initiating an unemployment insurance system. On this basis, in April 1993, the State Council issued the *Regulations on Unemployment Insurance of State-Owned Enterprise Employees*. In November 1993, the unemployment insurance system was officially adopted in the *Decision on Issues Regarding the Establishment of a Socialist Market Economic System* of the Third Plenary Session of the 14th CCCPC, and put onto a track of fast development since then. By the end of 2002, the unemployment insurance covered a total of 102 million people.[17]

The funds for the unemployment insurance system come from unemployment insurance premiums contributed by enterprises, interest proceeds from the unemployment insurance fund, and subsidies from the government. Normally, the rate of enterprise contribution is no more than 1 percent of its payroll, and no individual account is established. In the late 1990s, as the problem of lay-offs in SOEs aggravated, it was no longer possible for the unemployment insurance system alone to guarantee the basic living standard of laid-off workers. Therefore, the central government adopted a "triple-support" financing plan for laid-off workers. The central government, the local government, and the enterprise each contributed one-third to the payment of basic living expenses for laid-off workers. As unemployment insurance revenue was inadequate to meet expenditure, especially when a considerable portion of the living expenses of laid-off workers had to be covered by the unemployment insurance, in May 1998, it was determined at the Meeting on Reemployment of Laid-Off Workers of State-Owned Enterprises convened by the central government that the rate of unemployment insurance contribution would be increased from 1 percent to 3 percent of payroll, of which 1 percent would be borne by individuals.

In recent years, the unemployment insurance has been declining. According to official statistics, in 2002, the number of people participating in the unemployment insurance plan decreased by 1.73 million compared to 2001.[18] Recently, some scholars suggested that the unemployment insurance be incorporated into the minimum living guarantee system for urban residents. In practice, however, the unemployment insurance fund is used in many regions to pay for reemployment training and employment services for the unemployed, but these are the functions not covered by the minimum living guarantee system for urban residents. Therefore, the future of the existing unemployment insurance system remains uncertain.

8.3.4. Minimum Living Guarantee System

As the advance of China's economic reform demanded for a better social safety net, which was obviously impossible under the existing social security arrangement, the Chinese government decided to establish a minimum living guarantee (dibao) system for urban residents. In September 1997, the State Council issued the *Circular Regarding the Establishment of a Minimum Living Guarantee System for Urban Residents across the Country*, requiring that a minimum living guarantee system for urban residents in cities and towns be established during the period of the Ninth Five-Year Plan to guarantee the basic needs of urban residents. Its main points are as follows.

1. The beneficiaries of the minimum living guarantee system are urban residents of non-agricultural residence status with a per capita household income lower

than the local minimum living standard, including the following three categories: (i) residents without a source of income, labor capacity, or supporters; (ii) residents receiving unemployment benefits or unable to be reemployed upon their expiration, with a per capita household income lower than the minimum living standard; and (iii) active employees, laid-off workers, or retirees with a per capita household income lower than the minimum living standard even after receiving wages, minimum wages/basic living expenses, or pensions, respectively.

2. The minimum living standard for urban residents is to be determined solely by the local governments on the basis of the local realities and the principle of securing basic needs while overcoming a dependency mentality. It should be parallel with the local cost of basic living and the bearing capacity of local government finance, and made known to the public after its approval by the local government. Adjustments should be made to reflect changes in prices of living necessities and improvement in the people's living standards.

3. Funds needed for the implementation of the minimum living guarantee system for urban residents should be listed by local governments at various levels in their fiscal budget and be incorporated into the special expenditure items for social welfare and managed as a separate account. Cities currently adopting the practice of sharing the financial responsibility for minimum living allowance between the government finance and the work units of the beneficiaries should gradually switch to the practice of government financing.

In recent years, various localities have achieved rapid development in the establishment of the minimum living guarantee system. Statistics show that by the end of September 2002, the number of poor residents enjoying the minimum living allowance nationwide had reached 19.63 million; the average minimum living standard nationwide was RMB 152 per capita per month; and the average minimum living allowance payment to beneficiaries nationwide was RMB 70 per capita per month.

In some well-off regions, attempts are being made to extend the minimum living guarantee system to rural residents. For instance, Zhejiang Province has implemented the minimum living guarantee system for all people in the province since October 2001.

8.3.5. Rural Social Security

China has a rural population of over nine hundred million. Under the People's Commune system, China's rural areas developed a social security system with the "Five Guarantees" (referring to care and material assistance such as food, clothing, housing, medical services, and burial for those without source of income, working capacity, or supporters) and a rural cooperative medical service (i.e., "barefoot doctors"). However, the degree of security was very low and the necessary expenses were borne mainly by collective economic entities. After the implementation of the household contracting system, the rural social security system lost its original source of financing (i.e., collective economic organizations) and fell apart. Under current conditions in the vast rural areas, there is virtually no effective supply of medical service resources. Restricted by low income, the farmers have no opportunity to enjoy the medical service resources allocated mainly to cities. Because of this, health of the rural population as well as the public health conditions in rural areas are compromised.

In October 1986, the Ministry of Civil Affairs decided to implement the rural pension insurance in regions with a fairly developed rural economy, with the community as the unit. However, the development of rural pension insurance was not successful. At the end of 2001, the number of people in rural areas participating in the pension insurance was about sixty million; by the end of 2002, the figure had dropped to around fifty-four million.

There are two basic problems facing the rural social security system: the first is the financing and management of funds to convert potential demand in rural areas to effective demand for social security, and the second is the allocation of social security resources to ensure an effective supply. The settlement of these two basic problems requires the development of a rural social security system on both the demand and the supply sides at the same time. This has been subject to the constraint of a number of practical conditions.

The gap between urban and rural areas has had a long history in China, and it will not be eliminated in the foreseeable future. Under this constraint, the rural social security system must be developed separately from the urban social security system. It should not aspire to be grandiose, but rather, with a focus on the key issues, develop an overall plan for steady progress. Diversified views can be found among the academic circles and policymakers concerning the development strategy for rural social security. One view believes that the rural social security should combine social security with household provision, jointly funded by the state, the collective, and the individual. Another argues that, in the rural society where the traditional mode of agricultural production has not yet completely changed, household provision is still the main way to resist various risks. Under such a traditional mode of production, the most appropriate model would be some kind of cooperative social security on the basis of voluntary participation by farmers, rather than the compulsory social security with social pooling. Hence, the development strategy for rural social security should be to guide rural communities to set up voluntary and informal cooperative security organizations.

One way to integrate the reasonable components of these different viewpoints is for the government to provide a suitable institutional framework to guide rural areas and farmers in raising and managing a rural cooperative social security fund and determining the specific social security benefits through the existing villagers' self-governing organizations. The social security financial aid provided by the government should be supplied to farmers in dire need through a mechanism with a positive incentive to increase its efficiency. The practice in some regions of providing farmers with a basic social security allowance by making use of an insurance mechanism is certainly a measure worthy of consideration.

As the income level of rural households remains quite low, it is impossible, without external assistance, for farmers to establish a rural social security system capable of providing protection against multiple risks. The development of a rural social security system will be a long-term process and should focus on the key issues. At present, however, the development of a medical service system including a public health system with social pooling may be more urgent than a pension insurance system.

Under the constraint of the present realities, rural medical resources should be allocated to institutional "growing points" with comparative advantage according to the theory of comparative advantage. For instance, the resources of traditional

Chinese medicine can be developed and utilized in favor of rural areas. Medical professionals can collect, sort out, and authenticate the resources of traditional Chinese medicine. Protection can be provided in the form of qualifications for practicing traditional Chinese medicine and patents for traditional Chinese treatments with real therapeutic effects. Such actions can, to a great extent, alleviate the problem of sick farmers being unable to afford treatment because of the high-priced urban medical service resources.

Notes and References

1. Urban "big collectives" refer to enterprises established by local governments at the district level or above. This kind of enterprise is called a "collective" enterprise but is in fact owned and managed by the government.

2. The State Commission for Restructuring Economic Systems, *The Social Security System Reform* (Shehui baozhang tizhi gaige), Beijing: Reform Press, 1995. This book collects some policies and schemes formulated by the State Council and its relevant departments during this period concerning social security reform and offers descriptions and explanations on the strategies behind these policies and scheme.

3. The Ministry of Labor and Social Security and the National Bureau of Statistics, *2002 Bulletin of Labor and Social Security Undertakings Development Statistics*, May 7, 2003, http://www.stats.gov.cn/tjgb/qttjgb/qgqttjgb/t20030507_77008.htm.

4. The so-called "cutting a chunk" refers to allotting a certain portion of state assets for repaying the government implicit debt to the pension fund for older employees of state-owned enterprises. When drafting the social security scheme m 1993, quite a few economists had proposed this suggestion. See Zhou Xiaochuan and Wang Lin, "Social Security: Economic Analysis and System Proposal (Shehui baozhang: jingji fenxi yu tizhi jianshe) (1993)," in Wu Jinglian et al., *Building Up a Market Economy: Comprehensive Framework and Working Proposals* (Jianshe shichang jingji de zongti gouxiang yu fang'an sheji), Beijing: Central Compilation & Translation Press, 1996, pp. 211-258.

5. "Recognition bonds" are government bonds issued by the Chilean government in 1981 during pension reform; its purpose was to repay the government's implicit debt to those employees who

had quit from the government pension plan. Some Chinese economists believe that China may also adopt this kind of method to solve the problem of "empty accounts" of older employees (Zhou Xiaochuan and Wang Lin, ibid, pp. 244-245).

6. United Nations Development Programme, China Human Development Report: Human Development and Poverty Alleviation, 1997,

7. Beijing: UNDP China, 1997, p. 62. 11 Yang Yiyong, "Why the Collection Rate of Pension Insurance Fund Contribution Continually Declines? (Yanglao baoxian jijin shoujiaolyu weihe buduan xiajiang?)," *Economic Highlights* (Jingjixue xiaoxi bao), March 7, 1997.

8. The Ministry of Labor, *Report Outline Concerning the Unification of Pension Insurance Systems for Enterprise Employees* (Guanyu tongyi qiye zhigong yanglao baoxian zhidu de huibao tigang), August 26, 1997.

9. Lawrence J. Lau, "A Proposed Pension System for the People's Republic of China (Guanyu Zhongguo shehui yanglao baozhang tixi de jiben gouxiang). For main contents of this article, see Comparative Studies (Bijiao), Vol. 6, Beijing: CITIC Press, 2003, p. 328.

10. Wu Jinglian, "Major Problems to Be Solved in the Reduction of State Shareholding (Shenme shi guoyougu jianchi yao jiejue de zhuyao wenti)," *Caijing* Magazine (29, 2000).", 2002, No. 1.

11. Martin S. Feldstein, "Social Security Pension Reform m China (Zhongguo de yanglao baozhang zhidu gaige)," *Comparison of Economic and Social Systems* (Jingji shehui tizhi bijiao), 1999, No. 2.

12. Guo Shuqing, "To Establish a Fully-Funded Basic Pension Insurance System Is the Best Choice (Jianli wanquan jileixing dejiben yanglao baoxian zhidu shi zuijia xuanze)," *Comparison of Economic and Social Systems* (Jingji shehui tizhi bijiao), 2002, No. 1.

13. The Ministry of Labor and Social Security and the National Bureau of Statistics, *2001 Bulletin of Labor and Social Security Undertakings Development Statistics* (2001 Niandu laodong he shehui baozhang shiye fazhan tongji gongbao), February 10, 2003,

14. Song Xiaowu et al., *China's Social Security System Reform and Development Report* (Zhongguo shehui baozhang tizhi gaige yu fazhan baogao), Beijing: China Renmin University Press, 2001, pp. 95-99.

15. The Ministry of Labor and Social Security and the National Bureau of Statistics, *2002 Bulletin of Labor and Social Security Undertakings Development Statistics* (2002 niandu laodong he shehui baozhang shiye fazhan tongji gongbao), May 7, 2003, http://www.stats .gov.cn/tj gb/qttjgb/qgqttjgb/t20030507_77008.htm.

16. Janos Kornai and Karen Eggleston, *Welfare, Choice and Solidarity in Transition: Reforming the Health Sector in Eastern Europe*, Cambridge: Cambridge University Press, 2001.

17. The Ministry of Labor and Social Security and the National Bureau of Statistics, *2002 Bulletin of Labor and Social Security Under takings Development Statistics* (2002 niandu laodong he shehui baozhang shiye fazhan tongji gongbao), May 7, 2003, http://www.sta ts.gov. cn/tjgb/qttjgb/qgqttjgb/t20030507_77008.htm

18. Ibid.

CHAPTER NINE

MACROECONOMY IN THE REFORM

Most Eastern European socialist countries have been plagued by inflation as they sought to reform their economic policies during the transition to a market economy. For a long time after China started reform and opening up at the end of 1978, inflation occurred again and again, and each was worse than the previous one.

9.1
Macroeconomy and Macroeconomic Policies under Inflationary Pressure (1979-1994)

In a planned economy, the government controls the entire national economy with no distinction between macroeconomic and microeconomic issues. With the transition from a planned economy to a market economy and the enlarged autonomy of microeconomic agents, macroeconomic issues have become the focus of the government. Table 9.1 shows the price indices change since 1978:

Table 9.1 **Price Indices Change since 1978** (year-to-year growth, %)

Year	Retail Price Index	Consumer Price Index (CPI)
1978	0.7	
1979	2.0	
1980	6.0	
1981	2.4	
1982	1.9	
1983	1.5	
1984	2.8	
1985	8.8	9.3
1986	6.0	6.5
1987	7.3	7.3
1988	18.5	18.8
1989	17.8	18.0
1990	2.1	3.1
1991	2.9	3.4
1992	5.4	6.4
1993	13.2	14.7
1994	21.7	24.1
1995	14.8	17.1
1996	6.1	8.3
1997	0.8	2.8
1998	-2.6	-0.8
1999	-3.0	-1.4
2000	-1.5	0.4
2001	-0.8	0.7
2002	1.3	-0.8
2003	-0.1	1.2

Source: The National Bureau of Statistics, *China Statistical Yearbook* (Zhongguo tongji nianjian), Beijing: China Statistics Press, various years.

The fifteen years between 1980 and 1994 saw four rounds of severe economic fluctuation in China, which all began with expansionary macroeconomic policies, especially an expansionary financial policy. The result was an overheated economy and surging prices for commodities. When the overheated economy and inflation caused severe negative effects both economically and politically, macroeconomic policies were switched to contractive ones, and economic stability was restored after varying adjustment periods.

9.1.1 The First Round of Economic Fluctuation (1978 -1983)

With the end of the Great Cultural Revolution in 1976, the leaders of China's central government failed to give priority to adjustments and reform, but rather following the tradition of extensive growth, that is, high-target, high-input and low-efficiency. Formulated in February 1978, the *Ten-Year Planning Outline for the Development of National Economy* during 1976 to 1985 set targets of, between 1978 and 1985, constructing or expanding 120 large projects and building 14 large bases of heavy industry all over the country. Within the eight-year period, China's gross value of industrial output was supposed to grow at an average annual rate of 10 percent or more, according to the *Outline*. To make the new leap forward a reality, the principle discussion meetings of the State Council held from July to September 1978, emphasized the need to obtain foreign advanced technology and equipment in large quantities. Within a few months after the meetings, China signed contracts to import nine large-scale chemical projects costing a total of RMB 16 billion and another twenty-two projects costing a total of RMB 60 billion, including Baosteel and one hundred sets of integrated coal-mining equipment. Such huge investment and so many large-scale projects simultaneously undergoing construction caused a fiscal deficit which increased quickly and extensively. While the fiscal surplus was RMB 1.01 billion in 1978, the astounding deficit was RMB 20.6 billion in 1979, or 5.2 percent of GDP, generating substantial pressure for monetary expansion. The annual growth rate of the cash supply (Mo) soared from 9.7 percent in 1978 to 24.4 percent in 1979 and 25.5 percent in 1980; the annual growth rate of bank credit balances rose from 10.2 percent in 1979 to 18.3 percent in 1980. Under such macroeconomic conditions, prices of commodities began to rise although most were still under administrative control at that time. The retail price index jumped from 0.7 percent in 1978 to 2.0 percent in 1979, then went to 6.0 percent in 1980.

In view of this situation, the Financial and Economic Committee of the State Council, founded in March 1979, put forward the "Eight-Character Guideline" of "readjusting, restructuring, straightening out and upgrading." However, this guideline could not be enforced for some time. The Central Committee of the Communist Party of China (CCCPC) decided in the winter of 1980 to "further readjust the national economy" more extensively in the next year.[1] This time, the readjustment of the national economy was carried out in the general milieu of "insisting on the dominance of the planned economy."[2] During the three years between 1979 and 1981, the following contractive measures were taken: (1) investment in fixed assets and capital construction projects was scaled down, (2) outlays for national defense and administration expenditures was cut, (3) bank credit was put under tight control while savings accounts of enterprises were frozen, and (4) RMB 4.8 billion in government bonds were issued to enterprises by administrative order.

Table 9.2 **China's Macroeconomic Situation during 1978-1983** (year to year, %)

Year	1978	1979	1980	1981	1982	1983
GDP Growth	11.7	7.6	7.8	5.2	9.1	10.9
Increase in Retail Price Index	0.7	2.0	6.0	2.4	1.9	1.5

Source: The National Bureau of Statistics, *China Statistical Yearbook* (Zhongguo tongji nianjian), Beijing: China Statistics Press, various years.

Because this round of economic fluctuation involved certain characteristics related to changes in the pattern of interests resulting from economic reform, it was considered the first economic cycle after the inception of reform and opening up.

9.1.2 The Second Round of Economic Fluctuation (1984 -1986)

In September 1982, the 12th National Congress of the CPC formally set the strategic goal of China's development, i.e., to quadruple the gross value of industrial and agricultural outputs by the end of the twentieth century. A corresponding strategic focus and implementation plan were also established. According to the original plan, during the twenty years between 1980 and 2000, the first ten years would involve laying the foundation, and the second ten years would see the economy take off. However, starting in early 1984, many local governments started vying with each other, raising the target at every level, and demanding the enlargement of their investment to "quadruple ahead of schedule." Although leaders of the central government later repeatedly called for calm, some local governments adopted strategies of "starting your projects while those of everyone else are suspended" and "keep advancing amid criticism" based on their past experience. These local governments kept expanding, making it even more difficult to check the overheating of the economy. In September 1984, the Third Plenary Session of the 12th CCCPC explicitly set the goal of reform as establishing a socialist commodity economy. In those days, the public readily embraced optimistic sentiments, believing that they would be able to carry out reform with a free hand, and the Chinese economy would soon take off. Meanwhile, October 1984 happened to be the grand celebration of the thirty-fifth anniversary of the founding of the People's Republic of China. Some leaders advocated the concept of "being able to earn and being willing to spend," so many government agencies and enterprises scrambled to raise salaries and to distribute bonuses and consumer goods such as clothing, adding more fuel to the flames of an overheated economy.

In addition, a technical error was made when measures to expand the autonomy of specialized banks to grant loans, which were supposed to be implemented in 1985, were formulated. The error was the stipulation that the central bank would use the total of actual loans granted by each specialized bank in 1984 as the base quota in setting the credit quota of that specialized bank in succeeding years. Therefore, every specialized bank, to raise its 1985 credit quota, competed with each other to expand the scale of bank credit by setting targets for every lower level and deliberately fabricating a larger base quota. Branches of specialized banks not only approved all loan applications from enterprises but also visited enterprises to solicit applications, requesting enterprises to borrow more.

The combined effect was that the money supply increased rapidly. Total amount of bank credit in 1984 increased by 28.8 percent on a year-on-year basis, and

December of 1984 saw an increase of 84.4 percent compared with the same month the previous year. The supply of cash (M0) increased by 49.5 percent on a year-on-year basis. At the end of the first quarter of 1985, M0, M1, and M2 increased by 59 percent, 39 percent, and 44 percent, respectively, compared with the same period the previous year. As could be expected, starting with the second quarter of 1985, prices rose rapidly.

In late 1984 and 1985, economists and policymakers had different opinions about whether the economy was overheated and contractive policies were necessary. As a result, the government was unable to decide on policies in a timely manner. Only with the intervention of Deng Xiaoping did different opinions on how to deal with inflation among the Chinese leaders converge.

Then the State Council demanded that all local governments formulate plans to stop further rises in prices. At the same time, the State Council decided to send out inspection teams to all provinces to supervise the reduction of capital construction projects. Beginning with the third quarter of 1985, the growth rate of investment fell every month. Meanwhile, the People's Bank of China adopted a contractive monetary policy, and in addition to enhancing control over credit quotas, it raised both deposit interest rates and lending interest rates twice in succession. Accordingly, the interest rates for working capital loans and capital construction loans both increased. As a result of these changes in both administrative and economic measures, the money supply in the second half of 1985 began to fall. In the first quarter of 1986, annual growth rates of M0 and M2 dropped to 14 percent and 13 percent, respectively, and the growth of the price index and GDP also fell quickly (see Table 9.3).

Table 9.3 **China's Macroeconomic Situation during 1983-1986** (year to year, %)

Year	1983	1984	1985	1986
GDP Growth	10.9	15.2	13.5	8.8
Growth of Investment in Fixed Assets	15.3	26.1	51.4	14.6
Increase in Retail Price Index	1.5	2.8	8.8	6.0

Source: The National Bureau of Statistics, *China Statistical Yearbook* (Zhongguo tongji nianjian), Beijing: China Statistics Press, various years.

As early as the end of 1984, when signs of an overheated economy first appeared, economic policy advisory agencies and economists launched a fierce debate on the macroeconomic situation of the time. Economists advocating expansionary macroeconomic policies argued any attempt to use macro control measures to suppress aggregate demand and to limit money supply would not only harm highspeed growth but also cause damage to the interests of all parties and, subsequently, weaken the support for reform. Contrary to this point of view, other economists argued that overall reform of the economic system, including the price system, should have the prerequisite that aggregate demand more or less matched aggregate supply; that the economic environment was rather easy going; and that national financial resources were sufficient to avoid severe inflation when the government debuted the next round of major reform measures. Therefore, according to these economists, the party and the government should decisively move to reduce aggregate demand, increase aggregate supply, and rapidly implement the first batch of supporting reforms when the economic environment was improved to a certain extent, so the new economic system could start functioning and help the national economy enter a positive cycle as soon as possible.

The International Conference on Macroeconomic Management, also known as the Bashanlun Conference, sponsored by the State Commission for Restructuring Economic Systems, the Chinese Academy of Social Sciences, and the World Bank, September 2 to 7, 1985, played a leading role in correcting theoretical economic misconceptions. At the conference, James Tobin pointed out that China was facing the risk of severe inflation. He proposed that China adopt "triple-contractive policies," that is, a contractive fiscal policy, a contractive monetary policy, and a contractive income policy, instead of the combination of a contractive monetary policy and an expansionary fiscal policy that is usually adopted by Western countries to avoid a crisis when they face moderate inflation. The Bashanlun Conference also made the leaders of the State Council fully resolved to implement stabilization policies.[3]

The policy derived from this debate was drawn by the National Congress of the CPC in September 1985. Of the decisions made at this meeting, at least two directly pertained to macroeconomic policies.

1. Reform should be given top priority and should be well-coordinated and mutually supportive of development. Fundamentally speaking, reform serves development. For the time being, arrangements for development should be favorable for the advancement of reform. In order to pave the way for reform, the economic growth rate should be set at a reasonable level. Every care should be taken to prevent blindly vying with each other and going after the growth of output quantities and output values so as to avoid tension and dislocation in economic activities and to create a good economic environment for reform.

2. Equilibrium of aggregate demand and aggregate supply should be maintained and accumulation and consumption should be kept at an appropriate ratio. The key issue here is that while the government should make appropriate arrangements for the livelihoods of the people, it also bears responsibility to keep tab on the country's financial strength to determine the reasonable scale of investment in fixed assets, realizing balances in the country's financial position, credit position, tangible resources, and foreign exchange, as well as an overall balance among them.

The argument made by this meeting was a profound summary, based on experiences and lessons since the commencement of reform, of how to correctly deal with the relations between reform and economic growth and between reform and economic environment. Unfortunately, before long these lessons learned at a high price seemed to be forgotten, and thus, much more severe inflation began in 1986 and broke out in full in 1988.

9.1.3 The Third Round of Economic Fluctuation Between 1987 and 1990

According to the Chinese government's original plan, its policy for economic affairs in 1986 was to keep stabilizing the economy so as to prepare for "radical reform measures" in 1987. However, at the beginning of 1986, the Chinese economic growth rate was slowing down, and in February, GDP growth was reported as zero. At that time, the government decided to loosen control over bank credit. As a result, starting in the second quarter of 1986, the money supply increased sharply, which led to inflation resurfacing in the fourth quarter of 1987. But at this time, leaders were convinced of the misperception that "inflation cannot be harmful, but only be helpful." They believed that the economy in 1987 achieved growth with efficiency and high speed without any risk of inflation. Thus, in mid-1988, the annual growth rates of M_1 and M_2 reached 33 percent and 29 percent, respectively.

In early May 1988, the Standing Committee of the Political Bureau of the CPC decided to complete the "crashing through the pass of price reform and wage reform" in the following five years. At the end of May, at a high-level meeting on implementation of this decision, economists Liu Guoguang and Wu Jinglian, based on the macroeconomic situation at that time, proposed "improving the situation first before crashing through the pass of price reform." Their reasons were that: (1) the upward movement of prices that started with agricultural products in the fourth quarter of 1987 was spreading to other sectors; (2) the "bottleneck constraints" of transportation and supply of capital goods were becoming more and more severe; (3) sporadic panic buying appeared everywhere and was continuously spreading; (4) a negative growth rate of bank savings appeared in April, indicating that the inflation expectation had begun to take shape. However, at the same time, the misperception that "inflation cannot be harmful, but only be helpful" was at the peak of its powers. Some economists took their observations of economic situations in Latin America as an example, pointed out even inflation rates of a thousand percent or more would not necessarily throw obstacles in the way of economic prosperity. As a result, government leaders concluded that crashing through the pass of price reform could be achieved despite hyperinflation and high growth rates.[4]

In the second half of 1988, things did not develop as government leaders had optimistically expected. The Political Bureau of the CPC in early June officially decided to start "crashing through the pass of price reform and wage reform," and inflation expectations immediately appeared among the population, followed by a swift rise in prices. The retail price in the whole country rose by 80% in August, 1998, and the retail price index increased by 26 percent year-on-year in the second half of the year, and panic buying was common in cities. Speculative buying and selling of allocated supplies and foreign exchange quotas and corruption became widespread, aggravating the public discontent, turning economic problems into political ones, and leading to political unrest.

To control explosive inflation, in the third quarter of 1988, the government began to precipitately scale down investment in fixed assets; suspend approval of off-plan construction projects; clean up and reorganize newly created business entities, especially trust and investment corporations; strictly control the procurement activities of government institutions; tighten control over prices; and set price ceilings for critical capital goods. Following the "forced-landing" policy of macroeconomic adjustment formulated at the Central Working Conference in September 1988, the People's Bank of China adopted a set of contractive monetary and credit policies, including stringent control over the scale of bank credit and, at one point, suspending granting bank loans to township and village enterprises. It also raised the reserve ratio on deposits of specialized banks and adjusted its interest rate policy. Because of the surge of inflation, increases in prices of goods far exceeded deposit interest rates, making real interest rates fairly large negative values. To slow down the decline of real interest rates, nominal rates of interest were raised twice in September 1988 and February 1989 by the central bank. To further stabilize the financial situation and to protect the interests of depositors, the central bank instituted an inflation-proof interest rate system for deposits with maturities of three years or longer.

Although these tough measures succeeded in lowering the inflation rate in a rather short time, it did not get there without any cost. In the third quarter of 1989, the money supply index fell to its trough, the annual growth rates of M_1 and M_2 fell to -1 percent and 13 percent, respectively. Accordingly, retail prices fell as well, and the growth rate of the retail price index dropped to 0.6 percent on a year-on-year basis in the third quarter of 1990. At the same time, however, markets became sluggish; industrial production declined; enterprises operated below capacity; unemployment mounted; China's financial position deteriorated; and the economy slipped into recession, resulting in an unprecedented situation of an "over-cooled" economy (see Table 9.4).

Table 9.4 **China's Macroeconomic Situation during 1986-1991** (year to year, %)

Year	1986	1987	1988	1989	1990	1991
GDP Growth	8.8	11.6	11.3	4.1	3.8	9.2
Increase in CPI	6.5	7.3	18.8	18.0	3.1	3.4

Source: The National Bureau of Statistics, *China Statistical Yearbook* (Zhongguo tongji nianjian), Beijing: China Statistics Press, various years.

9.1.4 The Fourth Round of Economic Fluctuation (1991-1995)

In the third quarter of 1989, while the government managed to check inflation and reduce the price index, sales turnover began to decline; inventories piled up; and enterprises' production was in disarray. In the fourth quarter of 1989, the People's Bank of China, at the behest of the State Council, started to inject a great deal of credit capital to "start-up" the economy that seemed at a standstill in its trough. The bank also substantially reduced deposit and lending interest rates in succession in March and August 1990, and April 1991. At the same time, the bank also reduced the inter-bank base rates for deposit and lending for financial institutions. However, because people had an expectation of low inflation and were under the influence of the psychological propensity "to buy when prices go up and not to buy when prices go down," the growth rate of GDP was merely 4.1 percent in 1990 although the growth rate of M_2 was as high as 28.0 percent. In 1991, with a continuous injection of substantial amounts of money, the growth rates of M_1 and M_2 reached 23.2 percent and 26.5 percent, respectively, and industrial production, led by the non-state sectors, started to bottom out.

In the beginning of 1992, Deng Xiaoping made his famous "South China speeches," calling for accelerating reform and development. His speeches boosted the rising momentum of the economy and set off a surge of development all over the country.

In the positive national economic climate of 1992, various localities, departments, and enterprises all showed great enthusiasm. They initiated various measures to boost reform and opening up in their regions and units and played a very important role in enlarging the scope of market functions. However, the central government seemed to be passive toward promoting reform, and failed to take actions supporting reform in key sectors including government finance, banking, and state-owned enterprises. Reform in these sectors could not proceed without the facilitation of state agencies.[5] At the same time, as a result of the adoption of an expansionary monetary policy to spur economic growth, local governments at various levels devoted their attention to setting up development zones and launching infrastructure investment projects, setting off another round of economy bubbles in the form of crazes for development zones, real estate, bonds, stocks, and futures. The economy quickly got overheated, and in

1992, M1 and M2 increased to 35.7 percent and 31.3 percent, respectively.

However, during the year between mid-1992 and mid-1993, many economists voiced different views regarding the macroeconomic situation. Some believed that the national economy had good momentum, and effort should be made to maintain this momentum. Others argued that signs of an overheated economy were already obvious, and appropriate measures should be adopted to rectify it. A popular analysis divided people into two factions according to the orientation of their macroeconomic policies. Those who believed that the economy was not yet overheated and nothing should be done belonged to the "reform faction;" those who believed that the economy was already overheated and timely remedial measures should be taken belonged to the "conservative faction." This analysis failed to conform to reality, however. In fact, the real situation at that time was much more complicated than this simplistic "dichotomization." Even people who apparently held the same views regarding the economic situation (whether it was overheated or not) might be widely different in their assumptions and policy propositions. Roughly speaking, there were actually four different viewpoints at that time. The first opinion attributed the overheated economy to the "over speed" at which the marketization reform had been pushed forward. The implication was that the reform effort should slow down, and control by plan should be tightened. The second opinion agreed with the first about the fact that the economy was overheated, but in contrast, proponents of this view insisted that the root cause of the overheated economy was that reform of key sectors had not been fast enough. They advocated for decisive measures to stabilize the economy and to accelerate reform. The third opinion was that the situation for economic development was excellent, and it should be maintained at a fast speed to avoid the occurrence of an overheated situation and the risk of inflation. Proponents of this view were affirmative about economic affairs in the preceding period and believed that what had been done should be continued. The fourth opinion was one of dissatisfaction with the progress of the reform, but proponents believed that the prospect of economic growth was still promising. They argued that inflation was inevitable for any country undergoing breakneck growth, so austerity measures should not be taken because they might reduce the momentum of fast growth.

Not until the spring of 1993 did the risk of inflation become too palpable to be veiled anymore. When the retail price index jumped up more than 10 percent compared with the same period of the previous year, and the six-month period between November 1992 and May 1993 saw the market exchange rate of RMB against US$ depreciated by 45 percent, inflation was obvious. In June 1993, the top leaders decided to adopt a "sixteen-main-point plan" to restore macroeconomic stability. The specific measures could be classified into three types: (1) administrative measures that included setting a definite time limit for banks to call back loans granted against rules and regulations, stepping up the control of credit quotas of specialized banks, reexamining investment projects, etc.; (2) economic measures that consisted of raising interest rates of bank deposits and lending twice, resuming inflation-proof bank savings, selling government bonds, etc.; and (3) execution of reform to get rid of microeconomic bases for inflation and to construct a macroeconomic adjustment system compatible with a market economy, including reform of state-owned enterprises, reform of the fiscal system, reform of the banking system, etc. Due to the grim macroeconomic situation at the time, priority was given to the emergency measures that could be effected quickly to stabilize the situation.

It took only a short period to deter the momentum of the overheated economy. The growth rate of M_1 dropped from 34.0 percent in June to 15.6 percent in October; the growth rate of investment in the state sector fell from 74.0 percent to 58.0 percent; the growth rate of the capital goods price index declined from 53.0 percent to 31.4 percent; and the exchange rate of the US$ for RMB decreased from 11.5 to 8.7.

Table 9.5 **China's Macroeconomic Situation during 1992-1996** (year to year, %)

Year	1992	1993	1994	1995	1996
GDP Growth	14.2	13.5	12.6	10.5	9.6
Increase in CPI	6.4	14.7	24.1	17.1	8.3

Source: The National Bureau of Statistics, *China Statistical Yearbook* (Zhongguo tongji nianjian), Beijing: China Statistics Press, various years.

9.1.5 Why does Inflation Frequently Occur During the Transitional Period?

Why does inflation frequently occur during the transition from a planned economy to a market economy? Many economists have studied this issue. They believe the reasons for this occurrence mainly are as follows.

1. Hidden inflation is unveiled. Hungarian economist Janos Kornai said in 1980 that a planned economy was a kind of shortage economy.[6] The normal state of a planned economy is that aggregate supply is insufficient to satisfy aggregate demand. However, as prices of most goods under planned economic systems are fixed, aggregate supply shortage usually does not manifest itself as increases in prices; instead, supply shortages remain hidden by administrative suppression and find expression in rationing systems and additional search costs. In this case, during the process of marketization reform and price liberalization, administrative suppression of prices loosens, the hidden inflation becomes apparent, and continuing increases in prices are unavoidable.

2. During the transition, the fiscal system is affected by many factors that increase expenditures and reduce revenues. On one side, preexisting macroeconomic control measures of a planned economy gradually weaken and become ineffective, but at the same time, the regulating mechanisms of a market economy have not yet been established. As a result, the government control over aggregate fiscal revenue and expenditure is weakened and budgetary revenues decreased. On the other hand, to neutralize opposition to reform, the state needs to increase resources used to pay for the costs of reform. The above two factors together likely to lead to increases in fiscal deficit, shortages of supplies, and instability of markets, and thus increased inflationary pressure in the early stages of reform.

3. During the transition, achieving sound macroeconomic control is a difficult task. First, a sound macroeconomic control infrastructure is a prerequisite to sound macroeconomic control. But at its early stages, such an infrastructure does not likely exist. Second, to let officials- who are used to operating with administrative orders in a planned economy but unfamiliar with modern economics- undertake macroeconomic control more often, could not get unsatisfactory results, to put it mildly. Finally, during the transition, macroeconomic decisions are usually made by political leaders. When weighing long-term versus short-term interests, they tend to prefer the shorter view.

When choosing between the need to maintain macroeconomic stability versus promoting faster long-term growth with efficiency and expansionary macroeconomic policies, the macroeconomic authorities often choose the second item as a priority over the first.

9.2
Macroeconomy and Macroeconomic Policies under Deflationary Pressure (1997-2002)

Since the beginning of the East Asia financial crisis in July 1997, the macroeconomic environment in both China and the world underwent dramatic changes. Recession replaced inflation to become the major problem faced by all countries of the world. China in 1997 started to suffer from insufficient aggregate demand, a sluggish market, and a declining growth rate. However, in China, these economic changes occurred for more complicated reasons than in other East Asian countries.

9.2.1 Causes of Insufficient Aggregate Demand

In the second half of 1997, China's national economy began to feel the pressure of insufficient aggregate demand. Many factors contributed to it: First, there were the lagging effects of austerity measures after 1993. For the past twenty years, in general, China's economy had followed the development pattern of upsurge-inflation-remedy-contraction-stagnation-recovery-expansion. The austerity measures that were implemented in the summer of 1993 had achieved significant success by the winter of 1996, and the inflation rate was nearly zero in 1997. Just as policy measures adopted by other countries to stabilize commodity prices usually had some lagging effects, China started moving toward deflation in 1998. Second, in the strategic restructuring of the state sector, it was necessary to discard some redundant production capacity. For example, in three years the textile industry had to reduce its capacity by ten million spindles, or 25 percent of the total capacity. As a result, state-owned enterprises had to lay off a great many workers. In 1997, the number of laid-off workers from state-owned enterprises totaled 12.75 million, and only a minority of these people managed to find new jobs. In 1998, another substantial number of SOE workers were laid off. Furthermore, during these years of reform, some township and village enterprises owned by local governments experienced slowdowns. All of these caused reductions in aggregate demand. Third, in the process of reform, particularly the reform of the housing and social security systems, the removal of old systems where the state took care of everything occurred much faster than the establishment of new systems. This discrepancy made the general public increase their saving and cut back on consumption, again, leading to a decrease in aggregate demand. The fourth reason was the impact of the East Asian financial crisis. Because of continuing economic and financial turbulence, neighboring countries suffered from severe depreciation of domestic currencies and diminishing purchasing power for imports. Consequently, demand for China's exports to these areas declined. Simultaneously, foreign direct investment in China from these areas substantially decreased. Overall, all these factors combined to result in economic contraction in China.

9.2.2. Policies to Increase Domestic Demand and Their Effect

In response to this situation, in early 1998, the Chinese government proposed policies that expand domestic demand to spur economic growth. These policy measures affecting both demand and supply sides of the economy were put in place after mid-1998.

9.2.2.1 Demand-side Policy

In early 1998, the Chinese macroeconomic authorities began to adopt policies to expand domestic demand. The first was a proactive fiscal policy, mainly in the form of investment financed by treasury bonds. Between 1998 and 2001, the authorities issued long-term treasury bonds for development totaling to RMB 510 billion, mainly invested in infrastructure construction, such as superhighways, transportation systems, power generation, and large water conservancy projects. In a relatively short time, this action succeeded in stopping the downward trend of investment. The second policy was for the total amount of supporting funds for projects financed by treasury bonds-in the form of commercial loans from the four state-owned commercial banks-to match the sum total of fiscal allocation funds. The third policy was a moderately expansionary monetary policy to supplement the fiscal policy. The central bank reduced deposit and lending interest rates seven times in succession and increased the money supply.

This economic policy of creating aggregate demand directly by the government had advantages in that it could quickly increase demand and stop downward investment trends. For example, after the East Asian financial crisis started in 1997, the CCCPC and the State Council in mid-1998 proposed to increase investment by RMB 160 billion. After the formalities of legislation, the fund was quickly allocated down through the government hierarchy by stages. However, to increase demand by this method, particularly on a perpetual basis, also resulted in some negative effects. First, government investment tended to "crowd out" private investment. Second, in competitive sectors, the efficiency of government investment would be lower than that of private investment. Third, and the most important, the treasury bonds issued for government investment would have to be redeemed eventually by increasing tax revenue. As a result, private investment would be hampered, worsening the investment environment. As a result, round the beginning of 2000, economists began to recommend that the proactive fiscal policy be gradually reduced.[7]

9.2.2.2 Supply-side Policy

As early as 1998, some economists suggested that under conditions of insufficient aggregate demand and slow economic growth, in addition to the expansionary fiscal policy on the demand side, supply-side policies should be adopted that would increase the involvement of enterprises. Although this proposition neither gained consensus among economists nor was formally declared, the Chinese government in practice did adopt supply-side policies because of the urgent needs for reform and the development of economic entities. First, according to the requirement of the 15th National Congress of the CPC that the layout of the state sector should be adjusted by "advancing in some areas while retreating from others," hundreds of thousands of small and medium-sized SOEs were transformed into non-state enterprises with a market orientation and clearly identified property rights. Second, the macroeconomic authorities adopted a series of measures to improve the business environment for non-state enterprises. These measures included setting up the Small and Medium Enterprise Department under the State Economic and Trade Commission to specifically facilitate the development of small and medium enterprises (SMEs), and emphasize the need for improving finance and credit services to SMEs. In response, credit guarantee companies or funds were established in all provinces and major cities to help improve financing options for SMEs. These measures improved the operating environment for non-state enterprises, spurred private investment, and enabled non-state SMEs to grow rapidly in some regions. Third, the authorities accelerated adjustments to the layout of the state sector and the reform of state-owned enterprises. Industries dominated by large state-owned enterprises, such as petroleum, telecommunication, railroads, and electric power, were reorganized, and incorporation of these enterprises was carried out. The macroeconomic authorities also completed the following tasks: (1) separated government administration from enterprise management and set up a new framework of government regulation; (2) eliminated business monopolies and promoted competition between enterprises; (3) set up the basic framework of corporate governance based on shareholder diversification upon the completion of incorporation and listing in overseas or domestic securities markets. All these measures increased the strength of enterprises by enabling different forms of ownership, improved financial positions, and better investment opportunities.

As time went on, however, the relative effectiveness of the demand versus the supply side policies changed. By 2001, supply-side policy effects had surpassed those of the demand-side policy. The supply side had become the major engine driving rapid economic growth of China, as the following shows:

1. Non-state enterprise growth enabled private investment to become the major part of total investment. A survey of the Development Research Center of the State Council showed that between 1999 and 2001, growth rates of fixed asset investment in the collective sector, the individual business sector, and the "others" sector increased faster than that of the state sector. Contrasting vividly with slowdowns in state investment growth, the average growth rate of domestic private investment in fixed assets reached 20.4 percent, 11.8 percent, 22.7 percent, and 20.3 percent, in the four years between 1998 and 2001, respectively. These rates were not only higher

than those of the state sector during this period, but also higher than the growth rate of the total investment of society.

As domestic private investment gathered momentum, the dependence of the total societal investment growth rate on government investment was decreasing, and the capacity of autonomous investment was growing. According to a report by the National Bureau of Statistics, in 1999, 2000, and 2001, the share of treasury bond investment (including total investment funded by national debt funds and total investment funded by supporting funds) in the total investment of society in fixed assets declined by 8.1 percent, 8.8 percent, and 6.5 percent, respectively. The growth rate of budgetary investment funds also declined by 54.7 percent, 13.9 percent, and 13.2 percent, respectively. Concurrently, the growth rate of total investment of society rose by 5.1 percent, 10.3 percent, and 13.0 percent, respectively.

In summary, strong autonomous private investment was driving the rebound of total investment of society (see Table 9.6).

Table 9.6 **Growth of Investment in Fixed Assets by Sector** (year to year, %)

Year		1998	1999	2000	2001	2002
Average of All Sectors		13.9	5.1	10.3	13.0	16.9
State Sector		17.4	3.8	3.5	6.7	7.2
Collective Sector		8.9	3.5	10.7	9.9	13.4
Individual Business Sector		9.2	7.9	12.2	15.3	20.1
Others		11.6	5.3	28.5	28.9	36.2
In Which	Shareholding	40.4	27.3	63.9	39.4	47.1
	Foreign	-16.2	-12.6	-8.4	7.8	19.1
	Hong Kong and Taiwan	42.4	-8.7	6.2	22.4	11.5
	Joint Ownership	-50.9	61.8	-3.2	-0.2	46.2

Source: The National Bureau of Statistics, *China Statistical Yearbook* (Zhongguo tongji nianjian), Beijing: China Statistics Press, various years.

2. Although the international economic situation was worsening, China maintained a high growth in exports. In 1999, the government granted permission for non-state enterprises to export their own products. In 2001, although the three major world economies of the United States, Europe, and Japan showed no signs of recovery, and

the absolute volume of global trade was dropping, China's exports grew substantially, and its share of global trade significantly increased.

9.2.3 Changes in Macroeconomic Situation

As a result of efforts made by the Chinese government since 1998, the slowdown in economic growth was stopped by 2000. By mid-2000, the economic situation was turned around (see Table 9.7).

Table 9.7 **China's Macroeconomic Situation during 1997-2002** (year to year, %)

Year	1997	1998	1999	2000	2001
GDP Growth	8.8	7.8	7.1	8.0	7.3
Increase in CPI	2.8	-0.8	-1.4	0.4	0.7

Source: The National Bureau of Statistics, *China Statistical Yearbook* (Zhongguo tongji nianjian), Beijing: China Statistics Press, various years.

Even in 2001 and 2002, when the external economic environment was unfavorable and government investment in total domestic investment was decreasing, China's GDP growth was still at eye-catching rates of 7.5 percent and 8.0 percent respectively, proving the effectiveness of the supply-side policy that invigorated the economy.

9.3
Challenge to the Stability of China's Economy

In more than twenty years of fast economic growth, many deep-rooted economic and social problems had not been solved. This backlog of problems made the microeconomic efficiency of enterprises low and the macroeconomic efficiency of the society low, which was epitomized by the relative inefficiency of the banking system. The negative consequences of high growth based on low efficiency were the mounting nonperforming loans (NPLs). At the same time, the unavoidable cost of economic transition was often expressed as "contingent losses" on the banks' balance sheets. For this reason, China's banking system during transition was very vulnerable, and tended to be the blasting fuse of economic and social crises. Some scholars even predict that, during the next twenty years, it is almost certain that China will have a financial crisis.[8]

9.3.1 The Root Cause of the Problems in the Chinese Financial System

In recent years, China's economic growth has been sustained by investment (see Figure 9.1). The new round of growth acceleration since the second half of 2002 was mainly induced by investment. Between January and August of 2003, the complete total investment of society in fixed assets jumped by 30 percent, up 10 percentage points, compared with the same period in the previous year.

Figure 9.1 **Growth of Total Investment of Society in Fixed Assets** (in real terms)

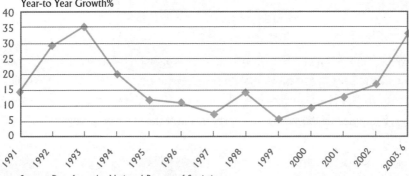

Source: Data from the National Bureau of Statistics.

Figure 9.2 **Rapid Growth of Loans**

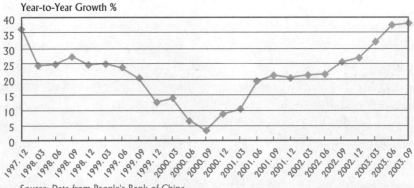

Source: Data from People's Bank of China.

288

The increases in investment were sustained by increases in loans (see Figure 9.2), Between January and August of 2003, loans in local currency granted by all financial institutions recorded an eight-month increase of RMB 2.1681 trillion, exceeding the previous year's 12-month increase of RMB 1.848 trillion.

In 2003, some economists studied the financial process of Chinese economy increase[9]. They point out that at present, because the age structure of the Chinese workforce is still on the young side and the Chinese people have a tradition of saving, the savings rate in China is very high, with savings comprising roughly 40 percent of GDP. Most Chinese resident savings are in the form of bank deposits. Banks use these deposits to make loans to enterprises (around 65 percent of total bank loans was made to state-owned enterprises), enabling them to make huge investments to support fast growth. A report of Standard & Poor's Ratings Services pointed out that since 1995, the growth rate of total lending by the Chinese banking system has been higher than the GDP growth rate of the country. By the end of 1995, total outstanding loans amounted to 88 percent of the GDP that year; and by the end of 2002, this amount had reached 138 percent of the GDP for that year. This means that the banking system was injecting more and more loans into industrial and commercial enterprises. With banks as intermediaries, China's high saving rate is turned into a high investment rate, and this further turns into high GDP growth rate. In this process, however, low efficiency in resource allocation leads to a huge waste of funds, and high-cost, low-efficiency growth leads to further accumulation of bad assets in the banking system.

The grounds for the conclusion of Paul Krugman, who in 1994 predicted the East Asian financial crisis, was that economic growth of East Asian countries was achieved almost entirely by heavy input of resources instead of enhancement of efficiency.[10] In his book, *The Return of Depression Economics* (1999), Krugman once again discussed this issue. He said that in 1994, he foresaw the East Asian financial crisis because Asia had fallen short in productivity growth, so that the area would eventually experience a period of diminishing returns. He pointed out that, as of 1997, Malaysia's investment amounted to 40 percent of its GDP, twice as much as that of the 1970s, whereas Singapore put 50 percent of its income into investment. However, even such high investment rates, which could not be higher, were still insufficient to sustain high-speed growth. For the whole region of Southeast Asia, this is demonstrated by the fact that the incremental capital-output ratio (ICOR), the indicator of the required investment growth rate needed to maintain a certain output growth rate, kept rising. The rising ICOR meant that the efficiency of investment kept falling, and the continuation of such conditions would definitely lead to the outbreak of a financial crisis.

It is alarming to note that since 1994, China's ICOR have continued to worsen (see Figure 9.3). Between 1998 and 2002, the required investment for every additional RMB in China's GDP jumped by 1.5 times the investment required for incremental GDP growth before 1994.

Figure 9.3 **Increase in ICOR in China**[11]

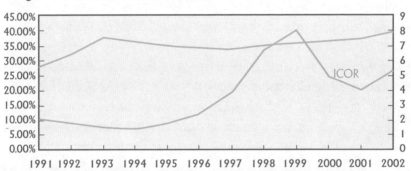

Source: Data from China International Capital Corporation Limited (CICC) and CEIC Data Company Limited (CEIC).

The evil consequence of this continuing high-cost growth is the huge increase of bad assets in the banking system. According to Chinese government figures, as of the end of 2002, China's four major state-owned commercial banks collectively had recorded a bad asset ratio of 25 percent. If the bad assets of RMB 1.4 trillion that had been turned over to four asset management corporations were included, bad assets would have been 45 percent of the four banks' total assets. This ratio came close to the Standard & Poor's Ratings Services 2003 estimate of the bad asset ratio of China's banking system,[12] and far exceeded that of Japan-and that country was being dragged down by its nonperforming financial system. The Standard & Poor's Ratings Services report further estimated that the Chinese government would have to

當代中國經濟改革

spend as much as US$518 billion, equivalent to 40 percent of its current GDP, before it could completely eliminate all these nonperforming loans. Some scholars dubbed this kind of economic growth under this kind of financial process as "borrowed growth,"[13] that is, growth sustained by money borrowed from bank depositors.

Of course, if certain conditions are met, "borrowed growth" can keep going on. Such conditions include (1) a high savings rate, (2) the monopoly status of state-owned banks, and (3) control of foreign exchange under a capital account.

What China has to attend to is that in the coming five to ten years, these conditions will definitely change. First, according to the commitment made when it joined the World Trade Organization, China will allow foreign banks to operate local currency (Renminbi) business free from any restrictions after 2007. It is predicted that in the future, many major customers may switch to foreign banks, so state-owned commercial banks, which currently carry the mountainous responsibility of supporting the growth of the economy, will lose their major sources of funds needed to keep their businesses going and to "dilute" their nonperforming loans. Second, a fully open China cannot everlastingly retain stringent control over foreign exchange under the capital account. If local businesses continue to operate with low efficiency and low profitability, and if the authorities relax exchange controls, Chinese citizens are very likely to invest their cash in better investment opportunities overseas. Third, as a result of China's one-child policy, the aging of the population will come faster in China than in other countries. Around 2010, China will arrive at a turning point due to an aging population when saving deposits in banks will start to drop and withdrawals will rise. As accumulation of social security funds in China is disastrously falling short, and the phenomenon of empty individual accounts of social security is ubiquitous, the problem of bank asset quality will become even greater than it is currently. Under such conditions, if necessary precautionary measures are not taken, a financial crisis like the one experienced by Japan and other East Asian countries will be hard to avoid.

9.3.2 Essential Measures Needed to Avoid a Crisis

To avoid a crisis, the Chinese authorities should take measures in two areas: first, accelerate reform and strengthen the system to reduce the possibility of a crisis;

second, establish an anti-crisis mechanism so the authorities will be able to limit the damage to a minimum if and when a financial crisis occurs.

About the first recommendation, other than the measures made to stabilize banks (the core of the financial system) that have been discussed, what should be undertaken are the other reforms discussed before: (1) adjust the layout of the state sector, reform state-owned enterprises and enhance their governance; (2) establish a social security system for all citizens; (3) facilitate the development of non-state enterprises; and moreover, include what will be discussed in next Chapter; and (4) build a basic framework for property rights and the rule of law.

As to the second recommendation, some financial experts have proposed[14]:

(1) formulate professional standards for financial institutions based on international experience and strictly enforce regulations according to these standards; (2)clearly define duties and responsibilities of different regulatory institutions, such as the China Securities Regulatory Commission, the China Insurance Regulatory Commission, and the China Banking Regulatory Commission, to reduce or eliminate overlapping functions and conflicts of interest;(3)improve the coordination among the central bank, financial regulatory institutions, and other government departments;(4)establish and improve a crisis management mechanism; (5)improve the reporting system management and public disclosure of financial information; (6) strengthen relevant departments of the central bank to enhance its ability to maintain financial stability; and (7)strengthen the study of financial stability problems by government departments and private institutions.

Notes and References

1. Chen Yun, "Economic Situation and Economic Lessons (Jingji xingshi yu jingji jiaoxun) (December 16, 1980)," *Selected Works of Chen Yun* (Chen Yun wenxuan) (1956-1985), Beijing: People's Publishing House, 1986, pp. 248-254

2. Chen Yun, "On Planning and Market Issues (Jihua yu shichang wenti) (March 8, 1979);" "Several Important Guidelines on Economic Construction (Jingji jianshe de jige zhongyao fangzhen) (December 22, 1981);" "Enhance and Improve the Work of Economic Planning (Jiaqiang he gaijm

jmgjijihua gongzuo) (January 25, 1982)," ibid, pp. 220-223, 275-277, and 278-280.

3. China Society of Economic Reform, *Macroeconomic Management and Reform-Selected Speeches of the International Conference on Macroeconomic Management* (Hongguan jingji de guanli he gaige-hongguan jingji guanli guoji taolunhui yanlun xuanbian), Beijing: Economic Daily Press, 1986.

4. Liu Hong, *Academic Critical Biography of Contemporary Chinese Economists: Wu Jinglian* (Dangdai Zhongguo jingjixuejia xueshu pingzhuan: Wu Jinglian), Xi'an: Shanxi Normal University Press, 2002, pp. 247-270.

5. Wu Jinglian, "Go All Out to Build Up the Basic Structure of a Market Economy (Quanliyifu, jianli shichang jingji de jichu jiegou)," *Reform* (Gaige), 1992, No. 2, pp. 4-11.

6. Kornai, *Economics of Shortage*, Amsterdam: North-Holland Publishing Company, 1980.

7. Wu Jinglian, "Economy Turns for the Better: Stronger Reform Measures Are Needed (Jingji zoushi chuxian zhuanji, haixu jiada gaige lidu) (2000)," *Reform: We Are Passing a Critical Moment* (Gaige: women zhengzai guo daguan), Beijing: Joint Publishing, 2001, pp. 76-82.

8. Lu Zhongyuan, "Analysis of the Situation of Private Investment (Minjian touzi taishi fenxi) (2002)," in Ma Hong and Wang Mengkui (eds.), *Research of Development in China-Selected Works of Development Research Center of the State Council* (Zhongguo fazhan yanjiu-guowuyuan fazhan yanjiu zhongxin baogaoxuan), Beijing: China Development Press, 2003, pp. 109-121.

9. Qian Yingyi and Huang Haizhou, "Financial Stability and Development in China after WTO Accession (Jiaru Shimao Zuzhihou jinrong de wending yu fazhan) (2001)," in Qian Yingyi, *Modern Economics and China's Reform* (Xiandai jingjixue yu Zhongguo jingji gaige), Beijing: China Renmin University Press, 2003, pp. 160-176.

10. Shen Liantao and Xiao Geng, "The Financial Reform and Development, and Construction of Infrastructures with Firm Ownership (Zhongguo jinrong gaige yu fazhan jianli wengu de chanquan jichu sheshi)," *Mimeograph*, August 2003. See also Shan Weijian, "Huge Paradox of China's Economic Growth (Zhongguo jingji zengzhang de juda beilun)," *Caijing* Magazine (Cai-jing), 2003, No. 17.

11. Paul Krugman, "The Myth of Asia's Miracle," *Foreign Affairs*, November/December 1994, pp. 62-78.

12. In June 2003, Standard & Poor's, in a report entitled China Banking Outlook 2003-2004, estimated that the proportion of non-performing loans in China's banking system had reached 50 percent. In spite of the substantial increase in the total outstanding loans of Chinese banks, Standard & Poor's in September 2003, revised its estimate to 44 to 45 percent.

13. Shan Weijian, "Huge Paradox of China's Economic Growth (Zhongguo jingji zengzhang de juda beilun)," *Caijing* Magazine (Caijing), 2003, No. 17.

14. Huang Haizhou and Wang Shuilin, "A Few Suggestions for the Reinforcement of the Stability of Financial System (Jiaqiang Zhongguo jinrong xitong wendingxing de jidian jianyi);" Tang Min, "Build an Open-Style Anti-Financial-Crisis Mechanism, *Caijing* Magazine (Caijing), 2003, No. 20.

Macroeconomy in the Reform

CHAPTER TEN

CONSTRUCTING A GOOD MARKET ECONOMY

Having undergone over twenty years of reform and opening, China has achieved a high-speed economic growth, and the outline of a modern market economy has appeared in front of the people. However, in the transitional period, a patch of people with authority in resource allocation tend to make exorbitant profits by exerting their powers. Therefore, to construct a good market economy which will benefit the whole society has become an acute social problem.

Charles Dickens described the British society in the Industrial Revolution in this way: "it was the spring of hope, it was the winter of despair; we were all going direct to Heaven, we were all going direct the other way."

10.1
Enlarging Income Disparity among Social Strata

The enlarging income disparity among different social strata is the focal point of various social contradictions during the transition from a traditional society to a modern one. In China's double transitions from planned economy to market economy, and from a traditional society to a modern one, the income disparity among social strata has kept enlarging significantly.

10.1.1 Income Disparity Enlarged

In the early 1980s, Deng Xiaoping proposed a policy of "letting some people get rich first"[1] and the original intention of this policy was to let those who were working diligently or good at doing business get rich first and then to lead the great majority of people to gradually attain the goal of common prosperity. However, in the process of reform, the income disparity among social strata enlarged greatly (see Figure 10.1).

Figure 10.1 **Ratio of Per Capita Disposable Income of Urban Households to Per Capita Net Income of Rural Households in China**

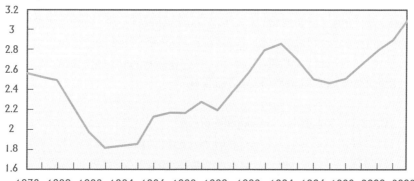

Source: The National Bureau of Statistics, *China Statistical Yearbook* (Zhongguo tongji nianjian), Beijing: China Statistics Press, various years.

According to estimates by the World Bank, the Gini coefficient calculated for combined urban and rural areas of China rose from 0.3 in 1984 to 0.35 in 1989.[2] In those days, the extent of inequality still could be considered to be at a medium level. In the 1990s, it reached a high level, beyond 0.4. Two studies had come out with similar results. One was done by the Income Distribution Task Group of the Economics Research Institute of the Chinese Academy of Social Sciences, whose estimates showed that the national Gini coefficient had increased from 0.382 in

Constructing A Good Market Economy

1988 to 0.452 in 1995, based on two random samplings of households.[3] The result of the other study was that the Gini coefficient had increased from 0.38 in 1988 to 0.45 in 1995.[4] Based on the information provided by the National Bureau of Statistics, the Economic Research Institute of Nankai University calculated that the Gini coefficient of residents' income had increased from 0.35 in 1988 to 0.40 in 1997; when tax evasion, official corruption, conversion of institutional consumption, and other sources of illicit income were included in the calculation, the actual Gini coefficient of residents' income had increased from 0.42 in 1988 to 0.49 in 1997.[5] Some scholars estimated that the actual Gini coefficient of residents' income in China exceeded 0.5, ranking China among countries of high income inequality in the world.[6] Judged by another indicator of the level of income inequality among all social groups, in China's neighbor, Japan, the total income of the richest 20 percent of all families was about four times as much as that of the poorest 20 percent, whereas, according to research done by Renmin University of China, in China the same indicator was 11.8, exceeding that of the United States (considered to have a high level of income inequality) by about 11.[7] The continuously enlarging income gap definitely posed a threat to social stability.

10.1.2 The lowest-income population

The lowest-income population in China consists of:

1. The laid-off employees of state-owned enterprises comprise one group of the lowest-income population. The financial condition of state-owned enterprises had been deteriorating since the mid-1980s. The majority of ordinary employees of state-owned enterprises fail to see any great improvement in their income. In the initial stage of reform, state-owned enterprises facing financial difficulty were kept running mainly by subsidies from the government. In the mid-1980s, they switched to bank loans, and in the 1990s, when neither the treasury nor state-owned banks were able to "transfuse" enough "blood" to them; state-owned enterprises faced operation difficulties and even repayment crises. The deteriorating financial position of state-owned enterprises directly threatened the livelihood of their employees as well as the functioning of the social security system. Each year in the 1990s saw a

great number of SOE employees get laid off. After the outburst of the East Asian financial crisis, China suffered from sluggish exports and decreasing demand, and the problem of laid-off SOE employees worsened. The registered urban unemployment rate was 3.6 percent in 2001, 4.0 percent in 2002, and 4.2 percent in the first half of 2003.[8]

2. Peasants without nonagricultural income comprise another group in the lowest income population. Since the beginning of the reform and opening up, the poverty-stricken population in rural China has been substantially reduced (see Table 10.1). According to a report by the Rural Survey Team of the National Bureau of Statistics, the poverty-stricken population in rural China was reduced from 250 million in 1978 to 34 million in 1999. However, in sharp contrast with the rapid increase in the income of urban residents, the increase in the income of rural residents has been very slow. At the inception of the reform, the implementation of the household contracted responsibility system with remuneration linked to output raised peasants' income considerably. Because a large number of rural laborers were absorbed by the development of township and village enterprises on the basis of leaving agricultural jobs but not rural areas, and a large number of peasant workers left both agricultural jobs and rural areas, income of the rural population increased quickly. However, after 1985, income disparity between the urban and rural populations started to widen. Although income disparity between urban and rural residents narrowed in the first decade of reform, the gap widened rapidly again in the late 1980s. The disposable per capita income of urban residents exceeded the net per capita income of rural residents by RMB 209.8 in 1978, by RMB 286.3 in 1980, by RMB 341.5 in 1985, by RMB 823.9. in 1990, by RMB 2705.3 in 1995, and by RMB 3643.7 in 1999.[9] By 1993, the gap in the level of consumption between farming and non-farming residents had widened to the same level as the record high in 1959.[10] After 1997, due to the inefficiency caused by the stagnant reform of urban industry and commerce, the low utilization of the capacity of urban enterprises, and the high incidence of layoffs, cities were unable to create enough new jobs to absorb rural surplus laborers coming to work in nonagricultural industries. Therefore the stock of rural surplus laborers was on the rise rather than on the decline, resulting in more and more rural laborers crowding into less and less farmland. According to a speech made by Qiu

Xiaohua, Vice Director of the National Bureau of Statistics in March 2003, the income gap between urban and rural residents in China might have reached a ratio of 6:1, while the same ratio in most countries in the world was 1.5:1.[11]

Table 10.1 **Standard of Poverty Line and Rural Poverty Reduction in China (1990-1999)**

Year	Chinese Official Standard			International Standard (US$1 per person per day)	
	Poverty Line (RMB per Person per Year)	Rural Poverty-Stricken Population (Million)	Poverty-Stricken Population versus Rural Population (%)	Rural Poverty-Stricken Population (Million)	Poverty-Stricken Population versus Rural Population (%)
1990	300	85	9.5	280	31.3
1991	304	94	10.4	287	31.7
1992	317	80	8.8	274	30.1
1993	350	75	8.2	266	29.1
1994	440	70	7.6	237	25.9
1995	530	65	7.1	200	21.8
1996	580	58	6.3	138	15.0
1997	640	50	5.4	124	13.5
1998	635	42	4.6	106	11.5

Source: World Bank, *China: Overcoming Rural Poverty* (Joint Report of the Leading Group for Poverty Reduction, UNDP and the World Bank, Report No. 21105-CHA), Washington, D.C.: World Bank, 2000, p. xiii, Table 1.

10.1.3 The Level of Contentment Decreased

In the process of reform, the mistakes in implementing the policy facilitated the income disparity enlarging. Some corrupt officials with authority in resource allocation and others with connections for rent-seeking became nouveau riches, but the ordinary working people, including employees of state-owned enterprises and especially peasants, benefited little from the reform and their living standards were hardly improved or were even reduced because of the repeated emergence of inflation. In sharp contrast, neither soaring commodity prices nor surging securities prices caused any harm to those "wave riders" backed by power; instead, they got a chance to "fish in troubled waters," that is, gain advantage from other people's financial problems.

Income disparity leads to the decrease in the level of contentment. At the early stage of reform and opening, not only did non-state sectors experience rapid development, but the policy of power delegating and profit sharing adopted in the state sector succeeded in benefiting almost everyone as well, creating a sense of contentment within the whole society. As reform deepened, however, some social problems were not alleviated but aggravated. In recent years, the level of contentment has decreased sharply.

According to a research project in 2000 entitled "Social Stratification, Public Attitude, and Social Stability" by the Sociology Institute of the Chinese Academy of Social Sciences, people did not have an obvious sentiment of optimism, and 20 percent of those polled expressed a pessimistic attitude. When asked about the reform of the health care system, 36 percent believed that they would lose and 29 percent believed that they would either gain nothing or lose. When asked about the reform of the employment system, 14 percent believed that they would lose and 46 percent believed that they would either gain nothing or lose. In addition, according to other research conducted at the end of 2002, the number of urban residents who were discontented with their living standards reached one hundred to two hundred million, representing 22 to 45 percent of the total urban population; and the number of those who were very discontented reached thirty-two to thirty-six million, representing 7 to 8 percent. The discontented people were mainly those disadvantaged in the processes of economic transition and restructuring, including the laid-off and unemployed, peasants, low-income people, people with reduced income, and others. The conclusion of the research was that unfair distribution of social wealth was the ultimate root cause of social instability.[12]

The gap between the rich and the poor has enlarged to such a critical extent that it has undermined social stability and obstructed further reform and development of China.

10.2
Increases in Corrupt Activities

Lord Acton (1834-1902) said: "Power tends to corrupt, and absolute power corrupts absolutely."[13] Because mechanisms to check and balance power were not established early enough in the transitional period, it was possible for some people to take advantage of this special situation by exploiting their unrestrained power to gain exorbitant wealth in the name of anti- or pro-reform. And this is an important reason for the income disparity in China.

10.2.1 Main Forms of Corrupt Activities

Corrupt activities can be categorized into three major types by their economic sources: (1) taking advantage of the power of administrative intervention in market activities to make deals between power and money; (2) taking advantage of opportunities in the adjustment and change in property relations in the transitional period to misappropriate public property; and (3) taking advantage of the imperfections and anomalies in the market system to make exorbitant profits.

10.2.1.1 Taking Advantage of the Power of Administrative Intervention in Market Activities to Make Deals Between Power and Money

After the inception of the reform and opening up when the party and government organs and nonprofit institutions started to be allowed to establish their affiliates in commerce, whoever got permission to establish a "labor service company" or a shop would be sure to rake in a huge sum of money, and thus the phenomenon of the industrial, agricultural, military, educational, and commercial circles all engaging in trade came into fashion in China. When enterprises were granted autonomy to a certain extent, they were allowed to sell the part of their products exceeding the planned quotas at the negotiated prices of the market rather than the allocation prices of the plan. Hence, for the same goods, market prices were much higher than planned prices. In 1985, this dual-track system of pricing was established as a formal system. Because of the huge gaps between market prices and planned prices, goods could be acquired at low prices and then resold at market prices to make exorbitant profits. The secret of making a fortune by profiteering was power, and therefore people referred to those engaging in profiteering by buying and selling as "bureaucratic profiteers."

By the early 1990s, rent-seeking activities were still rampant, although almost all controls on commodity prices had been lifted and rent-seeking by selling approval documents of commodities was no longer profitable. Around that time, two new targets for rent-seeking emerged: bank loans and land. Hence, the bulk of bureaucratic profiteering activity shifted from commodity rent-seeking in the 1980s to production factor rent-seeking. Taking land as an example, in the era of a planned economy, all parcels of state-owned land were assigned through the plan to state-owned enterprises. In the early 1990s when China started large-scale land leasing, most local governments adopted the leasing method of private negotiation; thus, people who had personal connections were able to purchase prime sites at low prices and make a great deal of profit once the land was resold. If speculation in real estate could generate bubbles, even the second-hand buyer, or the third-hand buyer, or the fourth-hand buyer would be able to earn a sizeable windfall, until the last buyer with bad luck was trapped. In those days, Beihai City of Guangxi Province was a hotspot in land leasing and speculation in real estate that attracted funds in tens of billions from all over the country, breeding a crop of billionaires, corrupting a batch of cadres, and ruining countless public property after the eventual burst of bubbles.

The ratio between total value of rents and GNP is recognized as a standard measurement of a country's corruption. According to calculations by economist Hu Heli in 1987 and 1988, the total sum of rents in the Chinese economy reached the astounding proportions of 20 percent and 40 percent of GNP, respectively.[14] According to calculations by economist Wan Anpei, in 1992 when rent-seeking activities in the financial market and the real estate market were at their peak, rents in the whole country totaled RMB 624.37 billion, representing 32.3 percent[15] of the national income that year. Wang Shaoguang, Hu Angang, and Ding Yuanzhu classified corruption behaviors in the transitional period into four categories: (1) rent-seeking corruption, (2) underground economy corruption, (3) loss of taxation income corruption, and (4) public investment and public expenditure corruption. According to estimates, in the second half of the 1990s, these four types of corruption caused economic losses averaging between 13.3 to

16.9 percent of GDP; during 1999 to 2001, economic losses caused by corruption accounted for 14.5 to 14.9 percent of GDP.[16]

10.2.1.2 Taking Advantage of the Adjustment of Property Relationship to Seek Personal Gain

The transitional period was one of great changes in ownership structure and great adjustment in interest relationship. Because the original demarcation of property rights to public property was ambiguous and the redemarcation of property rights was to be done under the government's leadership, if the exercise of power is not subject to strict monitoring and restriction, some people with power can make use of their unrestricted power to misappropriate public property. The following are some common situations.

1. In the reform of state-owned enterprises, the government as the real boss of enterprise kept itself in the background and let the manager employed handle the properties of the enterprises.

For a long period of time, the main content of the reform of state-owned enterprises had been delegating power to and sharing profit with enterprise leaders (factory directors or managers), resulting in the problem of "self dealing" as it is called in management. In other words, as representatives of the owner vested with full authority, enterprise leaders were delegating power to and sharing profit with themselves.

One common practice was to transfer the profit from the public coffer of the state to the private coffer of the enterprise. After the commencement of the reform and opening up, state-owned enterprises were allowed to market the extra-plan part of their products themselves and to retain a certain percentage of the sales revenues of the extra-plan products to establish the "Three Funds," namely the employees' bonus fund, the employees' welfare fund, and the production development fund. Moreover, enterprises were allowed to make investments to set up their own labor service companies, tertiary businesses, etc. Therefore, the assets of each state-owned enterprise were divided into two parts: state assets belonging to the state and self-owned assets belonging to the enterprise. Both types of assets were under the control of the enterprise leader. As a result, various means of transferring profits from the public coffer to the private coffer were invented. Some large state-owned enterprises, especially those in foreign trade, speculated in high-risk-high-return international futures markets; any loss would be a loss to the state while any gain would be a gain to the private coffer or even individuals' wallets.

Another practice was to misappropriate public property through subordinate enterprises. When the era of highly concentrated planned economy ended, state-owned enterprises as well as party and government organs were allowed to set up labor service companies or tertiary businesses, whose original purpose was to solve the employment problem of employees' children returning to cities from the countryside. Before long, some people discovered the trick of appointing their trusted aides to establish subordinate enterprises and transferring profit to them. Since leaders of the parent organizations were representatives of the owner (the state) and vested with full authority, if they engaged in transferring profit, whether to the private coffers or to their own wallets, they would encounter little hindrance. Hence, it became a common practice for state-owned enterprises to invest money in organizing subordinate enterprises. Similarly, leaders of subordinate enterprises copycatted the same trick. Another rather popular way to misappropriate public property was, in the process of establishing the shareholding system, to sell floating shares to investors at unreasonably high premiums to "grab money" and to give free or very low-cost initial shares to those within the enterprise.

2. The concept of power delegating and profit sharing, which guided enterprise reform, provided large loopholes.

The root cause of the problem of state-owned enterprises was the ineffective enterprise system. However, for a very long period of time, the problems had not been addressed by the clarification of property rights and changes in the system. Instead, the enterprise reform had been limited to delegating power to and sharing profit with enterprises (mainly their leaders) in the hope of bringing their enthusiasm into play to improve the performance of enterprises. There were substantial drawbacks in such approaches as "enterprise contracting," "authorized management," and "authorized investment" adopted by the government during the process of power delegating and profit sharing. The practice of the owner of state-owned enterprises (the state) authorizing management to exercise the property rights started when the enterprise contracting system was introduced into commercial and industrial enterprises. Modern economic theories consider the possession by the owner of residual control (ultimate control) and residual claim (claim to profit) as the basic requirement for the clarification of property rights. The basic principle of the enterprise contracting system is "fixing the base quota, guaranteeing the remittance, retaining what exceeds the quota, and making up what falls short of the quota." The substance of this practice was that, during the contract period, the owner (the party awarding the contract) relinquished complete control and claim to the portion of profit exceeding the base quota of the contract. This enabled the employed agent (the party awarded the contract) to become the real master of the property rights of the enterprise. Such an institutional arrangement of property rights made it possible for the party awarded the contract, by virtue of this control, to misappropriate public property by various means. This ambiguous institutional arrangement of property rights created a tremendous hotbed for managerial corruption. The enterprise contracting system later evolved into a formal system of authorized management, written into the *Law on Industrial Enterprises Owned by the Whole People*. This law interpreted the separation of ownership from management as the separation of the ownership of the state from the occupation, use, and disposition rights over the enterprises exercised by the factory directors or managers as the representatives of the state. The law provided the factory directors or managers as employees with some sort of legal basis to handle the enterprises' properties according to their own interests and desires.

3. The enterprise system of transformed enterprises had inherent imperfection and the internal management system had huge loopholes.

A transformed enterprise (previously part of an existing state-owned enterprise) often adopted the form of a corporation, in which the owner of the state shares and the state-owned corporate shares was clearly defined; thus, appearing as if property rights were clearly established. Although the original state-owned enterprise (sometimes called a holding company, a group corporation, or an assets management company) acted as the investment institution authorized by the state to exercise the rights of the shareholder with a controlling interest, the authorized investment institution itself was an independent enterprise. Furthermore, the managers of the enterprise were at the same time representatives of the owner, vested with full authority. Therefore, the real owner was absent and it was impossible to develop checks and balances between the owner and the management, allowing insider control to continue. When the managers of the authorized investment institution were not only representatives of the owner vested with full authority but also employed insiders, some of the leaders of the authorized investment institution could utilize their authority to seek gain for themselves or members of their cliques. One common practice was for the authorized investment institution as the parent to deliberately "hollow out" the listed company as the subsidiary by delaying payments for goods delivered or occupying the working capital. In the absence of the owner, internal financial control of enterprises was lost. Once the last link was broken, the whole chain of principals and agents was broken. The problem was caused by the ambiguity about who was the owner in the last link. As a result, state-owned securities and futures companies sometimes engaged in "rat trading," where secret accounts were arranged so that any gain would go to the secret accounts, while any loss would come from the state's account. Although at the turn of the century, state-owned banks had written off RMB 1.4 trillion of non-performing loans by establishing four asset management corporations. Yet by 2002, RMB 1.8 trillion of non-performing loans had shown up again in their books. A significant part of these astoundingly huge losses could be attributed to corruption in the state sector of the economy.

10.2.1.3 Taking Advantage of Market Imperfections and Anomalies to Make an Exorbitant Profit

In almost every market, information available to the two parties of a transaction is asymmetric, and the party with superior information can take advantage of the party with inferior information to gain profit. Thus, to put the market mechanism into action, it is necessary to regulate markets and transactions. The market economy in China is still in the process of being established, and we encounter not only problems caused by the inherent contradictions of a market economy but also problems caused by the nonexistence of market relations. Consequently, there are ugly behaviors in a primitive market economy, such as bullying competitors and dominating the market, as well as ugly behaviors in a market economy without the rule of law, such as deceiving and misleading consumers. In the securities market, illegal practices such as false statements, insider trading, and market price manipulating are rampant but punishment for these kinds of illicit market behaviors is not very severe. As a result, some lawless persons have easily accumulated substantial wealth by taking advantage of the chaotic market environment; but few of them have been punished according to the law.

10.2.2 In the Name of Reform

Such huge profits from rent-seeking have nurtured a large and powerful group of vested interests. Unlike the old group of vested interests who were nostalgic for the "good old days" of the planned economy, this new group of vested interests did not want to revert to the system of a planned economy or to see the establishment of a normalized market with fair competition. Instead, they wanted to maintain or even intensify the existing disorder and administrative intervention in the marketplace so they could continue rent seeking and making a fortune by taking advantage of their privileged status. They tried their best to find fault with and create roadblocks to the real reform necessary to establish a normalized market.

For example, in the name of reform, they paid the utmost tribute to land leasing to replicate the tragedy of the enclosure movement. They used their financial know-how to take advantage of numerous medium and small investors and they used reform of property rights to take over public property. All these were supposedly the panacea enabling the country to be prosperous and the people to be rich. Because these people had the credentials of being early participants of reform and they continued to wave the banner of reform even as they actually blocked or distorted reform, they could easily mislead the masses, making them believe the deceit to be truth. These actions were very damaging in two ways. First, they could take reform down the wrong path and hamper the construction of a sound market economy. Second, they led those who were ignorant of the truth to believe that the various despicable practices of the primitive market economy were the outcome of reform, while actually they ran counter to social justice. These actions turned people against reform and encouraged the sentiment and even the actions to restore the old economy.

These two processes would adversely affect the smooth progress of reform and social stability during the transition period. Although it may seem that the first social force (in favor of a planned economy) and the third social force (striving to maintain the status quo of the existing system) were opposing each other, they were in fact supporting each other. Both sides have quoted the existence of the other side as proof of its own correctness, in order to gain public support. Frequently citing those who used reform as a front to embezzle public property- but were in fact damaging reform- the first social force denigrated the real reform to muster public support for their conservative propositions. The third social force, which waved the banner of reform to seek personal gain, used the existence of conservative power as a "scarecrow" to instill fear in the general public and to confuse the principal boundaries between the two completely different criticisms of the existing system, which were based on two different sets of starting points and end results. Their goal was to oppose correct measures to further advance reform, to mislead the general public, and to make those dedicated to reform (but ignorant of the truth) believe that China would return to the old path of a planned economy if their propositions of false reform (which actually confounded right and wrong) were ignored. During this complicated transitional period, it was common for people to feel uncertain about their understanding of reform, resulting in vehement debates about the right direction to go and the right policies and measures to adopt.

10.3
Active Promotion of Political Reform

The great income disparity and the rampant corrupt practices urge us to achieve social justice in the transition, which is closely related to the exertion of Constitutional right, the effective supervision over the government, and the cultivation of a civil society. It has become a pressing issue to promote the political reform in order to prevent the market economy from deteriorating and to establish a good market economy which will benefit the whole society.

10.3.1 Making Government Affairs Open and Protecting the People's Right to Know

The monopoly of decision-making rights by government institutions and their officials often rely on their monopoly of public information. All information generated during the process of executing official duties is a public resource, which the general public must have in order to understand public affairs and the government's working situation and to monitor government officials. Therefore, modern countries usually have legislation to ensure open information and a "sunshine government", except for information related to national security and information exempted by law, all public information must be available to the public. Only when a system of transparent information is established can government agencies and their officials be monitored by the public. However, the totalist government of the past more often perceived the administration of public affairs and information that reflected this process as internal secrets of the party and the government. The operation of such a system over a long period of time has formed a whole set of established practices for handling crises: disregarding citizens' right to know, maintaining the approach of "being relaxed outside but tense inside," stringently keeping secrets and seeking resolution of the crises within the government without the public's knowledge. Hence, access to information has become a privilege and some corrupt government officials are able to turn what should be public information into their private information and to use it as a tool for rent seeking. Taking advantage of this kind of nontransparent system, these officials can not only seek personal gain and deceive the public but also can blindfold higher authorities. In recent years, many corrupt officials were able to muzzle public opinion by abusing their power to hide the truth so that their wrongdoings of riding roughshod over the masses remained unexposed for years. In a modern society, mass media such as newspapers, magazines, television broadcasting, and the Internet are major means for society to exchange public information and for citizens to exercise their right to know and to monitor granted by the constitution. If mass media cannot play the role it should play, society will be in a state of information blackout, resulting in serious negative economic, political, and social consequences.

10.3.2 Separating Party Leadership from Government Administration and Separating Government Administration from Enterprise Management

Generally speaking, each country's party in power has three alternative ways to exercise its leadership in political life. The first is for the party in power to exercise its leadership by state power, that is, by drawing up the constitution, amending the constitution, and participating in other law-making activities of the representative institution of the country, and by implementing these laws by organs of state power. The second is for the party in power to circumvent state power and directly exercise the functions that should have been exercised by the representative institution and organs of state power. The third is for the party in power to control the government, making all decisions while the government implements the decisions. Nicos Poulantzas, a French scholar studying Marxism, once pointed out that "the political structure, in which the political parties and the administration of a country are entwined and integrated, does not have any connection at all with democracy or even with socialism."[17] Because the Leftist party line historically combined party leadership with government administration, government administration with enterprise management, and violated the principle of the rule of law of socialism, Deng Xiaoping repeated many times that the principles of separation of party leadership from government administration and separation of government administration from enterprise management must be carried out in China's political life.

10.3.3 Democratic Election System

The construction of democratic politics in China started from elections at the grassroots level. After the Third Plenary Session of the 11th CCCPC, the party clearly proposed to "realize step by step the people's direct democracy in the governments and the social life at the grassroots level." In the early 1980s, peasants in Guangxi Province and some other places established their autonomous organizations of villagers' committees after the implementation of the "all-round responsibility system" in agriculture. The new constitution adopted and implemented in 1982 defined this kind of autonomous system at the grassroots level. In 1987, the *Law on Organization of Villagers' Committees (Trial)* was enacted, stipulating that the chairman, vice chairmen, and other members of a villagers' committee should be elected directly by the villagers.

The Report of the 15th National Congress of the CPC in 1997 pointed out that "all grassroots organs of political power and grassroots autonomous organizations of the masses in urban and rural areas should institute a sound democratic election system." In 1998, the *Law on Organization of Villagers' Committee* was officially put into force, which further defined the autonomous nature of villagers' committees and instituted sound procedures of direct election. As of 2001, villagers' committees all over the countryside had generally completed four rounds of regular elections; the degree of democratization and normalization had increased with each round, and millions of village officials had been switched from a nomination system to a direct election system.[18] In the late 1990s, a few cases of competitive election at the township level emerged in Sichuan Province and Guangdong Province. Then, in 2002, 40 percent of townships (about two thousand) in Sichuan Province adopted competitive elections to elect the town head and vice town head upon the completion of their office terms; some locations also adopted the competitive election of township party vice-secretaries. In cities, residents' committees of communities have ubiquitously been selected by direct election. However, due to the long-time absence of an election system and culture in China, the fundamental principles and significance of democratic election go beyond the understanding of most Chinese; for example, some voters expressed an indifferent attitude as to who was going to be elected, just swimming with the tide; some elections were manipulated; and various problems of bribery and fraud in election existed. Therefore, it is necessary to provide the masses with civic education, incorporating details of democratic election into the syllabus of high-school civil education courses.

10.3.4 Instituting the Rule of Law

The rule of law is a fundamental characteristic of a modern political system, and is a critical issue that every country must solve in the transition toward a market economy and democratic politics. China does not have a tradition of the rule of law. In the era of feudalism, the legal system was just a tool in the hands of the emperor. During a period after the founding of the People's Republic of China, some government leaders had been interested in starting the rule of law; but after 1957, the rule of law was condemned as the view of bourgeois Rightists. The press not only repeatedly propagandized the writings of Lenin that "proletarian dictatorship is a dictatorship that is bound by no law" but also advocated Mao Zedong's "supreme instruction" of defying all laws, human or divine.[19] Although leaders of the party and the government have been emphasizing administration according to law and institution of the rule of law in recent years, the ideological inertia is still a hurdle to be overcome. Furthermore, steps to institute the rule of law are necessary in the following aspects.

First, establishing the supremacy of the constitution. The *Constitution* is China's fundamental law; all other statutory laws, bylaws, or governmental orders of the administrative apparatuses must comply with the *Constitution*. The main content of the *Constitution* is the protection of citizens' fundamental rights. First of all, property rights, be public or private, are under the protection of laws and free from any infringement. At the same time, the scope of the government authority must be defined to prevent the government from abusing its authority and infringing upon citizens' fundamental rights. Corruption is manifested by the abuse of entrusted public authorities to infringe upon property rights and economic interests of citizens. One of the factors that allow rent-seeking activities to become universal is overly pervasive government control with too much discretionary power in the hands of government officials. A basic requirement for instituting a constitutional government is prevention of the existence of any entity with absolute, unconstrained power.

Second, instituting a transparent legal framework. Under the rule of law, the legal system must be transparent. There are three basic requirements of transparency. The first is that the public should extensively participate in the process of legislation and have a chance to take part in the drafting of laws. The second is that laws should be made known to the public. Right now, many government organs treat laws and regulations as their private information, and outsiders are not allowed to know about the existence of laws and regulations relevant to them or their specific contents. This allows corrupt officials to control the situation officially or under the table so they can pervert laws and infringe upon the interests of citizens. According to the modern notion of the rule of law, a law not made known to the public is an ineffective law. The third requirement for transparency is that citizens should be able to predict the legal consequences of their actions. For example, according to the principle of the

CONSTRUCTING A GOOD MARKET ECONOMY

rule of law, a law can only be applied to actions carried out after the law was issued; the law cannot be applied retroactively. Otherwise, citizens will not control their own destinies and will be forced to seek backdoor connections and offer bribes to officials who have a lot of discretionary power to make an exception in their case.

Third, ensuring judicial impartiality and judicial independence. Independent trial by judges and law enforcement with justice are basic requirements for institution of the rule of law. At present, judicial corruption and administrative intervention are major obstacles to realizing these basic requirements. To remove these obstacles, in addition to perfecting the system, monitoring by the public and by party committees at various levels must be increased. The political leadership of the Communist Party of China in its capacity of being the party in office and judicial independence required by the socialist rule of law are compatible with each other. First of all, the political programs and requirements of the party in office must be enacted into laws through legal procedures; every party member and every party organization can act only within the scope of the *Constitution* and law, and no one can be allowed to be above the law. Second, the monitoring function of judicial practice of party committees at various levels should be expressed as monitoring of the justice of legal procedures, not as intervening in specific judicial processes and decisions. Nowadays, another important threat against judicial impartiality and judicial independence comes from so-called "judicial parochialization." The outcome of a cross-region case of economic dispute more often depends on which region possesses the judicial jurisdiction of the case. In view of this, several corrective measures have been proposed. For example, the power of local people's congresses in the nomination procedures of local judges should be restricted. Moreover, some scholars have recommended the People's Supreme Court to organize circuit courts to handle cross-region cases. This is a feasible method to stifle local protectionism.

10.3.5 Correcting the Relationship between the Government and the People

The major drawback of the political and social administration system in the era of a planned economy was that the system of a "big totalist government" reversed the original rightful relation of government as servant and the people as master. As early as 130 years ago, during discussion of the experience of the Paris Commune, the founder of Marxism repeatedly reiterated that the most important issue was the need to prevent the "transformation of the state and the organs of the state from servants of society into masters of society."[20] Under the system of a big totalist government, although some party and government organizations and their officials had slogans of "serving the people" or "acting as the servant of the people" on their office walls and on their lips, in reality they remained in the seat of "master of society" and "chief" of the masses and were able to impose their own will on society in the name of state objectives and to make decisions on behalf of "people of all family names" under their jurisdiction on all issues, including issues critical to citizens' vital interests. In a country like China with a long tradition of autocracy, this completely reversed relationship was able to gain acceptance by citizens. For example, such social aberrances as local officials being called "parent officials" of "people of all family names" and white-collar officials being laurelled "parents of citizens" became the social norm. By virtue of their power and influence, some unlawful officials were unbearably arrogant toward people; they not only were free from the monitoring of voters and taxpayers but also considered people's petitions and visits to appeal to the higher authorities for help as illegal or rebellious actions, to be strictly forbidden.

It was the existence of these outmoded conventions and irrational practices that went against the grain of modern political civilization, that caused some government officials in charge to take very irresponsible actions- such as blocking the transfer of information, hiding the epidemic situation, and disseminating false information- on the vital issue of the SARS epidemic in 2003, while still believing what they had done was something right and proper and conforming to rules and procedures of the government. To rectify this reversed relation between master and servant, it is important to build a constitutional political order that clearly defines fundamental human rights and establishes a set of explicit constraints on the government's authority, in accordance with the *Decision* of the 16th National Congress of the CPC to promote political reform by promoting political civilization, developing democratic politics, and constructing a society with the rule of law. Officials of the party and the government who are vested with state power should be accountable for what they have done. The exercise of people's right to monitor and dismiss public servants should be ensured by legal procedures with operational feasibility.

As a country with "a strong tradition of feudal autocracy and a weak tradition of democratic legality," China has a great and formidable task to put into effect the rule of law in constitutional democracy. However, time and tide wait for no man. That is a vital step for China to stand on her own feet among multitudes of nations in this era of constant progress. Therefore, in this new historical period of comprehensively improving the market economic system under the rule of law, promoting political civilization, establishing a democratic system, and building a society under the rule of law will be the main theme of reform.

Notes and References

1. Some people in rural areas and cities should be allowed to get rich before other. It is only fair that people who work hard should prosper. To let some people and some regions become prosperous first is a new policy that is supported by everyone. It is better than the old one." See Deng Xiaoping, "Our Work in All Fields Should Contribute to the Building of Socialism with Chinese Characteristics (Ge xiang gongzuo dou yao youzhuyu jianshe you Zhongguo tese de shehuizhuyi) (January 12, 1983)," *Selected Works of Deng Xiaoping* (Deng Xiaoping wenxuan), Vol. 3, Beijing: People's Publishing House, 1993, p. 23.
2. United Nations Development Programme, *China Human Development Report: Human Development and Poverty Alleviation*, 1997, Beijing: UNDP China, 1997, p. 47.
3. Keith Griffin and Zhao Renwei (eds.), *The Distribution of Income in China*, New York: St. Martin's, 1993. See also Zhao Renwei and Keith Griffin (eds.), *The Study of Distribution of Income of Chinese Residents* (Zhongguo jumin shouru fenpei yanjiu), Beijing: China Social Science Publishing House, 1994; and Zhao Renwei, Li Shi, and Li Siqin (eds.), *The Restudy of Distribution of Income of Chinese Residents* (Zhongguo jumin shouru fenpei zai yanjiu), Beijing: China Finance and Economics Publishing House, 1999.
4. Azizur Khan, "Distribution of Income in China: Evolution of Inequality, 1988 -1995 (Paper for Workshop on Income Distribution in China) (1997)"; United Nations Development Programme, *China Human Development Report: Human Development and Poverty Alleviation*, 1997, Beijing: UNDP China, 1997, p. 47.
5. Cheng Zongsheng and Zhou Yunbo, "The Impact of Illicit Abnormal Income on Residents' Income Disparity and Its Economics Interpretation (Feifa feizhengchang shouru dui jumin shouru chabie de yingxiang jiqi jingjixue jieshi)," *Economic Research Journal* (jingji yanjiu), 2001, No. 4, pp. 14-23.
6. Wang Shaoguang, Hu Angang, and Ding Yuanzhu, "Social Instability behind Economic Prosperity (Jingji fanrong beihou de shehui bu wending)," *Strategy and Administration* (zhanlyue yu guanli), 2002, No. 3.

7. *China Market Economy Post* (Zhongguo shichang jingji bao), July 26, 1995,

8. According to the speech made by Zhang Zuoji, Minister of Labor and Social Security, at the press conference on November 11, 2002 at the Press Center of the 16th National Congress of the CPC, as of September 2002, the registered urban unemployment rate in China was 3.9 percent, or 7.52 million. If the six million people laid off and still waiting for reemployment were included, it added up to fourteen million, representing an unemployment rate of 7 percent.

9. Xu Rui'e, "Summary of Views on Income Disparities among Residents in China (Wo guo jumin shouru chaju guandian zong-shu)," November 14, 2002, http://www.drcnet.com.

10. In 1993, the average consumption level of nonfarming residents reached 3.2 times that of the farming residents, equal to that of the historical high in 1959. (See The National Bureau of Statistics, *China Statistical Yearbook* (Zhongguo tongji nianjian), Beijing: China Statistics Press, various years.)

11. http://www.cei.gov.cn, March 11, 2003.

12. Wang Shaoguang, Hu Angang, and Ding Yuanzhu, "Social Instability behind Economic Prosperity (Jingji fanrong beihou de shehui bu wending)," *Strategy and Administration* (zhanlyue yu guanli), 2002, No. 3.

13. Lord Acton, "Letter to Mandell Creighton of April 5, 1887," *Essays on Freedom and Power*, in Gertrude Himmelfarb (ed.), New York: Penguin Books, 1972, p. 335.

14. Hu Heli, "Three Policies of Anti-Corruption (Lianzheng sance);" "Estimation of Rent of China m 1988 (1988 nian wo guo zujin de gusuan," in editing department of Comparisons of Social Economic System (Jingji shehui tizhi bijiao) (ed.), *Corruption: Making Deals between Power and Money* (Fubai: quanli yu jinqian de jiaohuan), 2nd edition, Beijing: China Economic Publishing House, 1993, pp. 20-46.

15. Wan Anpei, "Analyses of the Major Features and Composition of Rents in the Transitional Period of Chinese Economy (Zhongguo jingji zhuanxing shiqi de zujin goucheng ji zhuyao tedian fenxi) (1995)," in Wu Jinglian et al., *Building Up a Market Economy: Comprehensive Framework and Working Proposals* (Jianshe shichang jingji de zongti gouxiang yu fang'an sheji), Beijing: Central Compilation and Translation Press, 1996, pp. 331-364.

16. Wang Shaoguang, Hu Angang, and Ding Yuanzhu, "Social Instability behind Economic Prosperity (Jingji fanrong beihou de shehui bu wending)," *Strategy and Administration* (Zhanlyue yu guanli), 2002, No. 3.

17. Wang Yan, "Promote Legalization of Political Life in China (Cujin guojia zhengzhi shenghuo de fazhihua)," *Methods* (Fangfa), 1998, No. 4.

18. Zhan Chengfu, "Several Issues Regarding Direct Election in Villages in China (Guanyu wo guo xiangcun zhijie xuanju de ji ge wenti)," *Research on Socialism* (Shehuizhuyi yanjiu), 2001, No. 4.

19. Xiong Xianghui, *My Intelligence and Diplomatic Life* (Wo de qingbao yu waijiao shengya), Beijing: The Central Party History Press, 1999, p. 220.

20. Friedrich Engels, "The 1891 Preface to Marx's 'The Civil War in France' (Makesi Falanxi Neizhan 1891 Nian Danxingben daoyan) (1891)," *Selected Works of Marx and Engels* (Makesi Engesi xuanji), Chinese edition, Vol. 3, Beijing: People's Publishing House, 1995, pp. 12-14.